INTERPRETIVE HUMAN STUDIES

An Introduction to Phenomenological Research

Edited by

Vivian Darroch
Ronald J. Silvers
Ontario Institute for Studies in Education

UNIVERSITY
PRESS OF
AMERICA

LANHAM • NEW YORK • LONDON

Copyright © 1982 by

University Press of America, ™ **Inc.**

4720 Boston Way
Lanham, MD 20706

3 Henrietta Street
London WC2E 8LU England

Library of Congress Cataloging in Publication Data
Main entry under title:

Interpretive human studies.

    Includes bibliographical references.
    Contents: Biography and discourse / Vivian Darroch and
Ronald J. Silvers — Transcript of a colloquium / edited
by Vivian Darroch and Ronald J. Silvers — Mapping a
region of social experience / Terrence Trussler — [etc.]
    1. Sociology—Philosophy—Congresses.
2. Phenomenology—Congresses. 3. Existentialism—
Congresses. 4. Hermeneutics—Congresses. 5. Education—
Congresses. I. Darroch, Vivian. II. Silvers, Ronald J.
HM26.I57   1982   301'.01   82-13636
ISBN 0-8191-2698-5 (alk. paper)
ISBN 0-8191-2699-3 (pbk. : alk. paper)

All University Press of America books are produced on acid-free
paper which exceeds the minimum standards set by the National
Historical Publications and Records Commission.

ACKNOWLEDGEMENT

Grateful acknowledgement is given to <u>Atlantis: A Women's Studies Journal</u> for permission to reprint "Narrative: A Range of Sense for a Verbal Vision" by Vivian Darroch, which appeared in their Spring/ Summer 1982 issue.

TABLE OF CONTENTS

v

PREFACE

"Interpretive studies," "existential inquiry," "hermeneutics," and "phenomenology" are terms connected with
a new direction that has been emerging in the social
sciences in recent years, a direction that demands a
substantial change in the social scientist's definition
of self as scientist and of science as activity. Like
all departures from "established" ways of thinking
about science, it commands the attention of those who
have been schooled in a conventional stance and who
sense a dissonance between that stance and what they
hoped their training would open to them. And like all
such departures worthy of committed attention, interpretive human studies is just that--a departure, a
direction for exploration, not a destination.

However, many who are curious about this exploration may find themselves in a quandary: Those immersed
in the endeavor, in the process of reviewing their
place as researchers, have reshaped their vocabulary
in such a manner as to articulate the central issues.
Those outside the endeavor then are confronted with
discourse in which the words seem freighted with mys-
terious connotations carrying meaning only to the initiated. How, then, does one find a starting point?

One could, of course, solve the problem by searching out a definitive text--if a definitive text were
not totally inappropriate to the subject. For interpretive human studies is not a system to be laid down,
a series of techniques to be specified, or even a
collection of closed definitions. It is, in a simplis-
tic sense, a way of bringing individual researchers
more fully into the service of their research in a
tension such that what is of the individual is disci-
plined by the analytical and synthetic necessities of
what can be shown as knowledge. Hence the impossibility of any ultimate "how-to" guide, for the "how-to"
is ultimately indivisible from the particular researchers.

What this book attempts to do is allow readers to
explore what interpretive human studies is about by
sharing the experience of some people who are themselves in the process of exploration. An important
part of the book is the transcript of a colloquim held
at the Ontario Institute for Studies in Education (OISE)
in Toronto. In that colloquium researchers who had for
some time been working from an interpretive stance

sought a language in common with interested students and faculty so as to bring to the fore, with considerable elaboration and example, many of the central concerns.

Another part of the book contains samples excerpted from our own work and from the work of graduate students who are moving toward interpretive studies from a conventional undergraduate orientation. The inquiries described in these papers address a variety of concerns in diverse areas of human studies; critical experiences in everyday life; the experience of being an immigrant; moments of time between an autistic child and a therapist; the place of "play" in knowing and friendship; women's friendships; the experience of having rheumatoid arthritis; children's conversations; and biographical narratives. In yet another part, our own papers attempt to exemplify a more fully developed point in our respective work.

While the order in which these sections are presented has a logic determined by our intention to engage readers in the processes of interpretive thought, we urge readers to enter the material in whatever order they find most satisfactory: one section may offer more if a later section is sampled first--but which sections, in which order, may vary for particular individuals.

Our intention in compiling this book has been to represent our interest in existence in life-worlds as we come to interpret the meaning of existence through reflection. Thus, interpretive inquiry may be seen as a "composite" of ideas from existentialism, hermeneutics (interpretive thought), and phenomenology. Existentialism is central, because the knowledge sought is dependent on the place of the researcher within inquiry and, thus, moves the inquiry toward ontology (the nature of being). Hermeneutics is central, because the inquiry seeks not only to interpret and recover the ground of meaning but to produce further meaning in the very act of doing the research. Phenomenology is central, because the practice of the inquiry is grounded in reflective thought.

We hope that this book will give readers a point of departure for their own explorations of a conception of social science that is capable of greater responsibility to both science and society.

The very format of this book has been formed by the context in which the work emerged: a graduate multidisciplinary program in the social sciences and education in which we attempted to formulate with our students the possibilities for an existential phenomenology in the human sciences. In attempting to offer paths for others, we found our own way; and in answering persistent questions and in responding to the doubts of those beginning, we found our own voices. In this context of seminars and dissertation projects, an outline of a process of research was discovered and clarified. This graduate program, which provided an immense variety of research projects within a pluralistic setting, brought us together not only with students but with our colleagues, both inside and outside of OISE, who as members of dissertation committees required us to specify to them the boundaries and principles of the inquiry. In all phases of our attempts we have received helpful responses from graduate students and colleagues and we are especially thankful to them.

Part of the work behind this book has been supported by the Social Sciences and Humanities Research Council of Canada Program Grant No. 431-770006. We are grateful to Shawn Moore for his skilled administration of that work and for his critical response to parts of this book.

Beverly Bingham contributed care and craft to the typing of all the drafts and reliability when it was badly needed.

Catherine Cragg responded to us warmly and understandingly as editor and friend. From the beginning she showed us how we could go beyond our first words and strengthen our manuscript.

Vivian Darroch
Ron Silvers

June 1982
Toronto, Canada

PART I

INTRODUCING THE INQUIRY

In the introductory essay that follows, we offer a statement which establishes and circumscribes the foundations for interpretive human studies. Here in this statement we attempt to explain why it has become necessary for us to select and formulate the principles which guide our research and how we have arrived at certain research practices. As we wrote it, we realized that this essay gathers together, in the act of writing, a clarifying and a making explicit for ourselves all that became manifest as we proceeded in the social act of inquiry.

This "introduction" was written at the conclusion of a period of work in our own independent research projects and in consultation with others pursuing research in interpretive studies. Therefore, we regard the statement not as a programmatic position but as a reflective conceptualization of an inquiry.

BIOGRAPHY AND DISCOURSE

Vivian Darroch
and Ronald J. Silvers

What Is Necessary and What Is Possible

Interpretive inquiry in the human sciences and education
as it will be addressed here is a form of inquiry in
which the researcher's biography is recognized to be a
vital part of what is studied. In saying this, we mean
that the researcher's biography must be analytically in-
corporated in her or his understandings of others, and
further, that in the communicating of these understandings the researcher's biography must be available to
others in a visible commitment to discourse. In denoting
interpretive inquiry to be this, we are placing it within
the domain of existentialism and are requiring that it be
informed by the principles and watchfulness of existential thought. For existentialism raises the question of
what is one's place in the world, and here what we wish
to show from the outset is that what is at issue in interpretive inquiry is the reconciliation between worlds
present in the work of research (that is, the world of
the researcher and the world of the other who is studied)
and the world of the receiver (reader) of that research.

While we have chosen to use "biography" and "discourse" to denote interpretive inquiry itself, we also
contend that the researchers' presences in the act of
inquiry and their articulation of those presences are
basic conditions for knowledge in the human sciences and
education. We submit that what is necessary is that
which is authentic in its relationship to the phenomenon
under study, social in the sources of meaning through
which investigations are pursued, responsible for judgments and interpretations made in the research itself,
and committed to what lies beyond the immediate appearance of what is under study.

What has led us to this position is our excursions
as researchers in human studies who, in encountering the
persistent mundane issues of the methodologies of social
sciences, sought to deal with the difficulties of what
was being studied and of what could be offered as knowledge. We began to realize that it was no longer sufficient in response to our difficulties to formulate
answers which referred back, as is typical, to methodo-

3

logical issues or technical problems. We begin to realize that the continued difficulties we faced were inherent in the nature of the self-other dialectic which is necessarily present in human studies, and in what we brought to the occasion of inquiry, that "what" being ourselves. Then as researchers independent from each other, we saw the need of reforming and re-forming inquiry itself. For us, our experience and the problems of relating and reporting the relationship of social science to everyday life pointed to what was necessary in two senses: in the limiting sense of what the limits of research are, and in the open sense of what is possible in human studies.

Now, from all of this contending with the work of research, we have come to realize also what is necessary and what is possible in our relationship with those whom we engage in research. We have also come to realize what is necessary in addressing our commitments to others in our research and in addressing our commitments to the moral nature of how we study those whom we study. What is necessary is that we recognize we can never speak on behalf of another, for we can only uncover and account for how we are speaking for that other. Only the latter is possible, because within inquiry it is the researchers who stand as the link between the world of the presence of the one studied and the world of the presence of the one receiving our work. In this way we realize that all that we attempt to note here is a task of clearing an opening in which it may be seen how we can and how we must engage others in the act of inquiry. Firstly, in the act of engaging others it is a question of how others appear to us. That is, the phenomenon we study is ostensibly the presence of the other, but it can only be the way in which the experience of the other is made available to us. Secondly, it is a question, as well, of how we appear to ourselves. For it is here that we provide an account of that link with the other which is ourselves. That account is a telling of our vision of the experience of the other and where in that vision we and the other are located. And thirdly, it is a question of how our reflections upon both appearances carry us beyond them. Our articulation of all of this to others is what we see as the challenge within the search which interpretive inquiry represents.

In offering these remarks as the foundations of our

work and as the source of inquiry, we have turned from a description of our experience in research to declarative statements. Those statements are necessary to mark our identity and the genesis from which we will explain this form of investigative research. However, for our purposes of establishing the features and principle of interpretive inquiry, we have chosen not to contrast interpretive inquiry to other inquiries (for example, inquiries which are reductive, whether based on quantitative or qualitative procedures or, perhaps, certain other phenomenologies). Nor have we chosen to outline the genealogy of interpretive inquiry, its lineage through previous writings. We have not done so because at each point in arriving at a formulation of interpretive inquiry we have depended upon a theoretic recovery of what we have found in our research experience, and it is that recovery we are attempting to share here. And that recovering speaks not for a reformulating of existing approaches in the human sciences, but for an attention to what lies at the center of research. Yet before proceeding we will mark by differentiation the distinction between the inquiry we will discuss here and what are called "ethnomethodology," "analytic phenomenology," and "phenomenologically based approaches."

In comparing interpretive inquiry with ethnomethodology,[1] the principle of difference is that of a conception of knowledge. In ethnomethodology, the point of departure is a notion of knowledge as "representative" of entities which exist independently in the world. The making sense of ethnomethodology is a seeking to formulate members' practices on the basis of shared understandings whose "validity" is based on "empirical" observations. In ethnomethodology, essentially there is no analytical incorporation of the biography of the researcher in the inquiry, no "recovery" of the researcher's own reflective thought. As will be discussed, the knowledge of the inquiry in interpretive human studies is nonrepresentative, nonaccumulative, not dependent on "realism" in the traditional empirical sense, and it must allow for the researcher's interpretation of meaning through the researcher's reflective

---

1 Among the formulations of ethnomethodology, the one which stands closest to interpretive human studies, and to which this work might be compared, is presented by James L. Heap. See his "Description in Ethnomethodology," Human Studies, 3 (1980) 87-106.

thought.

In that the basis of this work is reflective thought, the incorporation of such thought allows interpretive human studies to share thought in common with the work of analytic phenomenology.[2] However, the place of reflective thought in analytic phenomenology is different from the place of reflective thought in interpretive inquiry as we have defined it. In analytic phenomenology there is a seeking to formulate the "other's" voice (to which this inquiry also attends), but there is no seeking by the speaker to formulate the thought, the voice, of the speaker. The latter is critical to interpretive inquiry. That is, while analytic phenomenology takes as its task to find others' place of speaking, the inquiry and research here requires us to find our own place of speaking. Our emphasis on biography moves us away from "classical" thought and into existentialism.

Again, it is our emphasis here on our task of finding our place of speaking and our existential responsibility for our own voice in inquiry which separates this inquiry from more general inquiries in the human sciences which have come to be called "phenomenologically based approaches."[3] There is a proliferation of these latter approaches, and they have in common the important commitment of recognizing the realities of persons existing in their acts and the preserving of persons' lived-through experiences.[4] These approaches typically emphasize description, procedures of "theming," compilation of "profiles," and so on. Because such procedures depend on a knowledge which yet remains within the

---

2 The research practice behind analytic phenomenology may be found in the introduction to On the Beginning of Social Inquiry by Peter McHugh, Stanley Raffel, Daniel C. Foss, and Alan F. Blum (London: Routledge & Kegan Paul: 1974).

3 Perhaps one of the earliest, best-known, and most comprehensive presentations of a movement toward phenomenology is found in Psychology as a Human Science: A Phenomenologically Based Approach by Amedeo Giorgi (New York: Harper and Row, 1970).

4 Another early and valuable book in the human sciences which documents this commitment is Understanding Everyday Life edited by Jack Douglas (Chicago: Aldine, 1970).

confines of a traditional perception[5] which separates
the "knower" from the "known," these approaches perpe-
tuate an exteriorizing of those studied from ourselves,
the researchers. As well, because such procedures yet
have as their objective the establishing of an explanation of experience, these approaches (albeit qualitative
ones) return these researchers to the "reduction" from
which many say they wish to depart. It is our concern
that the attitudinal commitments behind these approaches
are not accomplished "in act" through the superordinate
principles and procedures which stem from their programmatic statements. It is in the superordinate principles
which guide our work where we depart from "phenomenologically based approaches."

The exceptions to our concern with phenomenologically based approaches would be that in many areas of
feminist studies (some of which are described as phenomenological) there are successful attempts to transcend/
surpass the dualism which concerns us.[6] Further, we
find some of the articulations of consciousness in
feminist studies to be articulations of the "consciousness" needed for this inquiry--a consciousness which is
mutable and ceaselessly moving, which deals substantively
with sentiment. And here we do not mean sentiment as in
the English "sentimental." Rather, we color the word
with the French connotations of sensibility--of fore-
seeing, experiencing, knowing.[7] Thus, this inquiry
allows the biographical treatment of sentiment, rather than
its objectification. By this we mean that we as researchers must recover the movement of our authorship of
thought and action by formulating its features within an
existential commitment to research and by locating this
commitment within a phenomenology of the human sciences.

Locating the Use of Interpretive Inquiry

By existential commitment we mean the effort to preserve

---

5 A perception which many in feminist studies would call
a patriarchal perception--and we would agree.

6 These attempts are dispersed throughout feminist literature. However, an exceedingly fine representation of
them is in the work. Gyn/Ecology: The Metaethics of
Radical Feminism by Mary Daly (Boston: Beacon Press, 1978).

7 Roland Barthes' Camera Lucida (tr. Richard Howard. New
York: Hill and Wang, 1981) treats sentiment substantively
in this way.

7

the interpretive presence of ourselves as researchers within our studies: in our relationships with those studied; in our explorations of communicative meaning; and in the transformation of our knowledge. It is only through this commitment that phenomenology may fulfill its promise in the human sciences to offer a path which turns away from a process of objectifying women, men, and children and "their texts" as things to be studied, from a process which reifies their actions and words as data and separates us as researchers from those we study. It is such a promise which may return us to what we call an "objectivating" process in everyday life which will allow us to achieve the social between ourselves as researchers and those we study. Whereas objectification is "to cause to become an object," objectivation signifies for us that process whereby our subjectivity manifests itself in a material world available to ourselves and others as a common world--a manifestation found in all social action.[8] Within objectification we lose sight of the objectivation of our subjectivity, failing to see our hand in and responsibility for what we create, for that creation is inherent in our interpretive understanding of the world. Existential reflection upon our objectivation returns to ourselves responsibility for our interpretations and authorship of social reality by recovering how we construct understandings and create meanings in dis-course--discourse here meaning a domain of language use. Existential reflection reveals our presence in the linguistic images we cast upon the world as a mani-festation of our consciousness.

Yet, the thrust of this reflection is to take us beyond the interpretation of consciousness into an inter-pretive domain of communicative meaning where the signi-fication of symbols in discourse are synthesized as meanings among equal participants who in their display of difference may enter into dialogue. The movement from the interpretation of consciousness to the domain of communicative interpretation is a shift from an initial exploration of the taken-for-granted (as an

---

8 For a discussion of the differences between objecti-fication and objectivation see Peter Berger and Stanley Pullberg "Reification and the Sociological Critique of Consciousness," History and Theory, 4 (1965), 196-211.

attempt to see how our previous understandings in discourse are constituted) to a subsequent creative synthesizing of meaning (to see how our understandings may be re-formed from the surface tension of linguistic images). In the former part of the movement we look at discourse in terms of the question "What is the foundation of our understandings?" In the latter part we consider discourse in terms of the undertaking "What communicative interpretations are possible?"

The practice of existentially recovering the process of objectivation in the life of research means that the manifested subjectivity of the researcher is the source material: from that source a work of inquiry commences (manifested subjectivity as narrated experiences of the researcher including the researcher's re-saying of others' words), and to it the theoretical knowledge of that inquiry must ultimately return (manifested subjectivity as reinterpretations and conceptualizations by the researcher). Thus it is that inquiry as we describe it here is not to enter into the world of the other to grasp the other's experience and understandings through an interpretation of the meanings of the other's discourse. Nor is this inquiry framed as a study of the negotiation of social reality among a group of others as perceived by the researcher--who, again, must enter into the experiences of the other. An existential commitment in phenomenology is a persistent effort to contend with the tangential relationships of researchers to those studied by constantly rediscovering and reformulating the meanings of the other for the researcher's self and the meanings of the researcher's self for the other. These rediscoveries and reformulations are the dynamic elements of a communicative relationship. And such a communicative relationship is the "use," the "practice" of this inquiry.

Interpretive Locatability in Discourse

The principal focus upon which this inquiry stands--irrespective of the particular topic of study under review or of the discipline in which it may be undertaken--is what we would term interpretive locatability in discourse. The phrase refers both to the problem of locating meaning within the in-between in the relationship of the researcher's self and the other (even where the other may be a former self of the researcher) and to the social achievement of communicative understanding between the researcher's self and the other. The "in-

between" in the location of meaning is exterior to subjectivities and interior to communicative relationships.
Leaving the domain of mind for the domain of communication identifies interpretive locatability in discourse
as a hermeneutic undertaking[9]--that is, as a search for
the meaning of a studied expression from discourse within the in-between (rather than in the mind of the other
or in one's own mind) and the achievement or, in its
pre-stage, the effort toward a hearing of the other
that resounds meaningfully within the researcher's self.
Such a leaving of mind and epistemology for communication and hermeneutics cannot be accomplished by a decision to move from one theory or field to another but
requires formulations of understanding accomplished
within a reflective inquiry of existential phenomenology.

So strong is our cultural attachment to mind that we
begin commonsensically to interpret others and ourselves
within an interpretive reference to interiorities and
subjectivities of intention, an interpretive reference
that reifies consciousness outside the self and other.
It is through the reflection of existential-phenomenological inquiry that we begin with this reification to
work backwards, to move back from that interpretive
reference to mind in order to surpass it in a consideration of communication. By backing up, we prepare in
reflection an uncovering of the ordinary everyday sense-
making of our own and others' interpretive use of
intentionality in order to free ourselves from the constraints of the intentional taken-for-granted of our
culture. Free of the constraints, we may move forward
through reflection to new formulations of understanding
as communicative participants.

Language of Interpretive Inquiry

Given that the consciousness behind this inquiry is
different from that behind reductive paradigms and
given that interpretive locatability is in discourse the
language of our interpretive inquiry, the way we express
our work and the way we explain how we work is a persistent source of interest for us and a difficulty to those
who first encounter such work. For in our focus upon

---

9 For example, Part Three of Richard Rorty's Philosophy
and the Mirror of Nature (Princeton, N.J.: Princeton
University Press, 1979).

the ordinary, the available and the concrete, we take interest in what is immediate to understanding in common sense. But in our attention to the immediacy of experience and in respect to understanding, we create a meta-language--that is, a language which may have a sense of "beside" that of which we speak, or even "across" from it, certainly of what is "situated behind" it. And our communication very often points to "beyond" that of which we are immediately speaking, writing. Thus we deal with the ordinary not through a language constructed from "scientific" terms which have been theoretically conceived, but through a form of discourse which permits a care in expressing or disclosing our relationship with the ordinary. Herein lies a paradox: in discussing the ordinary world with an unusual language, that language is found not in a finite set of terms to pin down the ordinary but rather in terms that show our relationship to the ordinary. As such, our discourse provides an interpretive source for recovering in our understanding what is ordinary so that that "what" is ordinary no longer. In addition, it provides an expressive search for the alteration of ourselves, for the "meta" of meta-language also means "change in, transformation of." And it is this which most marks this inquiry--changes in our understandings of the phenomenon we are studying and transformations in our understandings of ourselves. Our understandings, our ideologies, then become what is inscribed in our discourse and not a set of "external" beliefs or doctrines to be "adopted" by us and repeated. We are saying again that it is language which is offering meaning to ourselves.

And if the prominence of existential phenomenology is to be in envisioning the significance of knowledge in the moral judgment and choice which is expressed in the showing, understanding, and establishing of knowledge, then existential phenomenology requires a language which willingly will engage itself with the lives of people, as such lives are found, in a way which will allow the transcending/surpassing of our usual language.[10] That is, existential phenomenology requires a language which will accomplish more than the

---

10 The substance of this paragraph and the next two are excerpted from Vivian Darroch's "Notes for a Language for Phenomenology," Reflections: Essays in Phenomenology, 3, 1 (1982) p.34-48.

11

mirroring back of ourselves to ourselves. It requires
a language which will be adequate to the lives of those
it "speaks about" in that it will be a language which
will pass over that wide gap between our psychological/
social realities and our usual rhetorical and poetic
activities. The excavation and laying bare of specific
relations and specific effects of our involvement with
our "others" studied occurs in existential phenomenology
through subjective dialectic.

And subjective dialectic is alien to dialectical
materialism as the latter is usually presented--a conflict between two entities or forces being resolved by
the formation of a new entity or force. Subjective
dialectic does not hold implications for linearity of
thought and solution. In subjective dialectic the
language (writing and speaking) labors into being to
experience the life of dialectic in which images and
body (written and lived), in simultaneity, create. A
language for existential phenomenology must itself then
be a discourse which is existential; that is, a discourse
which is reactive through a lived departure from what
culturally is taken for granted. In certain other phenomenologies an epoche (that is, the conscious suspension
of the taken-for-granted) is assumed and purposefully
entered. But in existential phenomenology the "epoche"
is always lived, the taken-for-granted is always sus-
pended--because the shared understandings are never
embodied.

In certain other phenomenologies, the constructing
and contextualizing of meanings is within a cultural
context. In existential phenomenology, meaning dwells
and is (to be) "understood" within an existential con-
text--thus, the worlds of the words create order for the
worlds of the things. This idea, of course, is now
common, but it does point to where the truth of the
inquiry of existential phenomenology must lie. It must
lie within the process of its language (verbal or
otherwise, perhaps visual) which reports upon the
inquiry. And if the truth of the inquiry lies within
the contradictory processes of language, the language
of the inquiry must demonstrate that polyvalence.

Thus far our language here contains a number of
terms which emerge for us as we present our description
and analysis of what interpretive inquiry is. For
example, we have already referred to biography, discourse, and self-other and subjective dialectic, which

are not common terms of research in human studies. These concepts emerged in the work of our inquiry for us and for others who are concerned with an inquiry which existentially addresses the place of the researcher in it.

But the interest we have with language and the difficulty for others in first addressing this language is not in the special concepts we name. Indeed, we regard the issue of language as not in words which are special to a form of inquiry, but in how the words are used in articulating the research and explanation of that inquiry. We recognize that the language of interpretive inquiry is always circular in pointing back to the interpretive domain of the writer in an attempt to show what lies behind the words. This pointing or bending back means that what is described or explained is provided not as a matter of declaration but is a process of recovering what it was that permitted what was said to be said. Even here as we attempt to articulate what is special in the language of interpretive inquiry, we attempt to write reflectively. We realize that this means that our readers are asked to enter into an interpretive domain of reflective thinking--a thinking that does not merely follow the words of our reflections. Rather, readers are called upon to reflect upon their own interpretations of what is offered as interpretive inquiry.

The stance of the author in relation to readers structures the text of scientific writing in interpretive human studies as a form for the presenting of possible worlds for others' interpretations. The structure of the discourse in interpretive inquiry is a critical self-awareness and presentation of use which, as a form, requires from readers interpretive responsibility. The text's structure as self-referencing is a presentation of an other for the readers' selves and calls upon readers to self-reflectively explore their own interpretations. The establishing of the knowledge of interpretive inquiry thus depends upon <u>inter-interpretations</u>.

A Discourse for Communicative Relationship

The necessity of our showing our relationship to those studied is a necessity in showing the phenomenon we study. For the person, object, or event that we describe is in the interpretive domain that which <u>we</u>

13

designate, a phenomenon related to us. A showing of the phenomenon under study is thereby always a disclosing of an experience enfolded in our biographies.

The necessity of showing our relationship to the phenomenon of our study is exemplary of knowledge which is proximate to the other being studied. Such a knowledge preserves the bond between ourselves and that which we seek to know by recognizing that our knowledge is always a knowledge of our relationship through our biographies to the objects, to the events, to the people, to their biographies and their histories. Such a knowledge--which is the knowledge of reflective discourse--stands within the principle that we preserve the things we know as they show themselves to us. Hence the necessity that we show what we have found in the very way it has shown itself to us. Hence also the need for a way of discourse which will show to others what we ourselves have found, a discourse which risks a confounding of the ordinary by narrating the disclosure of the phenomenon in our personal relationship to it.

Such a discourse as an expression of an interpenetration of interpretive domains contains a tension between and a reflection of the experience within interpretive inquiry. The presence of the researcher is a presenting of his or her world as an interpretive domain which is always disclosed to have a distinctive reality and existential source. The researcher's presence is achieved in discourse where the interpretive domain is located in his or her biography as he or she proceeds on a quest to account for the providing of the presence of the other within his or her own interpretive domain. Thus, the problem of discourse for interpretive inquiry is how to provide and account for the presence (interpretive domain) of those studied along with the presence (interpretive domain) of the researcher. It is the preserving of both of these presences in discourse which makes possible an understanding among persons whose experience of life and reality are distinct from each other.

Thus, what we seek in discourse is an achieving of a communicative relationship between ourselves as researchers and those we study. Within our immediate world of circumstance we attempt to transform through reflective understanding and existential knowledge what it is that we first fail to understand and grasp in the lives of

14

others. For this new understanding we try to achieve a
relationship of reciprocity in providing not only for
our own presence but for a welcoming of the presence of
those who are studied. We look to discourse as the means
of going beyond our knowledge as social scientists.
Social science provides for the possibility of knowledge
through inquiry and theorizing. But social science is
confronted with the contradictions between the logic of
its own practices and the logic of the practices of
those studied, as when the particular rational practices of science are applied to the study of other practices of rationality of modern life.

Departure from Dualistic Thought

We are at each juncture in interpretive inquiry, and in
explaining it, standing in sharp contrast to and in a
"self-identity" separate from what is possible within
dualistic thought. We have introduced knowledge here as
the epistemology behind interpretive inquiry, and we
recognize that the introduction must forever lie in
contrast to a pervading epistemology of dualistic
thought which is manifested as additive knowledge. For
not only within the sciences themselves, but in the
objectification of what we know in the modern world,
additive knowledge stands in primacy.

By dualistic thought we refer to the division
between, on the one hand, that which we know or seek to
know (the objects of our attention) and, on the other
hand, the conscious subject who formulates the world of
objects. Within the physical sciences it is recognized
as a basis for distinguishing an objective world we
seek to understand through our objective procedures for
inquiry. Within social science it is established as
the source and necessity for objectivity within which
we remove the contamination, distortion, and bias of
the individual researcher in order to acquire a knowledge
of people and their relationships which corresponds to
the actual way they are and the real way that they
relate. The technical knowledge that we refer to is
an attempt to distinguish "what is really so" from what
our subjectivities and biographies and ideologies might
"make us think is so." It is a form of distinguishing
by virtue of technique (technique described or prescribed as the methods of the social sciences), which
sorts out through control, the elements of the subjective
and the ideological from the real. Interpretive inquiry,
on the other hand, as we have already emphasized, places

in doubt the distinction between the postulated and
the given.

The Place of Biography

We realize that our attempt to show interpretive inquiry
as a communicative relationship with what we encounter,
and not as a form of inquiry separate from ourselves,
brings us to a break with the traditions of what is now
conceived as modern social and educational science. But
it is not a critique of science that we seek. Nor is it
even an analysis of that science. Rather, our commitment to proximate knowledge in the realization of its
departure from dualistic thought is a commitment to the
source of our knowledge in experience; only in looking
to that source can we rigorously examine the understandings that we of necessity bring from within our biographies to any meaning of social life.

For within the understanding of the phenomenon we
encounter, particularly the unexpected that we encounter,
our bond is first and primarily a biographically based
knowledge. It is through the presence of the other that
we become aware of the other's experience and, further,
the other's understanding of experience as it will bear
upon and transform our own. For in naming our research
interpretive inquiry we pursue the understanding of
what is personal and what is social by an uncovering and
recovering of the other's understanding of experience.
But interpretive inquiry which is existential also begins
with the premise that we cannot share (hold in common)
the same experience. We cannot enter the subjectivity
of others; nor can they know our consciousness in its
interiority. Thus the mental construction of an experiment in imagination is ruled out. What can be shared
are the moments of experiencing. But the sharing of
these moments are not in the experience, but in our
existence. Thus the necessity of existentialism for
phenomenology in interpretive inquiry--for no other
interpretive phenomenology requires that we move to the
ontological domain of existence for understanding.

Though the temporal and essential source for understanding another's experience (that is, our ontological
domain of existence) must be within our own biography,
we must clarify that the reference to the "biography" of
the researcher is not to the researcher's "autobiography."
That is, it is not in the ordinary and unordinary personal and professional life of the researcher that the

16

experience of the other is understood. Rather it is in the researcher's biography as a cultural memory (cultural memory as the selection and signification of the structures of experience) that understanding as the meaning of another's experience (even where the other is the researcher herself or himself as a past "other") is made possible. For understanding, biography within interpretive inquiry refers to a cultural returning to what we hold with others as part of the collective form that we share with others. But this very cultural returning in understanding the experience of the other, which provides what we must have as a point of departure for understanding, is also what we must move beyond for knowledge itself. For in acquiring knowledge, we seek to recover how we know what we understand. The task of interpretive inquiry is thus a stepping <u>beyond</u> cultural memory, the very memory which provided an understanding of the phenomenon being studied, in order to bring that understanding forward as knowledge.

Therefore, we realize that we do not stop at "showing" and "understanding" within interpretive inquiry. A showing and understanding of the subjective dimension of the social world in the experience of others is insufficient. It is to the knowing, to the objectivation of that knowing as a knowledge of a cultural memory, that the inquiry is directed. It is by recovering and making explicit the sources of our knowledge in our biographies and through discourse with others that the tacit biographical nature of our bond to the lives and to the histories of others and to the memories of ourselves may be put forward, recognizable as knowledge.

The Knowledge of Interpretive Inquiry

However, because the knowledge of interpretive inquiry is <u>a work to produce meaning</u> and <u>not</u> a process of "recognition" dependent on a conscious intentionality, the knowledge that we seek in reflective thought continually runs the risk of being misunderstood as a personal, self-indulgent knowledge. Given the prevailing thought of modern society--with its centering on objectified inquiry as a removal of the biographical, as a transpersonal establishing of what is real in the world by removing the personal sources of inquiry--the knowledge of interpretive inquiry may be mislabeled as simply a personal understanding, an opinion or judgment of only a self. And it is possible that, in first turning to the articulation of reflective thought, an

17

attachment to subjective certainty will mask what the
phenomenon shows. The discourse may seem, at first,
to concentrate too closely upon the place of the researcher, or the first attempts at this inquiry may
appear to be simply replacing the experiences of the
other with one's own experiences. Often the confusion
of this knowledge with subjectivizing is found when
there is a continued commitment to the dualism of technical thought and to a correspondence theory of knowledge (a correspondence between the theories of science
and the reality of an "objective" world). In actuality,
however, as the inquiry proceeds the knowledge becomes
"subjectless," because the de-creating processes of
the inquiry ensure continual <u>reunion</u> with the "other"
and <u>with</u> the next <u>being</u> of the researcher.

In the knowledge that we seek within interpretive
inquiry, our attempt is to account to others fully and
rigorously for the place of biography in our bond to
the social phenomena we study. Yet that bond is established in the traditions which make our biographies
possible. For knowledge itself, we recognize, is not
simply the truth value of statements offered as knowledge. Knowledge is always a social knowledge established within a culture, a social knowledge in relation to another culture; or in knowledge's transformation of a culture. Although we will not detail it
here (because it is described in other parts of this
book), the knowledge of reflective discourse involves
a number of different voices for its articulation.
Among them are narrative voices, analytic voices, and
voices of synthesis. Briefly, a narrative voice is a
voice bearing witness to an occasion as a narrating of
one's own experience in that occasion. An analytic
voice is that of a witness to the witnessing--as a
telling of how one comes to narrate the experience in
the way that one does. A voice of synthesis is one
which gives coherence and integrity to the de-creating
which is consequent upon the dialectic of the other
voices--its center is at the making of a world.

The studies we have conducted and those of others
in which we have participated are ones which offer as
knowledge dimensions of lives and of biographies in
relation to what was formerly known and to what has
been promised by some theories in the social sciences,
in education, and in the humanities. The studies of
interpretive inquiries are, as with other theoretical
perspectives, a reference to established traditions of

knowledge, or in some cases a revealing of traditions immanent in themselves. They are all established in tradition in the history of knowledge itself, whether that history is disclosed as a cognate discipline or whether that history is established in other quarters such as myth, poetics, or language itself.

The relationship between the knowledge of a study in interpretive inquiry and traditions of knowledge in the movement of histories shows the significance of what is offered and the importance of the inquiry as a moral endeavor. For, rather than the limitations of dualistic thought, rather than the significance of knowledge in terms of its relevance to the solution of "social problems" (we add quotation marks to indicate the questionable character of consensus around the naming of problems), rather than the conception of knowledge as a remedial attempt to deal with people and their lives, we envision the significance of knowledge in the moral judgment and choice expressed in the showing and understanding, and especially in the establishing of the tradition of the knowledge behind and beyond the phenomenon being studied. And this showing and understanding is not accomplished through an inquiry which is declarative and imperative about its knowledge but through an interrogative reflection which draws attention to itself and invites answers to what it poses.

The significance of a study in interpretive inquiry is revealed in the way that study discloses and responds to the limits of the researcher's knowledge. The significance of an interpretive study is found in the way that study speaks to and reshapes the knowledge to which it is related. The significance of interpretive inquiry is in the way it may show its own presence in the transformation of knowledge, as a knowledge of shared existence with the lives of others. Thus the purpose of this inquiry becomes the transformation of consciousness for both those who are studied and the researchers who conduct the studies. This purpose points to fundamental changes in society at the level of people's understandings of their own experiences and changes in their existence in society as their existence is found in their lived world of experience. But it also points for us as researchers to a de-institutionalization of the structure of research.

What we have been attempting to describe up to now

is what we see lying at the center of research. This
center must be seen not as a reformulation of existing
approaches in the human sciences, not even of phenomenology itself, but as an attention to the recomposing of
research with a new center which is in contrast with
what previously we have taken to be inquiry. Institu-
tionalized research takes as its focus the study of
others as separated from the researcher by the practices of inquiry (practices of inquiry as "methodology").
Methodology, whether it be in the positivistic social
sciences or the phenomenological human sciences, is seen
to be what is professionally at play for the researcher
but not for the other who is the focus of study. That
is, as they are presently institutionally constrained,
we find the worlds of the researchers and worlds of the
persons studied to be separated by different interests,
different significances, different forms of reason.
What we are speaking for is a coming to another way of
research in which the research is organized around the
intertwining of dialectics between the researcher and
the persons studied. This intertwining would ensure a
mutual understanding of the inquiry itself as it proceeds (not merely a mutual consensus of what the inquiry
is "about"). And this intertwining must also be brought
to the occasion of the writing of the research--for
there is always the potential of alienation between
writer and reader.

The placing of the researcher within inquiry as we
have attempted to describe it contributes to ensuring
that the inquiry will not be destroyed by its very means--
the observing, the interpreting, the conceptualizing,
the synthesizing. The placing of the researcher within
inquiry also means that intentionality no longer holds
its central place in making sense of others. That is,
we will no longer "find" meaning by making recourse to
what persons think, to what is in their minds, to what is
interior to their consciousness. Rather, meaning will be
formed through the dialectics within and between us which
will shape us both--we the researchers and the "others."
Furthermore, the placing of the researcher within inquiry
means that moral conduct in the inquiry (what is ethical
in human studies research) has its source in the commitments of researchers to the knowledge of themselves.[11]

---

11 We thank Claus Wittmaack for his discussion
with us about the moral basis of interpretive inquiry.

The accounting for our knowledge of ourselves moves the ethics of this inquiry from the ethics of the realism and decisionism of recent history to an ethics of character, an ethics principally concerned with the self in its community.[12] And because our "knowledge" as researchers is inscribed in our discourse, it is the sustained attention to our tellings "about" others which will reveal and conceal our moral identities and so demonstrate how we, the researchers, are in relation to others we study.

The knowledge of this inquiry refers to the transforming of the very cultures within which we stand and for which we are responsible to speak.

---

12   For a wide discussion of character ethics we note James Wm. McClendon Jr.'s <u>Biography as Theology</u> (Nashville: Abingdon, 1974).

PART II

DIALOGUE ON THE CONDUCT OF INQUIRY

In the several hours of the colloquium presented here, colleagues and graduate students (about 85 persons) from departments which represent graduate studies in different cognate fields of the social sciences, as well as different foci of interest within education, attempted to outline the circumstances we all faced in undertaking interpretive inquiry. We directed the discussion of research particularly towards dissertation projects. We did this because it was our experience that the dissertation project, as an objectification of what is both necessary and possible in the social sciences and what is expected in the field of education, demands articulation in a language and through a dialogue which makes available to others how interpretive inquiry is a way of research. Discussion of interpretive research as dissertation project also requires articulating in a way which may allow others to move beyond their original way of basically understanding how research can and should be conducted.

Thus, we had all sought the colloquium as a natural setting to meet the questions and criticisms of fellow researchers whose commitments to theories and methodologies are different from each other's and from our own and who would address the descriptions and analyses we all might offer with a high sense of the differences they may hold. For many of us, too, the colloquium represented a critical search for a centering upon what is basic among us. We also found that a colloquium is the place in which we are called upon by students to provide those critical elements of explaining in fine detail what is entailed in interpretive inquiry. For students, in the clarity of their innocence, require us to show (not merely announce) what we know and how we search within research. And even more, in the context of apprenticeship, the doctoral student demands that the expression of the life of research, here interpretive research, be experientially grounded in the mundane of that with which the researcher must contend.

The colloquium, therefore, provided for a form of discourse, for an understanding of the knowledge of interpretive inquiry to come forth and show itself. This showing emerged through the attention given it: by practicing colleagues who hold to other paradigms and who wished to encounter the contentions and knowledge of the interpretive form, and by students who wished to encounter its possibilities.

We see the colloquium as a way not only of showing what interpretive inquiry is but of articulating for ourselves and for others the features and shape of this form of inquiry. The colloquium provides for searching and analysis in the presence of others, the others being those who previously have not undertaken interpretive research.

The colloquium, however, within the domain of interpretive analysis, is a mutual undertaking by interpretive practitioners and by those contending with such practitioners. The resulting transcript, then, can be read as an engagement of those with separate paradigmatic commitments in the mutual undertaking of an analysis of interpretive inquiry. That is, it is not information about a method that is contained in the transcript but a record of a search by different parties and for different motives. It is thus representative of different parties in dialogue where difference amongst them becomes the basis and life of their engagement, dispute, contention, and, most important, questioning. But the questioning is not only in individual queries, separate in the finite nature of their own respective commitments. The questioning is, as well, a mutual quest for knowledge.

And yet the concern here remains not only what the transcript may show but, indeed, how it may show what may be shown to a reader. We must try to provide for the opportunity of seeing the biographies of those present in that colloquium in the manner of their dis-course and what that discourse disclosed.

Thus, the questions that we asked ourselves are how may the transcript be read as a record of a dialogue about the practice of interpretive inquiry and how also is it to be for the reader more than a record? The task, as we see it, is this: How may the transcript be read so as to yield a meaning of interpretive inquiry beyond the occasion of the colloquium held on that day and with that group of people, and how may it become for the reader, within the engagement of reading, a "yiel-ding" of the meaning of this form of inquiry?

We feel that the engagement for the reader requires

from ourselves, as the editors of and participants in the colloquium, a disclosure which foundationally provides the starting points that we ourselves find to begin our research and descriptions of our work. We realize that for the transcript to engage the reader so that the reader can engage the transcript--that is, for the transcript to show itself in a way that it can be understood from its own life of experience and realm of reality with an acknowledgment of lives of experience and realms of reality different from its own--we must first begin to show the intimate sources of what we mean by research. We must show what we believe to be studiable, what we are committed to discover and analyze, what we are morally drawn to examine, and what we find necessary in the forms of expression by which interpretive research may be presented. We must first disclose (we profess that it is an intimate disclosure of theorizing) the foundations that we find in our turning and re-turning in our reflection of interpretive inquiry.

We have already said the colloquium which this transcript represents was dependent on how colleagues and students faced together the undertaking of understanding what interpretive inquiry is.

The transcript shows the dialogue as concrete. That is, the talk of the participants was always from a source of previous obstacles faced or obstacles anticipated (mundane issues which challenge any sustained work). The transcript also shows that it is out of such concreteness that there is a straining to reach beyond one's previous capacity to discuss research, to go to the issues of research independent of the proposal for a new form of thesis. The difficulty for every participant, including ourselves, was how to express previous disappointments and how to find words which would permit the grasping of what was being proposed by others. The search for the words was not an attempt for an eloquence either in a sophisticated knowing or in a primordial knowing. Rather, the search for the words was in the experience of entering into a communicative knowing of what may be asked and what may be encountered.

The search for those words will be recognized in the pages of the transcript in the halting character of the speech. But the character of that speech represents a search for a form of research, for a life of inquiry

itself and one's own place within it. It is from respect for this search that we have preserved the form
of participants' comments and the phrasings of their
speech. We have introduced minimal editorial comments,
shown in italic type.

In the course of transcribing the audiotape of the
colloquium, we found that we could not identify all of
the student participants by name. Thus, only Mark Egit
and Milada Disman appear under their own names. To
others we assigned fictitious names (Finkelstein, Korman, Patterson, Santos, Stoykoff, Traford, Train, Rouel)
so that the questions and comments of individuals can
be traced.

The faculty participants the reader will meet below
are members of the Ontario Institute for Studies in
Education and the Faculty of Graduate Studies, University of Toronto: William E. Alexander, Lynn E. Davie,
Edmund V. Sullivan, John C. Weiser, (and ourselves).
William (Bill) Barnard, a faculty member at that time,
now is engaged in private counseling and organizational
consulting in Toronto.

The Morning Session

VIVIAN DARROCH: Good morning. It's a surprise and a
pleasure to see so many of you here. We were uncertain
how many to expect. So welcome. I will say only a few
words which could orient how we might begin the day.
In a sense the meeting is very open and will depend on
your responses to the issues we will attempt to stimulate. I suspect that there will be a lot of issues
surrounding dissertation work that will be touched
upon, and, as best as I can, I will try and guide us
through them.

There were several staff and students who, for
quite a while, have talked about having an interdepart-
mental seminar such as this. The remarks that follow
represent the ideas of some. They don't represent a
consensus of what this topic is about, but I thought I
would say this in order to give you some kind of focus
so that you might better understand what objectives we
might accomplish here today.

In trying to make clear what we are here to do
today, it seems easiest to begin with what we are here
not to do--in other words, what we are here not to

26

represent. In terms of trying to find a specific name for this kind of meeting, it was difficult because, in terms of the way people go about expressing their interests, it appears a very unusual gathering. In terms of the calls we received after we first sent out the notice, some of you inferred by what we said that what we intended was that we would discuss qualitative rather than quantitative research. And while qualitative procedures may frequently be an issue, as a feature of the kind of work that we'll talk about today, it's not fundamentally what is at issue. As well, we are not here to discuss phenomenology theoretically or preceptively as opposed to another school of thought, and that we are not here solely to make a case that the kind of work that we might do might be a more humanistic research than another kind of science or another kind of work. To limit our talk here today to qualitative studies, to theoretical phenomenology, and to what may be more humanistic or not, and similar issues would take us off the track. That's not what we're to do today. There are a lot of people who see themselves as doing "qualitative work," or "phenomenological approaches," or things that they consider to be "very humanistic," which yet, in terms of the practices and commitments, that inform their investigations, keep them outside of the things that are concerning us here today. What concerns us here today is, and I'm saying this very broadly, the place of the researcher within the analysis. These are kind of the words I picked to characterize the work and to get us going. I'll say that again--the place of the researcher within the analysis. And, I can say now that the purpose of this meeting is to kind of explore and elaborate what this, as an issue, is, what it means in a practical sense, i.e., how it is made "real," and what this issue implies for dissertations. Just before I continue, I will elaborate a small bit right now about what this means because I can see one or two of you responding to this already with puzzlement.

Often, especially within psychology, which is my discipline, the researcher's place is considered "within methods." In psychology, anyway, this would be discussed in that whole literature about experimenter bias, which attests to the idea of recognizing the researcher's influence on and within his methods. The place of the researcher within analysis, however, is a different kind of consideration than the place of the researcher within method. I'm going to just talk

around that a bit more. For one example, in the
Institute, there is a Children's Culture Project--you
may have heard of it. These investigators study children's culture from the point of view of the conceptions
of adults. That is, their own analytic practices as
adults which are shared with or independent of the
children are what are brought to bear on the results
of their investigations; this, compared to that they
may have sought to discover only something about
"children." Alfred Schutz, for example, has written
about how all social sciences have to contend with two
levels of concepts--scientific concepts and everyday
concepts. Persons who write about this make the point
of the necessity of becoming knowledgeable of the everyday concepts that we carry around with us even in our
scientific work, for it is the two sets of interactions
which eventually come to bear on the endings of our
research. Another example of this would be, in the
Institute there's one person who's doing a dissertation
about patients with rheumatoid arthritis. This woman
is going into the research with, among other things,
her everyday concepts, which are: "we think of people
with disease--having a disease--we think of people
being diseased people"--two different everyday concepts--
and her research will inform and relate to these everyday concepts and then they, in turn, will inform and
relate to her research. There is a lot of emphasis--
the whole emphasis is that the construction of understandings is entirely dependent on the beliefs,the
current implicit understandings held by us and so on.
In one sense you may hear these examples as a variant
of the "location" of the reserachers being a limit to
their research. But I intend the examples to go beyond
that. I want them to begin to show that it is the knowledge itself which is under examination, an examination
which places the researchers' conceptions under the same
careful scrutiny as those of the people they study.

So, this is the principle to be seen as work that
is done within this approach of considering the researcher "within the analysis." And it is a principle which
throws open questions of "What is real?" "What is
truth?" Now, some of you might see what I'm giving as
being a preoccupation with individualism or some kind of
extravagance of subjective reflection. This is often
what my students are saying to me. But my point would
be, and I think this point will become clearer through
the day, that the analyses and syntheses which would

proceed in these examples that I have given is pressed
forward in a way that makes the researcher's private
world of thought into an issue brought forward to and
addressed in the research enterprise. So it transforms
a private world into a shared and public one. Of
course it is subjective reflection--but subjective
within the communities within which we live and are
responsible. The important thing then is to deal with
such reflection analytically, press it forward and
make the "private" world available to others for their
sharing. Of course it is subjective reflection; but it
is not subjective reflection as in introspection. It
is subjective reflection as a procedure of comprehending,
where totality--totality within person and community, a
synthesis of particulars -- is the major concern. So,
reflective thought, which simply is thought that bends
back to turn upon itself, is self-reflection to recover
and make articulate the embodied knowledge which we hold
as it is informing our conceptualizations of understandings about experience. It is that articulation
which expresses our thought to others and presents it
for dialogue, not as an authoritative thesis.

Interestingly, one of the things that distingui-
shes this kind of work--you will be aware of this especially if the students will talk about their work today--
is that the communicating of the research or the communicating of the analysis is not what we typically see in
the social sciences; it's not a "reporting" of the
analysis. Instead, the communicating of the analysis
is not treated as a separate activity from the analysis
itself. We'll particularly be paying attention to that
this afternoon. For this reason, many who have undertaken this kind of work turn to "language" itself. So
even some in communicating in this work may introduce
what in social sciences or education is the unfamiliar
mode of expression (e.g., "lyric" prose, non-sequential
discourse) but in doing so introduce it for analytical
purposes.

I think that I'm going to stop here. (I just have
a few more sentences. I want to look at my notes here--
I don't want to leave anything out.) I want to say
this, in closing, particularly for those of you here
who may be uncertain in any way about this kind of
work, and I'm going to say this to guide our discussion,
at least in the beginning. When we're discussing what
we do here today, I don't think we should see it as a
discussion of an alternative way of doing something, of

theorizing or researching. I don't think we should discuss it as an alternative methodology and certainly not as a radical way of doing research in the social sciences. I think all we're here today to do is to discuss a particular form of inquiry--that form of inquiry being one which is dependent on admitting the researcher into the analysis. As such, it is a form of inquiry, a way of scientific thinking, justification of which lies in its doing. And I think that's what a lot of the students will be addressing. Because its way of justification lies in its doing, it's not a methodology. It is not an "alternative" methodology. It is not something to be picked up and done unless one's own thoughts are already turning that way--and we have made the assumption that if you're in this room, your own thoughts are already turning that way, so that you'd be in that position. And simply because of the similarities of difficulties in doing this work, diffi- culties which some of us feel should be talked about, we thought we would call this meeting. And, as the chair, I will encourage these issues and the topics upon which the issues will turn, to be addressed analytically throughout the day.

Now, just before we get into the program, do you have any comments, or do you want to ask any questions before we go on? Essentially, this morning we will talk about this approach in general and the pursuit of topic, and this afternoon attend more to data analyses and communication of such work to others.

FINKELSTEIN: Could you give some examples of the kind of research going on in OISE at the present time where the researchers are placing themselves clearly in the analysis? I'm trying to visualize what that means and sort of carry it out as an example in terms of the medical model that is being applied in analyzing the case of the arthritic patient.

DARROCH: OK, I could address that briefly. The student whose research the question references--she, by the way, is a former nurse, which, in part, informs us as to the ground or source of her everyday concepts--she has the idea that alternately she sees arthritic patients as persons with a disease and, as an alternate possible construction, persons that are diseased persons. So, in her interviews with rheumatoid arthritic people, she is responding and listening to them from already understanding what she is bringing in terms of her history of being a former nurse. Now, she is not introducing to the patients ideas, she is really collecting their ideas completely free. After an introduction, she literally says nothing in the interview. But what happens then is, in terms of doing the analysis, it doesn't just become her interpretation of what they said from distance "way out here," but it becomes (and Bill Barnard is going to use this word in a few minutes) a dialogue between herself and the phenomena. So the dialogue, the exchange, the understanding for her, comes from looking at a bit of the material, transforming the concepts with the transformation returning to the material, the materials changing, and her always taking the responsibility for her presence there in terms of all that she knows (and doesn't know) she entered with. The key would be: you could be a former nurse, even come with the same concepts; but because of your place, your context, your understanding, the analysis would be different. So, it's not as if two former nurses with the same everyday concepts would produce the same analysis. Yet the different analyses would yield an arrangement of significances because organization emerges from emphasizing data, which here is what patients said, and what she the researcher, "responds" to what is said, and ideally a totality will emerge from such analyses.

FINKELSTEIN: Yes, it's articulating that framework before you go in?

DARROCH: I'm going to add one very important thing to that. You said "articulating the framework before you go in." That would be the mere beginning. The thing would be to be constantly "re-articulating" and take responsibility throughout the whole process for the decisions you make about changing the perspective with which you entered. So add that, because that would really be the most exacting part. And in a 'sense, often in other kinds of work, you acknowledge your framework only before you go in, but here the task is really to take it all with you to that occasion intact; to keep it with you, and to account for it continually-- even as it changes--as a source of understandings and changes in understandings.

What is present here between the questioner, who asks about "articulating the framework before going in," and Darroch's answer describing the analytic courses of interest throughout the study are two con-

*ceptions of research, two modes of approaching inquiry,
two forms of organizing study.*

*In the more traditional research in which we've
been trained and to which we are accustomed, the
questioner suggests a conception of design or preparation to do research in a process of projecting what is
known and what is asked about the phenomenon within the
present as a preparation for organizing the research in
the future. Here, an early, initial design of study
prepares and shapes the inquiry. Here, a theoretic
world is conceived within the organization of study and
projected into the future, as to what the phenomenon is
and as to what our practices of inquiry must be.*

*The tradition expressed in the other thesis, the
"other thesis" being the kind of research in which we
are interested today, is immediate and retrospective
with regard to the organization of study. Here the
researcher recognizes the encounter with the phenomenon
as organizationally basic, but not organizationally
prescribed. The researcher analyzes and articulates
that organization and eventually collects that organization into a totality that only then shows the design
of inquiry.*

Any other comments or questions? OK, maybe, then,
we should continue. The first topic will continue
possibly for about an hour or so.

We'll take about an hour, a little more, for the
idea of heuristic design. Bill Barnard has agreed to
sit up here with me and be the focus for this. None of
us has formal presentations--we just simply want to
provide a few words to get the discussion going.

BARNARD: Yesterday I didn't have any voice at all, kind
of a crackling voice (Barnard is referring to a sore
throat) and today it's coming back a little bit. But
I offered to share some of my thoughts and constructs
and images about heuristic research in the hope that
they will stimulate or evoke some responses in you. As
we go along, stop me, respond, steer me.

Those who have been in classes with me have heard
about "dialogue," as Vivian mentioned, so maybe I should
lay out my version of what I think it is and then we can
proceed from there. I draw the notion from Martin Buber,
whose work has had a major impact on me in the way I go
about teaching and learning--and living. Buber has

32

distinguished between two kinds of relationships--two
qualities of interaction, one being what he called
I/It, the subject/object kind of relationship which one
can have to anything in the world, including persons,
but generally just to "otherness." It's a stance toward the world. The I/Thou interaction of relationship
is one in which there is a direct and spontaneous and
mutual kind of relationship between yourself and otherness, i.e., the "thing" or "event" or "situation" which
stands over and against you. He paints the picture
that these are two life attitudes or life stances which
can be one or the other at any given point in time. He
places a premium on the subject-to-subject I/Thou
relationship in the sense that he sees that as the area
of creativity. It's the area in which one receives from
the other new categories, new frames, new positions; one
receives "otherness" when one is in that mode. In the
I/It mode, one categorizes, analyzes, and orients with
regard to the world as in science. No dialogue is
complete in Buber's sense, however, until one has
responded to this otherness. It completes the circle
or the dialectic to first of all expose yourself
directly in meeting to this otherness and then,
secondly, to place that otherness somehow in your
stock of knowledge or your stock of images to orient
yourself towards the world. But the constant cycling
in and out of these two modes, as Buber paints it, that
is, constitutes a mode of human existence. Buber's
fear--Buber called it a "crisis of humanity"--is that
most of us never achieve this I/Thou mode; rather we
tend to be fixed in the subject/object mode of meeting
other people, meeting our world in a way which categorizes it, and hence ourselves, as merely other. We
constantly thus experience our own identities, not as
the "question" that the other in the I/Thou mode implicitly faced us with, but rather as an element or a
feature of a process (I/It) that Buber sees as a life
that is dehumanizing. With that kind of a background
(there are a lot of implications in it), that five-
second introduction to it leads me to say that if one
is committed to being able to at least be responsive,
to be in dialogue with others--not just humans, but
sunsets and other kinds of things in the world--if one
is committed to being able to reach out, to connect,
to meet, in this notion of Buber's dialogue, it has
drastic implications for teaching and learning, for
living in general, for quality of relationship of all
kinds.

Given that kind of frame, one who approaches a research task can do it as Clark Moustakas did it, by representing from his own life experiences. Clark Moustakas, a psychotherapist at Merrill Palmer Institute in Detroit, has written about a phenomenon that he experienced and which he has labeled "loneliness." His response to that phenomenon was to record and to describe as well as he could afterwards what that life experience was like for him, and he published it. I'm sure that he must have had responses to the effect that this was not good, hard, serious research; it was not a number of things; but in fact it was a contribution for what it was like for one man to experience the phenomenon of loneliness. Others have responded in a variety of ways, but I borrowed the term "heuristic research" for my purposes from Moustakas's work. He described in his own processes the value of each of us describing for others, expressing for others, or bearing witness to the meaning of certain kinds of experiences that we have had. An illustration that I may borrow from Maurice Merleau-Ponty is the notion of the football player who is able to come off the playing field after the game and talk about what it's like to experience the smells of football, the feeling, the touching, all the direct inputs to the senses of "what it is like to play football"--the visual patterns of lines going by as he runs down the field, bodies looming up in front and tackling, and so on. That's a kind of knowing, a way of knowing, which is not available to the person in the stands. The person who sits in the stands can keep statistics on the game, can know that there were 37 percent fewer passes this game than last, and so on. The two modes of knowing are complementary to each other, but there is an input that the football player can make from direct experience which the person cannot make from the stands. And I use that story as an illustration of one who is meeting the situation, who is involved fully in the situation and who can report faithfully on those findings in a systematic way, in a rigorous way, following the direct life experience. It places a premium on life experience which is pre-reflective; it's the life experience before one reflects upon it to assign meaning. If we were to use William James's description of the stream of experience, it would be a kind of focusing on one particular episode of experience out of that stream and assigning some meaning, comparing that meaning to other people's meaning, talking about it, reporting it. Moustakas, for example, in his series of publications on the phenomenon of loneliness, received something like 10,000 responses to his books, which, as a good publisher, he also ploughed into later books and fed the series of books in its process; but he developed, in effect, a dialogue of sorts where people would say, "Well, the phenomenon you've described is very close to what I experienced in 1944 when such-and-such happened. And I experienced something else in 1957 which had the following variations." Moustakas's understanding of the phenomenon is also expanded through his interaction with others. So it's a knowledge building of sorts, but it's a knowledge building through direct meeting.

PATTERSON: It's not quite clear to me from your description what it means to understand; and secondly, why the concern about it?

BARNARD: Why the concern about understanding? Well, let me draw on Buber's concern first of all. Buber painted the picture that this notion of "meeting otherness" is the basis for what he calls "being human." In his philosophical anthropology, he paints it as the "moment of truth"; this moment of meeting is the only moment in his frame in which one experiences reality, and that's characterized by great sincerity, great trust, great openness. It's a direct exposure and encounter with otherness or reality. There is for Buber a religious "overlay" that goes with it, that it's the moment of meeting the infinite and it's a moment of meeting God. Others have come at it from the point of view of atheism or existentialism such as Camus and Merleau-Ponty. Both advocate similarly to Buber, but for other reasons, this meeting of otherness in a similar fashion. Maurice Friedman speaks of a "community of otherness."

It's this notion that truth is found at that intersection where man confronts "otherness" that gives rise to the importance of doing it, in that it's the only way that you have available to you as a human being to meet reality, to be grounded, to be in touch. From a philosophical position this would be Buber's ontology where he sees the "really real," if you want to put it in that way. Your present image is modified by the new messages coming in and so your images and concepts are constantly being modified; your understandings are being modified as you go along. But the whole worry that he had, as a lifelong preoccupation, was the decline of that process of understanding--de-humanizing of society, in that people were closed to each other, not able to receive from each other in that we tend to meet others within a closed frame. And traditional science for the most part is in a similar kind of closed process. We set our frame and our hypothesis, and then we encounter the other in terms of that. We aren't able to receive from the other what is truly there. We aren't able to expand our categories in the traditional scientific approach, we aren't open to the breaking and the shattering of some of our frames, our world views. Buber has painted it as a being able to risk, being able to allow, to expose your frame or your world view to another and allow it to be confirmed or disconfirmed or partially confirmed in the process. It is an openness to being transformed in the interaction. I think the characteristic of a heuristic design would be that it is one in which the researcher changes over time. The research has some given understandings, some going-in assumptions, which may or may not be modified during the process.

Barnard suggests heuristic research as a way of collecting the features of an experience, say of "loneliness." That collecting can then be used to compare the features of that experience for some to the experience of others.

This is a critical part of the analysis. It allows the researcher to more securely identify and locate in the phenomenon that to which he is uniquely responding. But we would suggest that in addition to the collecting of concrete features one also gathers together into a concept that which would show what stands behind the collected features which were first encountered. What we discover to lie behind is what provides for the particular concrete features that appear to us as that with which we resonate in social life. Thus, Barnard shows us where to start with the experience and how to locate the concrete of that experience. But in response to his pointing to the possibilities for transforming understandings through the research we are suggesting, an articulation of the conceptualization of what lies behind the collected concrete features is also required. For a phenomenon will only become intelligible when addressed through attempts at "totalization" (as a synthesis of particulars) which include the concepts behind where attention goes.

ROUEL: I wonder if you could tell me where Moustakas's approach was different, say, from Norman Mailer's journalism. Where does the rigor come in? Is there a difference?

BARNARD: I can't describe Norman Mailer's journalism.

ROUEL: Well, he seems to take a very personal approach to everything . . . he puts himself in the picture . . . he describes things from his point of view.

BARNARD: I think journalism as an approach certainly has some elements of similarity here. This becomes an interhuman interaction and not an inter-role interaction. It's an interaction in which there is a person risking his present understandings, his present world view in the interaction. He's exposing that world view to the responses of others, and if the process is complete, he is able to receive what those responses are from others. It's an absence of hiding, an absence of pretending, the dropping of those sorts of defenses, in effect. It's a kind of communion. Karl Jaspers writes about it as existential communication, or communication where the pretenses are all dropped and there is a direct exposure of one's present awareness or consciousness to that of the other, which is not what I perceive the human potential movement to have been up until now. I think it's not a case of "let-it-all-hang-out" sort of thing. It's a case of what is in fact said and selected to be said, is in fact a representation of your presence . . . your present understandings . . . your present world views. So, it would be characterized by a faithfulness. The rigor would be defined by the faithfulness of the person to be fully present and to select out what responses are germane to the unique interaction.

Here Barnard is addressing the source of what is necessary for what we have referred to above as attempting to study a phenomenon in its totalization.

In referring to existential communication with respect to what we might say or not about any topic which we are addressing, Barnard reminds us of the importance of coming to terms with the thematic commitments of our knowledge, commitments which represent us through our spoken and written words.

DARROCH: I want to add something here in slightly

different words, also too because I'm especially fond
of Norman Mailer's journalism. I think in the kind of
work we are considering here, which may at times appear
like oral history or journalism, the thing that has to
be present, if it is present as "personal," is that we
have to go beyond the mere description at which a lot
of journalists and oral historians just stop. Otherwise,
the analysis, if it is present, is present only in terms
of cultural expectations and cultural consensus. I
think the analysis has to be present from a personal
source within the speaker, the writer himself or herself. The analysis has to be there. It just can't
stop at some kind of reporting in the sense of description. It must also show what has been discovered
and how that "what" has been uncovered analytically by
the writer. Because this is important, let me try and
say it in other words too. By suddenly placing a premium on the personal, the question from the floor is,
"In what sense is our personal as person invoked?" It
is not invoked in a journalistic sense of our opinion,
our view, our particularistic judgment, our choice.
Rather, "personal" must be used with the emphases
analytically and synthetically on the personal understanding which is subjected to analysis (and synthesis)
and the personal commitment that we discover.

TRAIN: There has been a spate of oral histories that
have appeared on the market recently on Cuba, on the
Civil Rights Movement, etc. Could I make the distinction that that would not be considered to be heuristic
research despite the fact that a lot of it has been
done on tape because of the fact that there is no
evidence of there having been any change in the person
who has compiled the oral history between the beginning
of the book and the end of the book? Or would an oral
history in fact, in the compilation, become "heuristic
research"?

BARNARD: I don't think the mode, just because it's
oral, just because it's reported in that kind of a format, is what would automatically make it heuristic. Or,
if I can use that word "dialogical," since I'm using
Buber's constructs here. I think one can come at this
using other constructs; that just happens to be the one
that I'm drawing upon, the one that makes most sense to
me, and I'm just sharing it from that perspective. For
dialogue to be occurring, and if one is reporting some
beliefs and opinions as a result of a dialogical interaction or a study, it seems to me that the receiver of

that has to and can only try to make some judgments about the sincerity, the faithfulness to the data. There is a great difficulty from the outside of judging that inter-action, and I think for dissertation purposes it becomes very difficult.

DARROCH: Bill, given your comments about the researcher interacting with the data, let me add that I believe that heurism exists only when that interaction does indeed provide the possibility for the researcher to change his interpretation. And the responsibility for the researc-her is to show these changes to the other and to account for them through expressions which are increasingly translucent.

SANTOS: I would like to try to put the two statements that I've heard together, if possible. Vivian, you said, "constantly articulate framework before you go in and re-articulate it throughout your thesis." If we are constantly re-articulating our framework, and our frame-work at the beginning is different to a degree than the framework we are formulating as we proceed, where is this going to take us in terms of the evaluation of the thesis by others? I can see it making sense for those who use a phenomenological design, but where does it fit for those who aren't in phenomenology?

BARNARD: Well, there's an internal consistency that can be examined. Lots of the traditional criteria still apply. Clarity, internal consistency, a lot of the standard approaches to dissertations are still in place. But there is another dimension here--"faithful-ness" is the word that keeps popping up in my mind. How carefully is the person immersing his/her self in the data, working with the data to derive meanings, patterns, trends, issues, and reporting both what's happening inside, how that's coming together, what's emerging as well as the raw data as described? This is what I've found and this is the sense I make of it. There is a book that John O'Neil has produced over at York University that I happen to like a great deal, called Making Sense Together.

DARROCH: I would like to add that regarding the place of the researcher in analysis, the subjective respon-sibility in this way is independent of whether some-thing is phenomenological or not. Roger Pool talks of the subjective method, so to speak, as being a thinking

39

sui generis. I think he talks about concepts not being found but rather being surely formulated through consistent use of indirect communications. He suggests that phenomenology might be the nearest theoretical relation this kind of thought has yet in terms of the issue of responsibility. However, one could conceive that methodologies emerging from other orientations might also take up a responsibility for the researcher being in analysis in the way we are addressing it here.

SILVERS: I would think that the question would address any mode of analysis in social sciences. I wouldn't want to see it restricted to what has been mentioned as phenomenology. In fact, perhaps we could open it up and talk about what could be a "good science" or the most proper way of approaching science, so that we wouldn't see what we would be discussing here as somehow just an oddity, a specialty, something that just a few people do. And the reason for that is that in a sense all of us here are in the midst of a community of scientists. We might divide ourselves up by discipline, but nevertheless that is the community that we share. In so doing, when I would want to offer something to fellow members of my community, I would want them to be able to see what it is that I've found, what it is that I've concluded, and what it is that I did in order to come to the conclusions from what I started with. I would have to show them step by step; I would have to be as scrupulous as possible to report to them exactly how I moved in a step-by-step procedure from whatever materials I accumulated, e.g., data. And I would have to show in my very practices of analysis, in my modes of explanation, in my conceptualization, how I came to whatever statements, claims, principles, or generalizations I would then have to offer. In order to do that, I would have to show that movement. I think one of the difficulties we would have in any community, and it wouldn't just be in a scientific community, is that there are already ready-made conventions that are there for us; and for us those ready-made conventions are called methods. These are things that people have already accepted, agreed upon, are willing to use and reproduce for their purposes. But we also find within our work that we come upon procedures we cannot classify that way; in a sense (and I'm not being bashful about it, nor presumptious) we have created procedures that are not conventional. It then seems to me that we have to offer those,

that we have to be exceptionally careful in reporting
those, so that our fellow members of the community,
whoever they may be, can see how it is that we came
to those conclusions, those generalizations, and how it
is reasonable to accept what it is that we offer.

TRAFFORD: If we are doing a conventional thesis, isn't
that what we should put in our autobiography and pub-
lish our thesis separately in a conventional way?

SILVERS: I guess you're right in some sense--when my
colleague would say, "Look, maybe you're just at that
point reporting on something biographical and I'm not
too interested in that." But it would seem to me that
is the point at which my work begins: In order to show
how that same thing is not exclusively subjective,
individualistic, eccentric, etc., my work would begin
to try to show, offer, and convince how that really needs
to be seen to be part of the practices of inquiry. I
think that is the work in confronting the conventions
not in an offensive way, not in a way of saying "this
is right, or different," but by simply showing how
biography is analytically woven into the fabric of
interpretation and, further, how it is necessary to
recognize and retain the place of biography as a social
feature of research.

PATTERSON: Bill, might you say something about the
criteria you would see as being used to justify the
form that this "other" kind of research takes?

BARNARD: For certain kinds of phenomena, for instance
my own dissertation looking at the nature of trust, I
had to find methods to get at that phenomenon, and many
traditional methods were not available or I couldn't
find them and so my search was in terms of that particular phenomenoon. The method is secondary, it seems
to me, and has to be justified only in relation to the
research questions being asked. For certain kinds of
questions, certain kinds of methods are appropriate.
It's that internal consistency, it seems to me, that
makes sense for every dissertation. It must flow from
the research questions through the methodology to the
reporting of the findings.

DARROCH: It's very hard to define this quality of completeness that you're referring to . . .

BARNARD: I think part of the reason is that it's so

very difficult for various phenomena. Various approaches become apparent, and it's difficult to name them all in advance, in a sense. The claim at the end is that your methods have been adequate, that your choices are appropriate for this phenomenon. So, as you are in any other study, you're justifying these methods for this phenomenon and this report.

DAVIE: I'm having a little difficulty in this discussion, because when we asked the question "What are criteria for judging appropriateness?" the answer seems to be "If the procedures were appropriate." And it seems circular: the only two criteria so far, outside the sort of the circular "It's appropriate--it's appropriate" argument, are "clarity" and "internal consistency," which reminds me a lot of the story of the up-and-down staircase. Like the case of somebody taking a love note and correcting it for its English. And it seems to me that I, as a supervisor and then a colleague, can see how I would really resent having to judge people's work on an internal feeling whether I think I like it or I don't. It seems to me that it could raise all kinds of questions about the existence of an institution in which there are no external criteria to secure our agreement, except that I'm supposed to be judging whether it's appropriate. And how do I do this by whether it's appropriate or not? I don't find that helpful.

Lynn Davie critically raises a question of locating the criteria of judgment for selecting procedures in a study. Adequacy would be insufficient in his terms if it were described as something that is shown to be appropriate and sufficient after particular decisions are made. Criteria in the view Davie is speaking for here would require that principles to be applied for judgment of appropriateness be available before the selection of procedures are made.

Yet Barnard is pointing to another way in which the researcher attends to inquiry itself. That way locates its criteria of judgment for selecting procedures in the midst of the study itself, in the immediate occasion of interviewing, observing, asking, collecting, conceiving. That view, as the adequacy of research, is an awareness of the organizational complexity and the tacit decisions that comprise the social life of research, and that cannot be anticipated or ordered by

42

design, but must be attended to in the course of the investigation.

EGIT: But does "methodology" get yourself off the hook of having to deal with appropriateness? Like a methodology which I feel comfortable with, and if it does, therefore it's appropriate. That is, I don't see that you've gotten off the hook so easily. If, for example, in psychology, as a thesis supervisor you were given The Possessed, or The Idiot, or another of Dostoevski's works, would you then see it as adequate for a doctoral dissertation? The question is, first of all, could we have insights which are deep, which are meaningful, which are timely, but which are not authorized explicit criteria? By that I mean works that do not use methodologies that are implicated in edited volumes of methodology.

DAVIE: I am not asking for us not to question accepted methodologies any more than I would ask the same question for statistics. The question I'm asking is, "As a community of scholars, what ground rules can we use to interact with each other?" I don't want an answer right at the moment, but I want to know how we should or how we should not pursue this question. How do we discuss that issue about whether a piece of work is "psychology" or "literature"? Is that distinction important to preserve? It is important to me because I've not the training to judge literary works and therefore would have to excuse myself from that. That's all right, that's acceptable.

BARNARD: Lynn, another partial answer to that occurs to me. Some of us are involved in a study of Canada's penitentiary system and its approach to education, and one of the things during this process that we've been involved in is that we have been confronted with a study by Dr. Yokelsen and Dr. Samnau, who have a book--a three-volume work entitled The Criminal Personality-- which claims to be a phenomenological study and describes in great detail the nature of criminal personalities based on 23 years of direct experience with so-called criminals. Now, we're confronted with: "Is that our reality?" It is not in the regular sense. We're not able to use all the standard criteria for judging that work. But, in a sense, we can try it against the experience of others who have worked with criminals, some of whom say, "Yes, this fits my experience beautifully. I see it that way." Others see no value at all

43

in their view. Any claim has to be tested against
others' realities in our communities for a social construction of reality.

*The issue here, again, resides in the temporal orders of
two traditions of thought: What for the moment we will
call technical and classical. The former is a movement
in research of the present-into-the-future, of projection for design and decision, whereby the shareability
and evaluation of others is based on an articulation of
what is to come and what the inquiry is to do. But the
latter tradition, classical thought, is the realization
that the phenomenon is to be encountered, that the
researcher must realize what-is-at-hand and what-is-at-
stake, and in so doing make decisions that are potentially to be shared by others. That potential is made
available through accountability. Classical thought
within the movement of inquiry is a present-into-the-past,
as accounting for what is done in terms of how it was
done. Such a view is retrospective.*

*We may see then that the two traditions confront
one another, asking about an issue in two ways. The two
approaches (criteria vs. accountability) and the two
temporal orders projection and retrospection) not only
exemplify each as a form of thought, but as well show
how the conception of one tradition may be "heard" by
another.*

*Indeed, the tradition of technical thought is the
dominant one in social science and education. We may
recognize that the preentation of the classical mode and
questions from a technical source reveal the dominance
of the former as a basis for thinking about science,
which in the domain of another tradition permits a
re-thinking or critical attention. It is from a critical view that the nature of science is seen to be in
flux and in consideration by researchers.*

*In addition, if this discussion were to be pursued,
we would need to emphasize that within the inquiry being
spoken for here, science is the practice which produces
meaning; it is not a process of "recognition" and of
"representing" what might offer to share itself to us.
So, while its temporal order is retrospective, its
speaking will be prospective.*

DARROCH: Ron, you've been wanting to make some comments
these last few minutes.

SILVERS: Yes, I want to address the issue of criteria for judgment among competing forms of inquiry. I cannot simply assume that the good consensus of my colleagues is adequate to introduce a method. I must justify for a reader, I must justify for a hearer, what it is that I'm offering. That's number one. Number two--another kind of issue: "What do we do when we have more than one statement, more than one claim, more than one assertion?" Now what I'd like to do--I'd like to suggest that that is simply not, in the spirit of this approach, a methodological issue. That is, in fact, an analytic issue, and that is an issue for which we can work.

We can begin that work by asking the question, if I may be permitted and it wouldn't be redundant, "Why is that a question?" That is, why is it that when we have two claims on the same phenomenon, it would be seen as problematic because in different parts of history or different civilizations it would not be seen as problematic? But here in the discussion there is a taken-for-granted principle of resolving the multiple presence of claims. Here, already, we're getting to questions of what is truth, questions then which we deal with in terms of notions of reality and notions of epistemology. And we can get into those kinds of topics. But I don't think the whole discussion should go in that direction. What I simply want to say is that that is an issue for work, not simply an issue for providing a list of criteria by which you can make a judgment. So, I don't want to miss the question, but simply say that, yes, that's an analytic question.

Briefly, however, with respect to notions of "truth," "reality," and "epistemology," it can be inserted here that when there is the recognition by us of our place within our inquiry, then, necessarily, we depart from the idea of correspondence between what we describe (come to understand) and the "objects" within the world which we are describing. Epistemology, then, which assumes an order of things or an order of concepts upon which we may report, must be rejected and (following Roland Barthes, Michel Foucault, and others) truth is not guaranteed by a knowledge of its origin or source but is discursively produced. (Here we use discourse simply to mean a domain of language-use--a particular way of writing (talking) and thinking.)

STOYKOFF: I think there are two problems inherent in

45

what you're saying, from a thesis student's point of
view. One is in the context of the parameters of the
work. How do you achieve some commonality as to the
limits in terms of how far you go? A person has got
to make some judgments on how far the reasoning, the
inquiry, the amount of maturity of one's thinking, can
go for that moment. There's got to be some sort of cut-
off point. Otherwise, it would be a lifelong pursuit
and not a thesis. Do you get the point--how do you
get to an "end"?

The other catch to that, which I've been struggling with from a broader phenomenological standpoint,
is: "How often and how frequently should I really be
tapping into the 'thou,' the other's analysis of life?"
In a conventional sense from the point of the logical
positivist researcher, one acknowledges the existing
array of literature sources that support a particular
framework or provide certain frameworks in an area of
inquiry. What I started to experience from my understanding of phenomenology in terms of, perhaps, heuristic design (I don't know how far heurism goes with
this point I'm making) was that there has to be some
anchoring in what other people have been doing, what
other people have been thinking. And there again I've
got some problems in understanding material because if
you're saying a reasonable piece of work, as heuristic
research goes, is to represent oneself in one's inquiry,
is that in a sense a legitimate objective when there are
so many other people doing a similar effort in that
field that should be acknowledged and whose thinking
may have gone a little further than yours has so far?
Do you follow what I'm saying? The two points are:
Do we acknowledge the other purists, in a way, or the
other scientists? And secondly, how do we define the
limits of how far you go when you are doing something
like a thesis, a doctoral thesis?

This person in the first question raises the concern of
acknowledging the principled character of others' work
in relation to the principled character of their own.
This question inadvertently was unattended to in the
colloquium. So here we would suggest that in presenting
our work we must take into account the ideologies of
others' ideas of what the work should be, but we take
them into account dialogically. If knowledge is dis-
cursively produced, then it must be recognized that it
is a "product" in response to contradictions within and

*between existing discourses of ideology--ideology being
not a set of beliefs and conceptions but our experience
of the world and* inscribed in our discourses *(e.g. Catherine Belsey). Thus, our acknowledging of other is
grounded in our accounting for our responses to others,
discourses and in exposing our own contradictions in
and polyvalence of response to others. Such accounting
"brings" discourses together, but such a knowledge does
not seek an order outside of the reality of that dialogue.*

*The comments below of Sullivan, Davie, and Disman
respond to the second question about the definition of
limits of inquiry from different perspectives. Here we
also recall Barnard's earlier comments about exposing a
"world view to the responses of others, and if the
process is complete, one is able to receive what those
responses are from others."*

SULLIVAN: I'd just like to pick up on what was said by
several speakers before. The title of this conference
is "The Other Thesis," which is not just simply heuristic research, different research, but it's thesis
research that's different from what we talked about as
conventional research. And what I mean by that is,
that it is not just simply trying to establish some
very important convictions about being a researcher.
But I think that in doing a different kind of research
it has to be framed within the context of a subculture
about consensual agreements. And that subculture, at
the very least--and probably it would not be desirable
to have it at the very least--would be a committee that
would socially understand the reality that you're
working with, in fact can be a kind of critical reflec-
tor for you and in that kind of research. But I say
that that's the very least, because I think that in
this kind of context, this subculture, the possibility
exists of getting in such sectarian kinds of postures
that it becomes invidious intimacy.

The thesis is a public document that goes beyond
the intimacy of even the committee. This is very,
very clear in my mind just in terms of some of the
theses I've been concerned with that ultimately are
taken somewhat beyond and out of the context of the
importance that I or the student attached to them.
Just how far one has to accommodate to those things,
how one has to be constantly involved with something
that's counter or is known as the cultural versus the

subculture, is another practical question, but it is an important question when in some instances you do get conflicting interpretations. It is important to come up with your own interpretations, but conflict of interpretations on theses involves real practical questions that have to be dealt with.

The institution of a thesis therefore is not just simply heuristic research in the abstract. There is a set of social relationships within the committee structure that's different from just carrying out regular research. There is a set of social relationships that are involved with the larger institution outside the committee. That is, it's not simply "We're good scientists and everybody agrees on this," or however you want to put it. I think these are important and practical questions that one has to face at some point. I do think that one has to have at least a subculture conventionality so that in fact it can be seen and consented to that research has been and is the matter that is going on.

We interpret Sullivan's comments as taking consensus in science to be given a state of the community where conventionality set within the structure of relationship is a given state. In fact, science is not a community based on consensuality: it is a community based upon "consensibility," where consensus is a possibility created by the persuasive thesis of a scientist to his peers.

Sullivan goes on to say that the "other" theses could themselves have a conventionality unto themselves, as a subculture within social science. However, we feel that, particularly amongst those in a small subculture, conventionality of a limited domain should be rejected, for such a conventionality would then lead to the sectarianism to which Sullivan pointed and which is something to be feared. In place of adherence to even "other" rules, we instead would propose that each time a work or thesis calls upon others both within and outside that subculture, it be heard for its claims, for its logic, for its conceptualization. Its "truth" then becomes a truth not of "objectivity," but one that finally depends on the multiplicity of voices "surrounding" the "thesis." And this multiplicity of voices includes not only the many of indeterminate origin who may have created the "thesis" but also the readers of it who, most certainly, also constitute its meaning.

48

DAVIE: So you're saying it is the confines of the subculture laid upon the limits of the inquiry which
define the terms of how far we will go. The thing is,
you could go on ad infinitum in expanding your awareness
of what the phenomenon is. I could ask, "How am I to
decide or deliberate with other people who are on my
committee where the limits lie?" Do you do it on a
time cut-off point? Do you do it on expanded awareness?
I'm not hearing the answer in terms of criteria. I'm
saying, "How do you deliberate over the limits to which
you go in an inquiry when it's in the context of the
thesis itself?"

*Davie continues the important issue of the limits of
inquiry. However, we see him raise it in terms of the
will and control of the members of the subculture in
which the thesis is being proposed.*

*We suggest that limits would come to be discovered
within the commitments of the researcher, within the
researcher's biographical and cultural limits of understanding.*

*Limits are in fact an analytical interest held
which offer the beginnings of our inquiry. Far from
being a practical problem to overcome, the potential of
analysis being limitless, the issue is the limits of our
understandings. Thus, we begin with what we understand
and what we don't understand in the lives of the people
we study. Thus, as we arrive at a conceptualization, we
confront the difficulties of reaching beyond a set of
concepts we construct.*

*What we are attempting to say here, again, is that
a problem of research is within our view an analytic
problem requiring our inquiry and not a methodological
problem needing an a priori solution through organization, a solution of agreement, or a decision of strategy
for the making of consistent judgments, or for the planning of research.*

DISMAN: Theoretically speaking, I think that if there
would be an explanation about this question of limits
of inquiry with which everyone else would be able to
identify, it would mean that there is no necessity to
address phenomena at any time in the future. I believe
the limits should be derived from the dialogue between
researcher and topic rather than put on someone's back

49

by even a sympathetic committee. If my committee were
to suggest to me that I should stop whatever, I would
feel a bit uneasy, I would see myself in some kind of
trouble, because I would expect that I am more involved
with the phenomenon that I am dealing with. It would
trouble me that someone else has seen something that I
haven't been able to notice. I suppose that if limits
were derived from the dialogue between phenomenon and a
researcher, a question is how the researcher would
recognize when to stop. Maybe it's the point when you
feel that you know enough already about the phenomenon
such that you know what you're leaving out, when you
tacitly are able to define the boundaries which you
yourself have been proceeding from/with and have in
recognition transgressed.

SULLIVAN: I'd like to pick up on Disman's point,
because I really disagree fundamentally with it. First
of all, because I think a thesis committee is in fact a
community project, unless you just conceive of committee
members as sort of at best sympathetic appendages to
your ideas, your individual exploration or journey. In
fact, that's not the way my own role in thesis direction
is, or should be. When I find myself in that kind of
role it's not a very good situation to be in. But to
get back to the point. Even though it is your thesis
in a sense, developing your ideas, if it is not in dialogue and development with a committee, then I think it
really isn't reflecting the necessary kind of inten-
tions--because a thesis is a public document, not just
simply you and your data. I can tell you that if you
don't know about it now, you will know about it as the
process goes on, I guess. Rest assured of that.

      I'm just saying that the thesis set-up as an insti-
tution was here before you and it will be here after
you. Now, you can change it, but it's not a matter of
whether you like it or not. It's there. Now, I don't
know what you want to read out of that. When you're
doing "different kinds of theses" you will have to deal
with those things.

DISMAN: Let me explain. My thesis is that which I
enjoy doing and which I am doing because I want to have
it done, but also because I like it very much, getting
involved with it. In that dialogue with the committee
I would like to be able to put forward when and where I
stop as a result of my deep involvement. Secondly, I
would ask my committee for help and I would be very

grateful for it. But I still think I would not like it very much if someone from outside would say, "Now stop, don't do it." And I would feel that I would still have to go on.

Regarding Sullivan's comments concerning thesis committees, we should explain in reaction to these comments that, as we have already indicated, we would hope that the academic-scientific community is based on consensibility, not consensus, in that we are not governed by the prevailing agreement within a discipline. Rather, science is based on the ability to achieve understanding and agreement by explaining one's purposes and procedures of inquiry in such a manner that another can see how the thesis brings evidence, interpretation, and conclusions together.

Indeed, outside of new forms of inquiry which are in part represented in this seminar, the dynamics of consensibility may be seen to operate for any thesis committee in that the innovative character of each inquiry with its new claims and altered procedures necessitates the showing of how such claims can be made. The thesis is not a technical execution of procedures laid down by a community but an original work which, partly as craft and partly as theorizing, provides its own grounds for its acceptance. It provides its own grounds in the reasoning, justification, and methodological account which informs the reader of how the author arrived at the knowledge he or she did. It thus takes the immediate community into account, but a thesis is not limited to that community. Indeed, it is offered to and is a part of the tradition of scholarly inquiry. As such, it goes beyond the committee and beyond this point in history. To demonstrate this last point it is necessary to note that a committee is not a panel in an absolute sense of judgment as they may evaluate a thesis. Rather, a thesis committee, as it represents a scholarly tradition, is itself answerable and must be accountable to the candidate and others in the community. Disman's response shows her recognition of the responsibility which she would expect the committee to show to her and it also demonstrates her own commitments to her relationship to her phenomena and topic.

To this we would like to add that the public nature of the thesis ensures that this responsibility is a vital part of the institutional web of scholarship. It

51

ensures, among other things, that the existence of a
conventional, public reason for doing inquiry cannot
justify the exclusion of a newly proposed form of
inquiry.

DARROCH: Would anyone else want to address this concern, which is really a concern of conventionality?

WEISER: I'm not sure if this is in direct response,
but I want to make a couple of comments. Although my
experience with this type of work is that it is all
tied together and any artificial separation into stages
is, in a sense, artificial, I find it useful to make
some. I think it relates to some of these questions.
One of them is to talk about the phenomena. In terms
of whose experience you are talking about, there are
several kinds of people's experience; but to say "I'm
going to try and investigate other people's phenomena,"
then we need to talk about how I can convince you about
the legitimacy of <u>their</u> reporting. At what level of
contact with them<u>selves</u>, from what perspective, have
they reported to me, and how have I recorded that reporting? I think those are very legitimate issues.
If I ask you "What do you think about something?", I'm
asking you to stand in a certain place. But if I ask
you "What were you attending to, what were you aware
of in such a moment?", I'm asking you to stand in a
different place, and it's important to me--those two
places and an infinite variety of other places. In a
sense, if I ask "What do you think about separation in
Canada?", and you tell me your opinion about something
and I get ten of them and then I say, "OK, now I know
what the general opinion in Canada is on this issue,"
you would say I'm nuts. But if I get a thousand
people to say it and they all say the same thing, then
you begin to say "Gee, now I understand." Yet they
all may have been the same "lie," in a sense, of the
distorted perspective. You just get larger numbers of
the same distortion and it becomes the truth. There
are methodological decisions and ways of reporting and
talking about all this. They include my relation to
that data and interpretation as meaning and my explanation of where that comes from and why I've taken that
stance, which is public data at that point. That's no
different from any other kind of investigation. The
same problems are always there. Exactly the same.
So I think in terms of the questions of rigor, we
can break them down and deal with each problem and
justify and explain how you went about it and then

make a decision, and I think that's the important thing. Then you provide enough evidence that others can make a decision on the same question. It's always what we have to do.

We wish to emphasize that the questions that are asked of people and the comments, descriptions, and disclosures they make within research do not, in themselves, establish an interpretive social science of analytic reflection. The research that Weiser discusses is not what we envision as a tradition of interpretive inquiry. For we do not embrace a conception of a duality in subjectivity-objectivity, an illusion of the person studied and a reality grasped by the scientist, a fault as against an accurate expression of experience. Such dualities are counter to our formulation of the researcher, of the person studied, and of the knowledge we construct.

The important interest in the experience and accounts of people which Weiser speaks for is not limited to the classical tradition which is found in the "other" thesis. The way of that interest as an expression of thought may be revealed in quite different types of research. The distinctions we find, however, are contained in the superordinate processes of thought which guide the work, rather than in the processes of procedure which may be discovered through the thought.

EGIT: I'd like to make a related comment. The other kind of concern is the concern which deals with the relationship of the researcher and the data, and I would see that as central to what I would see the "other" thesis being. And it's very interesting that in research it is the methodology that makes us feel comfortable. With the "right" methodology we no longer have to say, "Look, I don't know if there's an outside world out there." This is comforting. That is, certain kinds of methods, certain kinds of analogues give us a comfort that we can then stand behind and understand why it is they have been designed this way. What I find interesting about us being scientific is what physical scientists recognize: "The central problem for the sciences is the relationship of the researcher to his own work." In this sense we're rushing in the direction that physical scientists are getting away from. We're putting ourselves there, and they say, you're doing what we did in the 18th century. That is, the very problem that the "other" thesis poses in some way, is the very problem at the center of science. What is the

53

relationship between us and the work that we do? Not
"Here, let me show you some variables; let me throw
them together and let me come up with an answer, and
let me posit the impossible." But rather, what in
effect have I as a person in the world to say about the
world, and why is that important? And what is it that
the importance can grow into and how is it that I look
at that engagement?

DAVIE: I would like to refer to what was originally
said--How do you choose what's appropriate except by
saying "It's appropriate"? And then Ron said something
to the effect of, "Well you've got to consider that
there is not simply one truth." This kind of research,
I think, has the fundamental premise that the truth is
a multidimensional thing that at most, because we have
linear lines, allows us to deal with a couple of dimensions. But there are many, many dimensions, so that in
selection, what is appropriate? I think there is a
guideline that can say, "What is appropriate is what
resonates for me as not too far from reality." At that
point, you can sometimes name for yourself why that
thing has for you some message of a truth or quality.
And it may be that the person when he was speaking to
you of that thing had glimmering eyes and the two of you
were somehow clicking away. You can in some ways record
that. There are reasons why this thing is frightening
as having a ring of truth. Or it could be that it
simply reflects something that you know of from your own
experience. And at that point, you're risking, as a
researcher, this kind of research is risked, by your
saying that you can have some claim to reflect truth
interacting with your subject throughout the research,
and then that you have the right to say that you have a
sense of what is true, and there are ways in which you
can record why you made those choices. But there are
many truths and your line of inquiry is valid, if you
can support and explain to me the choices you made as
you go along.

    As a person, I see that I have both a responsibi-
lity to me and a number of roles that I have accepted
as part of what I play. I have no difficulty with Ron's
comment. But when I am approaching it from the stand of
myself as Lynn Davie or the stand of myself as personal
scholar, I look at it, I make the judgments as to
whether it makes sense to me, whether it's consistent;
I reject it if it's not; if it differs from me I want
to know why it differs, and explore. I have no problems

54

with any of those.

What bothers me is in my role as public scholar to whom the people of Ontario have paid some money. May I exhibit that same self-choice in looking at, for example, RoseMarie's thesis? When she comes to me, and I say, "Well, you know, that glimmer in your eye is obtained over lack of sleep, not passion. All right, it is passion, but I'm really not into passion this week. Therefore, for me it is not valid. For you it is valid, for me it is not." The thing I am wrestling with is what do I do with my role which says there is a conflict between my conception and RoseMarie's. I would feel uncomfortable saying, "RoseMarie, go to hell, or to somewhere else and work with someone else." That situation is a conflict within the responsibility I accept as a graduate thesis supervisor. Yet there are things different from my way that are acceptable and reasonable. Now, without some personal criteria I have no way of relating to that except in a personal statement with all of its successes and all of its unfairnesses. And that's the point I have been trying to wrestle with.

DARROCH: Lynn, thank you for making this point, which really raises the conception of the "personal" again. For myself, I know I always conceive of the "personal" here in this work as a concept of the social. As such it is a requirement for an analytic process of discourse which allows us to move into the I/Thou to which Bill refers. I am uncertain what more to say now. I think this issue of what is the "personal" will continue in Ron's topic.

Our use of the term "personal" confronts a difficulty of its usage, its history, its legacy within social science. The personal is referring to what is biographically unique for the researcher, and therefore from our point of view necessarily present in the research, has been seen by traditional social science as that which is to be avoided, or even to be suppressed in research. For typically the term "personal" in social science is seen to be antithetical to what stands as social and can therefore be shareable and admitted.

Our use of the term "personal" for the place of the researcher within analysis is one of responsibility. To take on the personal is responsible in that one places one's commitments and understandings in view for not only evaluation by others but for others to see the

55

sources of our interests and constructs.

We believe that to prescribe criteria for judgment projectively for a study avoids responsibility insofar as it points away from oneself, the personal, to the community in terms of what the community would accept.

The presentation of one's concerns and under-standings is a social responsibility in that it brings the researcher into relationship with others. Personal responsibility as personal judgment and personal inter-pretation through accountability (retrospectively, making plain procedures and decisions of thought we discover) becomes a reaching out for the social. This meaning of the social situates us, the researchers, between ourselves as embodying the research undertaken and the community that we hold and address.

DARROCH: I wonder if we can move to Ron's topic of formulating the problem. But I also want to say that in the debate here on problems as you put them, we are beginning to theorize about another way to do research and so, in a sense, our conversations exemplify the very search towards which we seek to formulate a knowledge.

I'm thinking here out loud in terms of what's happening in terms of the kind of comments being made. Ron, you were going to address the idea of selecting the thesis topic. And perhaps we can keep the idea of the "personal" present before us as we listen to your comments.

SILVERS: I wonder if I may begin my talk by first addressing the last couple of things that were said. It seems to me that remarks made on behalf of what these theses might be are in no way an attempt to guard against and thrust through something which people would not entirely accept, would not see as scholarship, would not see as good science. However, I don't think those who attempt to do these theses could in any way adopt a fatalistic attitude about convention. What we're really doing--and we've been doing it for years; there's a history behind this--is talking about what is the res-ponsibility on the part of those who offer this sort of approach to try to wrestle with those conventions and address an audience which is historically located. That is, at this point, North American social science, here in the 1970s and 1980s. It is likewise the responsi-bility of those who hold to those conventions to at

56

least be able to begin to address those conventions critically, seriously, to see what it is that's being said.

For example, much of this thesis research (the "other thesis") proceeds on the basis not of assuming or adopting a givenness of a reality, but rather accepting a sense that reality is socially constructed. And therefore such issues as a correspondence between our statements about what's going on and about "what's presumably out there" does not hold. So when Lynn brings that up, we could begin addressing that, but we would have to begin addressing it analytically, which is what I was saying before.

But let me turn now to my general remarks. What I want to talk about briefly is the question of what is involved in choosing a topic within a thesis, and I want to direct my comments to something that people will recognize immediately for themselves, for their own work, for their doctoral dissertations, as being an entirely practical, immediate issue: practical in the sense of the kind of discussions that would be going on between themselves and their committee. I want to focus on the committee asking, "What is it that you're really after? What is it that you're really studying?" In trying to uncover this issue, I discovered what that work has been for myself, and I'll try to deal with it using the vehicle of my own doctoral dissertation. The reason that I'm doing it this way is that I want to start out by saying that the difficulty of choosing the topic is that the topic is not clear. But not only is the topic not clear to us at the beginning, at the commencement of the dissertation; I would like to suggest that the topic is not clear as we pursue the research through the dissertation and that in fact what occurs is that we find the topic being a revelation: the revealing of the phenomenon. As we move through the analysis, we come to recognize, more and more for ourselves, just what it is that we're dealing with, and as we uncover it we recognize that it is really something which is very personal to us. And that's going to be a difficult issue for others.

The title of my dissertation was "Artists and Asociability: Studies in the Ideology of Alienation." Longish tytle, typical colon in the middle. It kind of gives you a glimmering of what the dissertation might be. It was a historical study. If I can begin here with a sort of dialogue with myself, I start by asking myself what the dissertation was about. Artists? Well, the topic, yes, it dealt with artists, but the topic really wasn't artists. Art? Well, it dealt with art, but the topic really wasn't art. With respect to artists, I began my research by looking into what artists do, how they work, etc. But let me comment further in order to introduce this and to try to come to grips and reveal to you what it was.

The dissertation took an interesting turn in that there was an earlier thesis, a precursor dissertation, that was aborted. The former one was a comparison of artists and scientists which examined the process of creativity for artists and scientists. I started this because it seemed that what researchers in the past had done was show that both artists and scientists went through similar kinds of things in order to create. Interesting. However, I would then note that the kinds of descriptions of scientists' lives and descriptions of the pain of their work (or the difficulty of their work or the success and pleasure of their work) were quite different as we looked at artists. My notion was somehow in terms of what the two did and how they fit into society. I was concerned with the difference between the two: scientists were integrated in society; artists were alienated. If the two were basically involved in the same process of creativity, if they went through the same basic activities in their work, why the integration of one and the alienation of the other? This question I eventually tied in the completed thesis to that of different kinds of artists; I shifted from comparing scientists and artists to comparing different kinds of artists. Historically, the question focused on a comparison of those artists who were integrated and those who were alienated.

But let me return to the question here of what was the topic of my thesis. I did not simply inquiry about the process of the artist's creation, as described by others. What I want to say here is that what I was doing in the thesis was looking at what artists did, as they described their procedures of work, as they told about how they went about creation.

In one sense you might see this as a concern with methods. That is, in one way, you might begin to say, "Well, he's looking at the methods of artists, he's looking at the way in which they describe their methods."

58

(And I, if I had to describe my thesis at that time, I would say the same.)

Is this so? Was that the topic? Yes, but also no. And when I say yes, but also no, therein lies, looking retrospectively, what was one of the most important things for me in terms of what the topic was. And the reason I say that was important, is that the "yes and no" is an exclamation of an ambivalence. And what I want to say is that as we begin to locate a topic for ourselves and begin to find out what it is that we're studying and what it is that is our concern, we realize more and more that it is not simply a thoroughgoing concern in one direction or another, but it is in a divergent direction, and that divergence, that ambivalence, lies at the heart of what keeps us going, of what keeps that kind of concern, of what sustains us through the research and what sustains a piece of research.

Now, why I say "yes, but no," in terms of methods, is that when I began examining (and why I think I was even drawn to art) I found that there are certain artists who will describe how they work as not encompassing methods, but as practices coming out of themselves. You might consider this to be subjective, personal statements. Examples of these artists' practices would be found in the 1940s and 1950s with the abstract expressionists; if we go back to the Italian Renaissance, it would be Michelangelo. Now, if you were to say to me, "Were you interested in procedures that would lead to a certain kind of craft or work of art?", I would have to say, "Not really." When I began looking at what the artists were doing and saying about themselves and also describing their relationships to others, what I was doing was looking at the way they talked about their work, looking at the way they had a sense of how they work, as a way of doing and as a way of addressing the world. So it wasn't methods or procedures in the restricted sense; it was a larger issue that I was considering. But I must admit that I could only begin to comprehend this now, years later. If you had asked me in the midst of my research, I could only have given an incomplete answer. I could have said, "Well, it's something larger, but I don't know what that larger is." It's not just methods, it also has to do with the ability for someone to create and to create quite successfully, as successfully as someone who doesn't have methods. And yet that person professes, and I must acknowledge, that they do not follow methods in order to accomplish what they do. If I were to look back retrospectively, I would have to realize a second point of revelation in discovering my topic. The first revelation I mentioned is that we follow an ambivalence of concerns. The second revelation in discovering my topic is that my own thesis was in large part a combination of procedures which were not methodical. By that I mean that I could not show and demonstrate that the way I had investigated could completely be recurrent for others.

In the midst of my research, I realized that my own thesis both fell in and out of the notion of methods. It was an inquiry that was both methodological and non-methodological, similar to the artists I studied. When I began to realize that that was at issue, what was at issue for me was not only method and non-method; I was dealing with ambivalence as being in the world and with the question of one's place in the world. I was looking at artists, some of whom, like Da Vinci, scrupulously tried to work out methods, and others, like Michelangelo, who denied the possibility of them. I too embodying both, being a scientist but also beginning to address scientific conventions, began wondering for myself, what is this place of science that I have come to inhabit? And then, I think, at that point, I began approaching, began understanding more and more what that topic was. As I would do it, I would realize that the topic for me (and this only came at the end of the dissertation and not at the beginning) very much was that the pursuit and use of methods as techniques had to do with the place of rationality in our society. But I would have to say now as I revise my thoughts on that, it is a particular version of rationality in our society which concerns me deeply--a monistic conception of rationality in our society. So as I address my own thesis, as I realize what that topic was, it had to do with my personal self; it had to do with what my personal concerns would be. And even as I say that, I'm caught: I don't want to say really "personal," because somehow the notion, the word "personal," begins to exclude the social. Let me say, rather than personal, "intimate" or "private." And in so doing, let me end with something that one sociologist said, which I can offer to others as a way in which one chooses a topic and as a way one proceeds in the work. That was a statement quite a while ago by C. Wright Mills in a book called The Sociological Imagination, in which he said, "What is sociology? The transformation of private problems into public issues." Now, that's all that we ever do.

DARROCH: Thank you. We'll take about fifteen minutes if you like and maybe address the theme of the topic. Does anyone have a question, or a comment?

PATTERSON: If it is only at the end of the research that you come to identify the topic, how would you know what procedure to follow while you're working along?

SILVERS: You always have to deal with the tension of discovering both topic and procedure, and bringing them together. I don't think that there is just one set procedure that one begins with. The topic somehow begins to indicate a procedure and a procedure influences the identity of a topic. But the two are disclosed to us in our biographies, which in our research we transform into the "social" knowledge with which we will begin to address others.

KORMAN: Regardless of whether it's qualitative or quantitative, there seems to be some preconceived, predesigned, predetermined spout that funnels whatever my concepts or orientations are to a topic into reali-zable components, like the amount of data I can deal with and the amount of variables I can explore and the amount of time and money I have at my disposal to exist on, and all those other types of constraints. I am just trying to come to grips with that sort of embryonic stage that's pre-thesis. And it seems to me the thesis comes in at a point where I've got to become a realist. I've got to start coming to terms with the fact that I've got to get off my ass sometime and I've got to realize that moving on is just part of life--moving on to either becoming an academic or going in the whirl-pool of getting a job--no, no, I mean a real job. I'm trying to come to grips with the fact that there are these constraints. I'm sorry to keep coming back to that, but there must have been a point in your identi-fying the topic where you had to come to grips with it. Michelangelo, plus Da Vinci, plus five other artists, you had to come to grips with how much data do you go into. And does that have something to do with identi-fying the topic, or doesn't it?

SILVERS: Oh, I quite think it does. I don't think they could be removed from each other. I don't think it's at

61

all incidental or subsidiary in a secondary way. I
think very much what you're speaking about is that
somehow in doing our work, whether it is a dissertation
or a project after, we have to be organizationally
astute and apply our craft. The doing of our craft
would not be in sitting in a room removed from our
inquiry, but the actual doing of it in making mistakes
and in devising other ways. Very much I would falter,
I would make incorrect choices, I would have to recognize a waste of tiem, a diffusion of energy, a lack of
focus, etc., and begin to build it once again. What I
want to caution, though, is where the two are seen to
be independent of each other. Either the topic is seen
so important and so strong as to be independent of the
organization of inquiry or vice versa. I just heard in
one of my courses a description of a sociology student's
MA thesis and a problem that happened to her. She
wanted to do a study on the problems of a certain
immigrant group in Canada. She researched the material;
she went through the literature in terms of theoretical,
conceptual ideas; she put together an interview schedule; she worked out a proposal; she went into the
field; she collected the data; she came back, she did
a statistical analysis with computer operations; she
found out at that point that the problem of the immigrant that she looked for was not present as a phenomenon in the material she collected. What could she do
at that point? She continued her study as if the
phenomenon existed. Her topic was defined by the
literature and hence had to be there. Her experience
in the field had to be denied. Her analysis had to
proceed as if the phenomenon existed, and to do this
she had to do some fancy redefining of concepts to
acknowledge an absent phenomenon.

Now we're getting down to the sticky part. First
of all, I in no way want to suggest that hers was a
statistical problem. It has nothing to do with its
being a quantitative study. It has to do with her not
being able to make very critical and personal decisions
along the way. Her topic was not born out of her personal commitments; it did not emerge in increasing
clarity. Rather, she set a topic out of the necessity
of having to define the topic at the beginning. In
organizing her thesis, her defined topic, from the
literature dominating the study, the research became
a fiction. The research was not authentic for her: nor,
as she could not disclose that the topic was not to be
found as a phenomenon, was it to become authentic for

62

others. Only when we realize the organic quality of the
revelation of the topic for ourselves, and the organic
quality of the relationship of the topic to the phenomenon we discover, can our research become authentic and
fulfill our craft.

FINKELSTEIN: Is this a place for encouraging the candidate to constantly evaluate the data? We pay lip service
to that. But to evaluate critically in terms of whether
we are getting what we want from it, so that it's almost,
not exactly, pretesting. But it's that idea of continually evaluating if changes can be built into design. So
this really, I don't know if I'm expressing myself
clearly . . .

SULLIVAN: It's just not a question of my constant evaluation. You can't get into phenomena. Somehow I have got
to call a rhythm of withdrawal from the phenomenon in
order to reflect upon it. Because at some point you get
involved and do not reflect whether something close there
is going along the way you want. I don't think you can
really make any prescription as to when and where you do
that; it depends on the kinds of things that you're
working with.

DARROCH: It might be a small point, but I just want to
add it to this because I think it's important. It's not
a question of looking at the data to see whether you are
getting out of it what you want. This last, in fact,
represents a problem in the way this kind of work is
often seen. It would be, though, that there will be
systems of differences that you will recognize and which
you will attempt to resolve as you move back and forth
between your thought and your "data." But the idea of
getting what you want, that's like the old a priori hypothesis, it's verification, the affirmation of things,
which is not what this work is about. As William
Barrett discusses, the accomplishment of a presence of
a classical tradition is achieved not through "willful-
ness" but through "will-lessness."

*Following this point, we wish to note the contrast
between on the one hand "doing" scientific work for
purposes of the traditional attempt to secure information and substantiate claims as knowledge itself, and on
the other hand the work being talked about today, which
represents the "doing" of sicentific work as a search
which reveals our relationship with the world through our*

*understanding of the commitments and knowledge we pro-
duce as we participate in the world.*

End of Morning Session

- - -

The Afternoon Session

DARROCH: We were just having a bit of controversy at
the back about whether we would take a few moments to
address something or not, so before we get into the
topic of the data and what you do with that, we were
thinking what happened with some of the conversation
this morning. Some of the issues raised circled around
issues which we haven't addressed, so we're going to take
20 minutes to half an hour to look at the epistemological
bases from which a lot of people are speaking. If you
don't do that, then it will be very difficult to locate
people's responses about what to do with the data in
terms of what might be the objectives of the thesis
dependent on the kinds of thoughts and concerns here
today. So if you don't mind, we'll go ahead with that.
Some of you are nodding your heads. Great, we'll go
ahead. Now, we don't have anything really formal on
this either, but Bill Alexander is going to say just a
few words about it. People can respond. Again, the
idea would be to get an understanding in the sense of
what kind of realities, what kinds of knowledges you
are creating by different kinds of work. So in other
words, are you responding to some reality presumed out
there? Or if you're talking about constructing realities, which Ron mentioned this morning in passing, then
what does that really mean?

ALEXANDER: I'm confused, that's how all this started.
And what I'm confused about is I think I hear different
people with different sets of objectives--in terms of
what consitutes a search for knowledge or appropriate
knowledge, or a definition of knowledge. And I want to
check out to see if I really am confused or if I'm not
confused.

Now, it seems to me when I was listening to Bill
Barnard talk, that Bill was making the point that in
the research process it is sufficient if one develops an
I/Thou relationship, because in that I/Thou relationship
there exists certain truths. That is, the truth of
religious statement, it's the ultimate form of relation-

64

ship. So then, the question that I have for Bill is
"Is that an end in and of itself?" OK, what I heard
over there, it seemed to me that the position that you
were taking was there are lots of realities, an infinite,
an unaccountably large number of realities at least, and
that if the researcher puts forward one of these realities that's legitimate in and of itself; and therefore
I wonder, well, are there any grounds on which a person
can be challenged if we're willing to accept all realities as equally legitimate? I'm probably really over-
simplifying, which could help complicate this for me,
I guess. But then, of course, there is the traditional
point of view, which says what we're really about in
research is the construction of hypothetical, deductive
theories. We're concerned with the reduction of
variance, and the critical dimension of theory construction in that sense--in that "scientific" way-- is that
it's self-corrective. Let me just refer you to an idea
I've read which relates to what is a defense basically
of scientific theory: it goes something like "above all
let it be considered that what is more wholesome than
any particular belief is integrity of belief." And that
"to avoid looking into the support of any belief from a
fear that it may turn out to be rotten is quite as
immoral as it is disadvantageous." So, I'd like some
discussion and some clarification here as to what are
the objectives of the research effort as seen by various
people here. Did I misrepresent, folks?

Alexander's request for our objectives is a request for
understanding what we intend and what we propose. Al-
though his request is valid, couched in terms of the
language of objectives, it shows that some comments from
the morning were not heard, for the word "objectives"
signifies a way of research which some at the seminar
did not claim to do. Alexander's request signifies a
call for our choices through a willful rationality that
we do not wish to use. (Yet on the other hand, in a
general way we would say our "objective" is to transform
what we know (not only reveal it), to speak out of
silence (not only from an adding to what has been said)
and so on.

The differences of tradition as thought are most
pronounced here, as how the relationship to one's work
of research can be understood by others. Alexander
apparently hears that we are willing to accept all
realities as equally legitimate. This is a frequent
misconstruction, for its omission of the considerations

65

*to which we adhere creates the dubious arrangement of
a relative social world.*

*The considerations which are present in our work
include the primacy of experience of those studied as
a possibility of reality. That reality is located
within the biography of the persons studied, and within
the context of the circumstances of an occasion of the
structure and history of their society. The legitimacy
of the reality is recognized as situationally based.
But there is more. At no point do we release our own
judgments and realities. Indeed, the relationship and
tension between our understandings and the understandings of those we study is a principal issue, and
the knowledge we pursue is to account analytically for
the understandings of others in the light of our own
understandings. But always at issue, in awareness, is
the relationship of our* language *(of understanding) with
the* experience *(of other).*

ROUEL: From my point of view, I thought people were
saying the line of reality that one chooses to try to
represent is still at all times accountable to data. In
that sense it is not simply my objective reality, but my
assumptions outlined and then worked through constantly
and re-seen through the data.

ALEXANDER: But what is the objective? I mean, is there
an objective for accumulation of knowledge? Is that of
concern? I'm going to go and sit back there because
what I want to do is raise the issue, not monitor the
discussion.

DARROCH: OK, Bill. Thanks. Ron, you look like you want
to say something.

SILVERS: I wanted to address that, perhaps, through a
concrete example and try to point to various issues to
raise an example around this thought. One student I know
is embarking on the study of anorexia nervosa, which
apparently is a disease of mostly upper-class young
girls, and it's a disease which has very serious consequences, possibly death, by a purposeful starving of
oneself. But in the girls' eyes, that is, in the
patients' eyes, they don't see themselves as doing that.
For them the issues would then be they are too fat or
they are too heavy or something else in contact with
body image. And the reason that I mentioned this is that
that kind of topic, that sort of phenomenon, already
introduces an issue of the divergence of the way in which

we could see things. Let's say a divergence from one
standpoint either in the parent or the physician or the
psychologist, all of whom would be very troubled at the
actual physical deterioration of the girl. The other
side would be from the girl herself, who would see her
own physical condition as possibly obese or leading to
the obese and try to reduce her amount of intake in
food. For her there's actually a point at which there
is even a repulsion of food.

Now, the difficulty here is between the parents
or friends or physician or psychologist, on the one
hand, and the patient on the other. And the attempt to
convince the patient that she has a disease is often
difficult if not impossible. There's a cross-purpose
and cross-discussion where neither addresses the other.
I would see the possibility of a research of this topic
where we try somehow to put together how it is possible
to come to the view that makes it entirely sensible,
reasonable, practical, credible to do what the patient
is doing before we could actually begin to address the
patient. We must in fact entertain its possibility in
the world as a way of looking. Now, to do that, I
think we cannot have a perspective of a kind of dominant
reality for which this person's way of looking is somehow
obscured, diseased, deficient. When we begin with the
notion of a dominant, paramount reality for which
another is somehow in a subordinate position, we forever cannot come to grips with it, understand it, recognize it, resolve it for ourselves. So I hear Bill
Barnard saying that we must enter into the I/Thou
relationship in this case. And to enter into that
relationship we must realize the very grounds of our
differences as the reality, judgment, and morality that
we ourselves hold in contrast to another's. Now it seems
to me that there is an immediate consequence of this,
and then there is a kind of further consequence, a
secondary one in terms of the relationship. The immediate one is that through the research, the researcher
and, in this case, the patient will enter where they
share at least a common ground, an understanding. Once
that could be arrived at, it would seem the possibility--
and there's just one way to phrase it--the possibility
would be to locate a language, to locate a way of discourse, to locate a manner of communication that would
not be available before. Thus, in the I/Thou relationship, what is formulated is a way of speaking that we
did not have available before. That does not mean that
understanding an experience from the other side cannot

be an evaluative one; it means that new evaluations because of totally different perspectives (this time including both perspectives rather than the domination of one) are used. The by-product of such research would be that others would now be able to have a common language to address people with anorexia nervosa so that they would hear them and likewise be heard in conversation. There would then be understanding. This is an example of what a piece of work might be.

The work then is freed from even truth as intersubjectivity, for in releasing the positions (e.g., physician, patient) from which one (a reader) would normally understand the experience being inquired into (anorexia nervosa) a new discourse is created. The work then "lives" in the world for re-creating of meaning.

DISMAN: There is no what that I can possibly say that better. Now, I support your explanation of what this work might be. And if I can put it in four or five words, what I believe it is doing is giving power back to people and not holding onto the expert's view as educator--as researcher--as psychologist--as medical practitioner--and so on.

DARROCH: I think so too. I'd just like to add here that it makes me think of one student who asked something like, "In this work do you want to make everything that is mundane special? Do you want to make everything that we attend to in the work important?" It's another way of saying what you're saying. Because, yes, definitely, such specialness happens in the returning of the authority, well, not only to a person but to whatever the phenomenon might be. What we have in view is not the quest for the absolute, the finite, as to the experience and knowledge of the world, but the quest for the variety of the many different ways in which the world is experienced and known, the world's particularities and the relationship of our process of conceptualizations with that.

There are a couple of people who want to say something, but if I could just continue for a minute, I'd like to say that the way I see what Bill Barnard is saying is that his concern for relationship points to a way of communicating through which this kind of work may be accomplished. And in terms of the vision of the other theses, this work is unlike other work which from the outset seeks the universal in thematic, categorical reductive ways. I go back to what was said earlier in the morning. This work depends on the dialogue in discourse between the researcher and the other, be it person or phenomenon. And in that relationship begins the uncovering, unpacking, of what informs us. Now, a couple of people wanted to say something.

STOYKOFF: In terms of the goal or objectives of this kind of inquiry, I think the goal isn't all that different. We're seeking knowledge, we want to gain greater understanding; it's the way that we're doing it that's different. This kind of experiential knowing provides a different kind of knowledge, a knowledge of the person that's from the inside of their perspective, which is very different from the frame of reference that most people bring to research. To me that's the essential difference: what we do afterwards, how this helps us to be better practitioners, and better knowers, is the next step.

DARROCH: Good. Thank you. But I want to emphasize that it is not researching to seek knowledge. It is researching to seek understanding; to understand our own thoughts. And I use "understanding" here in the hermeneutical sense that our understanding shows how we participate in life. It is "being" interpreted. So it is quite different from knowledge as we use that word. Lynn, you want to say something?

DAVIE: Yes. I hope you don't see my participation in this conference as representing a point of view not sharing the tradition. I think these are comments about trying to understand what we're about. This is useful. Several of my students are currently involved. Some of my own work is in this tradition. What I'm trying to wrestle with is a clear understanding of what we, and myself, whoever, is about. What I really would like to know more about is the convincing. We talked earlier this morning about conventions, but it seems to me we are beginning to elucidate some of the conventions around these kinds of theses. But I would like to be convinced, as a reader, of what I have as an independent route to the data myself upon which to make decisions by.

SILVERS: It seems to me that you are raising the issue of the accuracy of what the researcher discovers and collects. This may be seen as a question of care of the researcher and the availability of the materials

for the review of others. But the main problem for us
is not what one finds as being true or not, I mean as
an accurate reflection of the social world, since we
see "fact" as a construction. Nor is it the issue of
validity, of what is true. What we are involved with is
in seeing the connection between what we claim to find
and how we account for our finding it in that way. Our
observations are not reproducible, but are organized
around our concerns. Our attempt is not an accurate
reporting of what happened, but a skilled version of
our understood meaning of what occurred.

*Here we find a tension between different views and
claims of reality for establishing what is truth and
what is knowledge.*

*At this place we would like to note that there were
several questions and comments which addressed the question of establishing validity in research. The question
raises the problem of truth, since there is not only
the claim of what is true for the researcher but, as
well, the fact that the view of what is real for the
researcher is* brought into question *as he or she confronts another way of understanding.*

*The question for many is, then again, what is
actually real, and in terms of the claims of the
research, what is valid as a relating of that reality?*

*But it is the position of our form of research that
this question of validity be seen analytically as one
of establishing for others what has been found to be
"real" in the world of the researcher. Our editorial
comments in the morning session which bear on "epistemology" and discourse may help contextualize our
position here.*

DARROCH: I'd just like to add something to Ron's
comment that might be helpful. It makes me think of
people always wanting to locate work somewhere. I
read a paper at a conference this summer and after I
was finished, one person said, "Is this (what I was
talking about) like gestalt therapy?" And another
person said, "What you're really talking about is the
importance of the right hemisphere of the brain." And
I thought that was interesting because I did not think
my work had anything to do with these two things. But
as I read what I was trying to express, people became

engaged with what was written, and then, of course, the location of the work had to be left up to them in the sense of what they were doing; and, in that sense, it was dependent upon them for figuring out a way to understand it, rather than for my directly telling them how to use it, either theoretically or practically. In that sense, the engagement also becomes the responsibility of hearer or reader. So the interest in interconnecting work is not to provide for a greater corroboration of ideas toward a greater truth, but rather to make something available as carefully as one can for others' responsible theorizing.

At lunch one of the students from Sociology, Mark Egit, consented to describe how he sees himself within his dissertation work. I'd like to ask him to come up now.

EGIT: This is how it all begins. I'll try and describe another way that I see of being in our data within our theses, and what I have to offer is, of course, whatever is happening with mine.

Where I see myself being present in the data is by way of that in me which drives the inquiry. That is, what is it that I'm doing and why is what I'm doing important to me?

The question I began to ask was, what is the world, how can I relate to it, how can I describe it, how is it that it has that kind of power over me? And how can I talk about it? I think in one of the classes here, someone came across the book, the Watson book on the DNA molecule, and I got to thinking about the DNA molecule.

The question becomes "How do you deal with realities of that kind?" For whatever reason I thought, "What is the hardest, the most penultimate strong thing, strong item that I would want to write against if I were going to go up against structures?" And what I found at that time was science. And I thought, let us take items from science and those are items which are seen as true, so whether it's the DNA molecule, whether it's thermodynamics, those are seen as laws, those are seen as immutable those are the things which you on the one hand may want to just play around with. On the other hand, those are immutable, they are not arguable, they are there. The question becomes "Can you undo?" What I try to figure out is, how to unstructure that which is seen as the

71

most real, that is, what is seen as the most structured
of all things? That is, the scientific product to show
that it only is another construction of reality, that
that which is seen as the most significant, the most
rigorous, really has no more rigor to it than does the
myth for Levi-Strauss. That is, it could have been
another one, and indeed, what part of a thesis is, is
to show how it could have been another one. Then the
question becomes "Then how come that one, and how come
we believe that one?" And in trying to answer this
question, in doing that, I go back all the way to my
problem with structures, my problems of the world presented to me as is. My problem with the world saying,
"Here is the way it is, here is the way we study it,
here's the way we'll teach it." And in a sense, always
being removed from that very world as we experience it.
So that intellectually you begin to grapple--you begin
to grapple not with the data, but with your world, and
you find yourself in the midst of that and you begin to
restructure your world. What does that mean? It means
not just for me and for scientists, it means that each
and every one of us has the ability to create the world
around us. Now whether or not that is true, the thing
is that is what I pulled out for myself in finishing,
at some point, the thesis and that is the important
thing for me beyond the thesis, the job, the dissertation; it's an answer for me and it gives me a certain
ability to face those very structures that are and were
troublesome for me and are troublesome for me to this
very day. But it gives me a handle. And working out
of that whole thing is like looking for a handle on the
world. And that for me is being in my thesis.

TRAIN: I really appreciate what you've said here. I
feel here from you in terms of what you felt. I can
hear you doing something for yourself, but I can't
hear you saying what you're seeing yourself contributing
to the general body of our knowledge or whether you are
even attempting to do anything in that vein. Would you
say something about this?

EGIT: It's very hard . . . and perhaps it's not for me
to say. That is, I can't go around saying about the
other guys. But I will deal with it from my point of
view. And in fact what would I do, and how is it they
would know the sign when I finish? In part what I
would do for my committee is try to put them in the
position that I was and try to resolve the issue for me
where they can see how intellectually I made my decisions.

What you do is set it up in such a way that the committee can say, "Yes, I can see what the issue was for you, I can see how you dealt with it, and I can see how you resolve it." And, hopefully, the committee would be able to see something more when they're finished than when they began. And therefore, my working out for myself gives me a clue to others, how to work it out for them, or simply to represent it to see what is going on in my working out. But not indulgent. Working in a sense of understanding something that had to be said, something that had to be confronted, and surely you can't ask more than that of anyone.

DARROCH: When you say not indulgent, it makes me think of the issue of relevance, and I think that's something we've been edging into and should clarify.

SILVERS: What we find within Mark Egit's remarks is a discovery of the significance of a work for himself and potentially for others, rather than the relevance of the work. Relevance would be a correspondence between the author's stated concern behind the research and the concerns of others. Social responsibility is not the parallel of such convergent concerns, but the revealing of what is a basic commitment, as significance, for the researcher. That commitment may then offer to others what may be seen as significant for them. The author may then offer the reader and others an insightfulness of what a concern could be and what a concern should be.

This work is not expected to be relevant in the sense of following a problem in society, but to be significant in showing the direction of concern.

DARROCH: Thanks, Ron. Mmm . . . I see that time is passing. I wonder, maybe you might suggest some other things you might want to express as a concern? Or we could think of drawing to a close. There might be things that you were expecting to come up that didn't come up.

FINKELSTEIN: I'd like to ask a question, a general question. Why at this time does this topic become topical in this Institute?

DARROCH: That's a good question. Actually many people are here. We had no idea how many would come in the end. Why now, rather than a few years ago?

SULLIVAN: I think it probably is the result of the momentum, partly of the 1960s, and it's just simply really having a certain kind of shattering effect on conventional social science. I think the momentum of that would not delve in any specific way in any particular discipline, until you really start to be able to say, "OK, I take that seriously for allowing us to see if there are any other kinds of modes of inquiry that we would want to do." It takes some time to put things together. I don't think that's a good explanation. But I would say if you don't like the emphasis on the absoluteness of discipline, which I think was what we were doing in the early 1960s--if you could go through that without having a challenge and then became involved in a lot of other things, then there developed a considerable amount of malaise with just simply conventional social research. It developed slowly but surely, and shows at this particular point.

DARROCH: In terms of topic I agree with you: it might just now be topical in the Institute for the reasons you say. But in terms of the nature of the work present in the "other" thesis it would be incorrect to see it as a historical consequence of the 1960s since the counter-culture generated its own form of radical social science which is not represented here. We may, however, see a similar spirit of attention in the work. But in terms of psychological thought this kind of work has always been done. So there is a longer legacy behind it as a way of research.

TRAIN: I want to try and answer this question, because I realize for me it's been a route that I can trace, reflecting on it, on what's been happening. I think there.are two things for me. One is that the tyranny of psychology is something that becomes a frightening thing, and I haven't understood how the conflict got into practice in terms of knowing and doing something about research. But when something like legislation can be proposed, where there is an attempt by psychological experts to decide what's "right thinking," that appears to me like a real cultural event. It's going to trigger a lot of questions of the most powerful force in terms of who are, what are, psychologists. So the questioning for me is only happening in the last little while, because psychology is more of an underdog than when I was an undergraduate a couple of years ago. The second thing is that in the 1960s the whole spiritual and emotional emphasis was on people themselves.

This came to the fore, but again it took time to integrate that into the way of knowing and studying and to understand that all that comes together around things like meaning, what is meaningful in research. It's taken time, to become integrated with academia.

The answer to the question of the historical presence and the "other" thesis at this time may be seen around the development of a different tradition of thought, which we have referred to throughout this transcript. That tradition is to be found in our own work. The emergence of the "other" thesis is an embodiment of a way of thought in which we find researchers as inquirers bonded to the phenomena to be understood and who at the same time, interrogate the phenomenon and themselves. That form of presence of the research is an achievement as a way of bringing the world into knowing and as expressing that knowing in thought. Such a tradition stands in contrast to technical thought, which is a rationality, a method of inquiry, and a conception of knowledge exemplified in positivism and related conceptions of scientific work and which is founded upon a duality of subject (inquirer) and object (phenomenon).

Within social science technical thought has had some four to five decades to see its promise realized. In the past decade, that promise has slipped substantially for many, particularly as an encouragment for those beginning their studies and research in the social sciences. Concomitant with this shift of interest, the movement of the classical tradition which began in Europe is beginning to take hold beyond philosophical anthropology and within studies in the human sciences.

True, the 1960s were important, but mainly to realize and address the significance of the concrete in the details of the variety of life-worlds and understandings that people hold, and to appreciate the importance of history in the lives of those people. The "other" thesis as a historical episode in human studies is both an example and a part of the current of one intellectual tradition meeting and facing another.

DARROCH: Thanks, I think we should close now. For all of us, it seems as if it was difficult to begin this discussion, easier to move through it, but now hardest to end it. Do you have any other comments or questions? I have to say that I really appreciate the energy that

75

you came with, because it made it a lot easier for me sitting up here, and now you at least, too, know some of the people in the different departments who are participating in this work. Thank you all for coming.

Close of Colloquium.

- - -

References

Note: Only one representative reference has been cited for each of the authors referred to in the transcript.

Barrett, William. The Illusion of Technique. New York: Anchor Press/Doubleday, 1978.

Barthes, Roland. S/Z. tr. Richard Miller. London: Cape, 1975.

Belsey, Catherine. Critical Practice. London: Methuen, 1980.

Buber, Martin. I and Thou. tr. Walter Kaufmann. New York: Charles Scribner's Sons, 1970.

Foucault, Michel. Power/Knowledge. ed. Colin Gordon. tr. Gordon, Marshall, Mepham, Soper. New York: Pantheon, 1980.

James, William. The Principles of Psychology. New York: Dover Publications, 1950.

Jaspers, Karl. "Existenzphilosophie". In Walter Kaufmann's Existentialism: from Dostoevsky to Sartre. New York: New American Library, 1975.

Merleau-Ponty, Maurice. Phenomenology of Perception. tr. Colin Smith. London: Routledge & Kegan Paul, 1962.

Mills, C. Wright. The Sociological Imagination. London: Oxford University Press, 1959.

Moustakas, Clark. Loneliness. Englewood Cliffs, New Jersey: Prentice-Hall, 1961.

O'Neil, John. Making Sense Together. New York: Harper and Row, 1974.

Poole, Roger. Towards Deep Subjectivity. New York:
    Harper and Row, 1972.

Schutz, Alfred. Collected Papers Vol. I. The Hague:
    Martinus Nijhoff, 1971.

PART III

RESEARCH IN THE INQUIRY

In preparing this section our purpose was to present the
life-worlds of researchers in the movement of interpretive inquiry as it represents the shape of knowledge of
that inquiry. We have chosen to include here papers in
which ordinary problems of research are encountered. We
find here the ordinary problems of all researchers in
human sciences: How do we begin? What do we choose to
study? How do we understand those whose circumstances
are so different from ours? How may the parts of our
research be gathered together? What language shall we
use to communicate to others about our inquiry? If we
are to account for ourselves within our inquiry how do
we accomplish it? In all the papers of others which we
have selected, we find the authors attempting to locate
the reasoning of their practices of inquiry. We have
made a similar attempt in our own essays which we have
included here. Although the papers have their sources
in different projects and in different fields, taken
together we hope that they may provide a sense of
inquiry seen as the attempt to form a certain kind of
relationship in which the researchers' responsibility
is to make themselves present, both analytically and
morally, to the persons being studied and to the persons to whom they then communicate about their inquiry.

MAPPING A REGION OF SOCIAL EXPERIENCE

Terrence Trussler

In his work, Trussler offers a way of moving from a des-
cription of everyday experiences through interpretation
of them to understanding what special dimension of
reflective life he may bring to his inquiry. Note-
worthy is his effort to show what is occurring in the
pre-reflective understanding of ordinary occasions.
But, more important, he is attempting to articulate and
develop further the moments of insightful awareness
which can emerge from ordinary occasions. Here he comes
to show that the evidence of moving toward understanding
depends upon critical experience being enveloped by a
tension of project (the "call" of the future) and social
tension (action between people).

These pages represent a series of events, understood to
be cohesive in retrospect, in which I was engaged in
locating myself in experience as an inquirer in ordinary
social life. In the absence of an explicit procedure, I
was attempting to follow, systematically, the path of my
attention as I found myself experiencing decisive
moments, spontaneous creation, vivid perception or insight in co-presence with others. Not that I simply
looked to these occasions. I was attending to ordinary
social life continuously. What I brought into the inquiry were the moments which occurred in my experience,
beyond the taken-for-granted understanding of my exis-
tence--an intensive shift into "hyperawareness." With
increasingly rigorous attention to the immediate experience, I began to describe and record these events while
mapping out features as they were reflectively available.

By incorporating my experiences in everyday social
life into my reflective inquiry, I became increasingly
aware of the dynamics of the movement in my own biography. What was subject for analytic scrutiny was the
path of my attention, the consequences of my actions,
and the reflective movement of my thought as I directed
myself toward understanding these dynamics. I was not
altogether comfortable with bringing my intimate social

---

* From "The Discovery of Critical Experience in the
Social Invention of Everyday Life," Terrence Trussler,
Doctoral Dissertation, University of Toronto, 1982.

encounters into the public realm of social research; yet my understanding of the limits of consciousness indicated that the path of my own attention was the only route to follow. The task that I had set for myself was to uncover the dynamics of what I now refer to as "critical experience" originating in everyday social experience. In undertaking the quest I recognized a new commitment to the social encounter as embodied in my experience, examining its dynamics in the movement of my biography.

I think of my fieldwork as a series of hikes into a relatively well known world. Not a long and protracted journey, for I engaged in smaller excursions into the proximate territory of social life as I experienced it with others in leisure. There are no visible trails in the territory of social experience. The features of the region I was uncovering were the dynamic structures and principles which inherently organize and orient our experience of social life. I encountered, however, the metaphysical markings of my predecessors, who had also examined social experience for its structures: Erich Jantsch, Joseph Zinker, Alfred Schutz, and David Buckholdt and Jaber Gubrium. Still, my task was to examine my own experience for its features as I encountered the region of social experience in which I was engaged. The predecessors provided guideposts in these invisible realms which were of inestimable value. I followed these vigorously in establishing my own markers, pointing to features of the social experience of leisure.

What I brought back for analytic scrutiny from these excursions were like photographs, still-life records, well exposed, portraying events which occurred when I traversed the region. My descriptions represent what I lived in my experience with the most careful attention to talk, action, and context which was available at the time. My focus improves, my attention shifts, and my experience is reoriented by the very action of these events as I lived them in their immediacy. As I uncover more of the dynamics of "hyperawareness" in these experiences, I discover more of the region of social experience, its features and structures. And I offer all of this as evidence, in the process of discovering critical experience as a dynamic principle which manifests itself as "hyperawareness" in these experiences I have lived in this region.

A leap into a world . . .

I was standing knee-deep in water when the notion

arrived. Rob and I were locked together in conversation,
having averted the impulse to dive into the lake. The
sun was hiding periodically behind cloud masses that
moved in the high winds of the upper atmosphere. Although it was late July, the air that day was chilling.
We craved the penetration of the sun before the splash.

We were alone on a beach that we often visit for
short canoeing adventures. I say short because we would
paddle across the lake on Friday afternoon of a summer
weekend, set up the tent, and paddle back across a mile
of water on Sunday afternoon. It was not strictly
"canoeing" which brought us here. The canoe was, however, more than symbolic. We used the canoe to paddle
across the water. We came to the beach to be on "the
land." The canoeing was linked with the way we practiced
being on the land.

Our conversation was rolling on. The sun would peek
out for enough moments that my back felt warmed. Then
just as the urge to dive in began to grow, a cloud would
pass and I would be chilled again. This was all somewhat
incidental to our conversation. We stood together in the
water on the beach, talking, listening, seeing, and
feeling--taking in the whole scene. We were only two
hours away from our lives in the city. Yet there was a
wilderness here that made us different. And this
difference was part of what we "knew" about being on the
land.

Rob and I have experienced the land with a kind of
reverence for much of our lives. There were the days as
children at family cabins. There were the summer camp
days when we took flotillas of children on canoes through
these lakes. We found a way to be at home on the land,
but the "way" was special. We developed a sensitivity
to the elements and the forest that you would not experience unless you were to live in the wild for a few
weeks. In the past, we lived in a tent for the entire
summer.

There is a power in this sensitivity. You begin to
feel cradled by the land, instead of threatened. The
silent, self-protective instinct of survival gives way
to wide-eyed wonder. Witness a violent summer storm
rolling across a lake from under a hastily made shelter
of sticks-holding-up-canoe. Billowing, steely-grey
masses and tympanic thunderclaps orchestrate a cartoon
symphony from under the canoe. There is unearthly

laughter as lightening flashes and the skies clack shut
around the burning arc.

Wonder brings worlds into perspective. And it was
talk of our other worlds that held us in conversation on
the beach. In the city, Rob was working as a counselor
in an outpatient clinic at a major hospital. I was at a
turning point in my career, and about to take on an inquiry, a decision that had been developing for some time.
We were speaking of a mutual interest--the special
qualities of experience that people undergo at moments
of insight, ecstasy, or crisis.

I had just completed reporting on my work at the
Art Gallery of Ontario, "looking-at-people-looking-at-
art." I was describing for Rob what was discovered when
the research group got deeply involved in the kind of
experiences that people have in art galleries. We had
seen that some people seemed to "fly," spiritually, with
a work of art, while others seemed to remain indifferent
to the same work. Individual taste did not seem to be
an adequate answer for what remained in question from
our experience in the gallery.

In our research at the gallery, one of the significant issues that we had dealt with was finding a way
to describe how people attend to what is around them.
We could not know what was in another's experience, but
we could describe a pattern in the other's way of
looking. We thought that this was a way of uncovering
the form of another's experience. By looking and
looking again in this way, we began to see that people
addressed the field of their attention in very different
ways. But how could we really know this from looking-
at-people-looking-at-art?

What we were looking at was a form, something
behind what was actually the experience of the visitors
at the art gallery. The form we were seeing was given
in the way in which people addressed the field-in-view.

We saw people "play" with their field-in-view to
find "something" in a work of art. They would move with
their whole body, back, and to the side, or stand medi-
tatively. There were others who, in rounding a corner,
would gasp ecstatically at a previously unseen work and
then move in closer, standing in "wide-eyed" bliss.
Still others would walk through a room where all of this
was going on and never stop or even slow down to take in
what was available.

84

There was the one experience in particular I remembered, with one member of the research group and three-art-panels-on-the-wall, that seemed the clearest example of what we were seeing. I was intrigued by moments of "hyperawareness" that we seemed to experience together on that occasion. I had a notion that there was some basic principle to be discovered in the dynamics of such experiences. What gave me this sense of "hyperawareness"? And what did it mean? It had been a level of experience that neither of us had previously shared together.

So, there I was with Rob, standing in knee-deep water, talking about special qualities of experience. Rob had lived through occasions of "hyperawareness" in his work. He spoke of the kind of tension that occurs when a clear movement-in-thinking comes across the face of a client. "The tension is between counselor and client. You can feel 'it' too because you are with him," he said. "You can hear movements of understanding in the changes of tone in the client's voice."

"How do you get at 'it'? That is the problem. How do you study an experience that is seemingly so uncertain? You 'know' even at the time that there is something 'magically' revealed in momentary process of experiencing 'hyperawareness'." We talked about the issues of conducting an experimental inquiry. We talked about predictability of such occurrences. And, as usual, we spoke to each other with great conviction held within the tension-of-the-moment in the knee-deep water on the beach.

We have made so many discoveries in these dialogues. They are a part of our way-of-being on the land. There is something about the background of the woods which gives such lofty conversation an ideal home. The land must hold some of the same truth we realize in our talk. We see processes taking form in the weather and the seasons. We experience ourselves as live creatures.

Out in the wild, the background of life processes reveals experience as part of the whole arrangement of life processes. The teeming confusion of life comes together in our thoughts. Husserl showed that thoughts are a relative latecomer in experience. This gives me the sense that thoughts are much like what we see of the land, developments. Thoughts are connected with the turning of attention in experience, patterns of movement.

85

The question seems to be whether we can perceive these
patterns directly. Or is there a way we would treat
attention which would give rise to more precise thinking
about experience? I think of the kind of attention that
goes with cycling, surfing, or sailing. In these experiences there is a wide-open way of treating movement and
the oncoming rush of events which reveals an elegant,
continuously balanced flow of attention. My hunch is
that this kind of attention could be put into action in
other occasions for the examination of experience
itself.

Thoughts about experience turned in conversation
with Rob on the beach. I "sensed" a development of
momentum. Our separate experiences fed the conversation.
We recalled some of the experiences which we had lived
together. I heard a lift in Rob's voice, a melodious
quality as he spoke. Our dialogue was like a dance of
words. We danced around a way of reaching and uncovering what is behind experiences of this extraordinary
potency--the moments of "hyperawareness."

I was interested in finding or developing a mode of
research into such powerful experiences as the one I had
encountered in the gallery. I was more interested in
the way such experiences of "hyperawareness" arise in
ordinary circumstances of everyday life. I had my
reasons. I had an idea that potent processes moving
in everyday social experience would be revealed. I had
noted, in thinking about this, that the way we bind our
experiences of the world together is patterned socially;
in other words, we pick up form in the experience of
others experiencing the world. This is tacit. We are
not particularly aware of how this happens; the way we
divert our eyes from each other when we pass along the
street, for example. I wanted to "see into" the processes of experience where these patterns are in a state
of transformation. I sensed a link between the process
of transformation and moments of "hyperawareness," but
I had no idea of how I "knew" this or how I could develop my understanding of this notion. So, as I stood
there talking with Rob, in the knee-deep water on the
beach, I was feeling we were on to something. I felt a
"tension" between us that was moving with our talk. It
was as if we were becoming very clear to each other as
we talked about this experience of "hyperawareness." I
was starting to percolate . . .

"When you examine social experience, there is an
altogether different perspective than the one we express

in ordinary talk. Consider politics and economics, for example. We refer to them in the same way that we refer to the weather. Something is happening to us--'out of my control.' We look for indicators like barometers to see what might be coming up next. Our efforts to predict are usually based on past experience and, like the weather, there is much uncertainty.

"Something else happens, though , when you begin to look at these processes from the standpoint of the ordinary experience of everyday life! The experience changes with this shift of perspective. What is revealed is that the processes we name politics and economics originate in ordinary social experience. We refer to them as having a life of their own, but the process of constituting their existence is given in social experience. Indeed, that so many people contribute to the process does give politics and economics a separate existence, but where do we give them reality but in the practicality of our everyday experience with others?

"Social experience is the encountering of other selves. We have a social habit, out of self-protection, of resisting 'seeing' the work that we do in constituting the encounter--its style and patterns. We prefer to see experience as 'happening to us.' Dare we move past our resistance and the sense of self we have invested in to acknowledge the work? What is the risk? Here is a crucial juncture from which we may begin to find another way of expressing self in the social experience."

I referred to the time we were lying in the tent watching the storm coming across the lake. Rob remembered the occasion immediately. We had both been beginning to doze off when the tent became illuminated with flashes of light. "Oh wow! There's a storm coming up!" We spread the flaps of the tent open and rolled over to see the oncoming flashes of light in the deep dark of the forest at night. The forks of lightening pierced the blackness and sent a jolt down my spine. I could hear Rob, "OHHHHHHHH." We made ourselves present for the occasion and shared the experience with unearthly laughter.

I had begun reading Erich Jantsch's Design for Evolution before our trip. Some of his ideas began to emerge in my talk with Rob.

"Erich Jantsch knew something about the way we constitute social experience to shape the reality of cultural existence in all of its forms. He dared to make
an obverse statement about his sense of it after a long
and distinguished career as a systems analyst and
theorist. After years of trying to fit the processes
involved in 'human systems' into a stable and rational
arrangement of patterns which could be predicted, he
turned completely around on his own thought. He discovered that the effort to make conditions fit a stable
set of explanations only created more uncertainty about
what was happening. The patterns defied prediction.
He had an insight which reoriented his view of the social processes he was examining. He began to 'see' that
man's intelligence had to be connected in some way to
the general pattern of evolution. The consequence of
this shift in perspective was a complete alteration in
the way he had been thinking of human enterprise.[1]

   "It was the _form_ revealed in social processes that
defied the rational system of explanation. Evolutionary
processes are uneven. Contrary to our ordinary thinking
of evolutionary process, there is not an even, sequential layering of events. A pattern develops in time,
but alteration in forms of life occur in random leaps.
New patterns are plucked from the old, but we are never
quite sure what aspects of the old go into the formation
of the new. Both the leap and the resulting consequences defy prediction. So, when Jantsch saw human systems
as processes with lives of their own, he turned his
attention to the pattern of evolutionary change within
them. What he saw must have been a little frightening
for a man who had invested so much of his career into a
rigorous system of explaining the major social processes.
He had to admit to himself that the 'life of human
systems' was unpredictable.

   "Jantsch found, however, a way to make use of his
insight. He believed that in order to study the change
of patterns in social organization, we would begin by
examining the processes of social experience. In
searching for ways to express knowledge that would only

_____

1 Erich Jantsch, <u>Design for Evolution</u>, pp.xii-xxii. I
have reworked the dialogue on the beach to do justice to
Jantsch and to present my interpretive arrangement of his
thought into the form of the inquiry as clearly as possible.

resist rational reduction, Jantsch proposed forms of
'experiential inquiry' that would embrace randomness.
Such an inquiry would account for the changes in experience and modes of expression occurring in the life of
the inquiry itself. The inquiry process would embrace
evolutionary patterns.

"The examination of social experience would be
accomplished in an exploration of the 'appreciated world'
of the inquirer. Jantsch referred to the 'appreciated
world' as the version of the world unique to the perspective of the inquirer. This version of the world
would be 'seen' in the social encounter or the encounter
with other versions of the world. Consciousness of the
'appreciated world' would result from mapping social
experience onto the 'appreciated world' of the inquirer.
Such an inquiry, Jantsch believed, would bring to consciousness the patterns of social process of evolutionary form. The expression of 'knowledge' would be a
creative process of 'design' following the form of the
inquiry itself. Jantsch thought of 'design' as an
expression of knowledge in which we would 'emancipate
ourselves from the grip of rigid reality' and find ourselves participant in the evolutionary pattern of life."[2]

The tension between Rob and I standing in the knee-
deep water reached a new peak. Something was beginning
to take shape in our talk. How would I design an
inquiry which would uncover what was behind potent forms
of experience? How would I embrace the potential for
experiences of "hyperawareness" in the act of conducting
an inquiry? How would I embrace the paradox of "knowledge" which defied rational prediction or explanation?
Rob struggled with me, making suggestions, sometimes
stopping in mid-sentence when the development of his
thinking was leading to a "set-up" procedure to examine
experience. How to set a course for the inquiry?

"Jantsch was concerned that much of 'knowledge' had
attempted to explain the grand design of human processes;
'great theories.' Such inquiries led only to another
static orientation which made human processes appear to
be non-human entities. Where a sense of movement would
emerge in inquiry was in finding movement in the self
living in a more or less static world. This approach he

_____

2 Ibid., p.121.

felt would 'bring into play the human faculty of grasping dynamic reality in a holistic way of becoming
sensitive to the evolutionary reality of human existence.'"[3]

"I 'see' that you and I have been doing this kind
of 'knowledge' in the woods. We watch the processes of
our presence in the forest. What happens when we build
a campfire and leave the charred remains of the wood?
Carbon will last for millenia and leave a trace in the
wild unless we take steps to burn wood completely to
grey ash. We watch the sweeping movement of cabins
encroaching on lakes where we would see no-one for days
in our younger lives. We grasp within ourselves the
consequences of our actions on the land and the presence
of other ways on the land. The 'knowledge' comes
between us. We have found a way of encountering each
other in our adventures in the wild."

"I don't know how yet, Rob, but I want to bring
what we are doing here into an inquiry. This is how 'it'
happens for us . . . the way our experiences turn out
when we get to standing around in the water like this
and end up talking this way for half an hour when we
should be swimming. Or like when you and I stayed up
to watch the storm. Or the time we first discovered
this beach. This is where they happen, these experiences of 'hyperawareness' that I can't even name yet:
when we're making things happen for ourselves like this."
I could see Rob's look, but I could not quite bring
myself to find an interpretation: partly knowing,
partly questioning, partly recognizing that I had just
made a decision and a commitment. It was a commitment
to turn my attention to an unknown path of inquiry.

I could see the edge of the broken clouds across
the sun opening up a clear sky. I began to wade slowly
back toward the shore watching the ripple of water form
around my ankles; my thoughts ran out to a blank tension.
Then I turned on my step and glanced at Rob, feeling a
grin form on my face, seeing it returned in his. And we
started running out across the shallows of the beach,
screaming "Yahhhhhhhhhhhh!"

---

3 Ibid., p.129.

References

Gubrium, Jaber F. and Buckholdt, David R. Towards
    Maturity. San Francisco: Jossey Bass, 1977.

Husserl, Edmund. Ideas: General Introduction to Pure
    Phenomenology. New York: MacMillan Publishing Co.
    Inc., 1931.

Jantsch, Erich. Design for Evolution. New York:
    George Brazillier, 1975.

Schutz, Alfred. The Structures of the Life World.
    London: Heinemann, 1977.

_____. Phenomenology and the Social World. North-
    western University Press, 1967.

Zinker, Joseph. Creative Process in Gestalt Therapy.
    New York: Random House, 1977.

APPROACHING A NEW INQUIRY

Eleoussa Polyzoi

*Polyzoi's materials are introduced here because we be-
lieve they exemplify how many students approach, and how
some are able to accomplish an initial understanding of
what interpretive inquiry is in relation to the phenomena
which interest them. When Polyzoi first entered this
research, one of the first aspects of it of which she
became aware was that the "content" of this inquiry and
its method must evolve concurrently. Hence, having topic
(the immigrant's life-world) but not having content or
method, Polyzoi asks the question "How do I organize my
research?" Having then determined certain steps for
organization, she moves into the necessity of conceptualization in the interpreting of her data. However, as
she confronts this necessity and grapples with interpretation inside the activity of inquiry itself, the
issue of "organizing" falls away for her. She is left
with only a consciousness of and attendance to her own
interpretive practices. It is here that she realizes
the "method" within her study and begins to explicate it.
Finally, in her interpretation we witness the "pull" of
the materials for Polyzoi--that is, the importance and
significance of them expressed for her as researcher.
Though Polyzoi does not comment upon this, her writing
expresses well what the comments of the immigrants mean
to her and how these comments illuminate the life-world
that she seeks to understand.*

In this brief paper, what I would like to outline are
aspects of my own analytical practice as it has evolved
in my doctoral dissertation over the past eight months.
I have chosen to describe this practice as a movement
from the traditional hypothetico-deductive framework, to
the qualitative yet still positivistic mode, and, finally
to the phenomenological orientation which I am just now
coming to understand.

The first and perhaps most entrenched phase of my
own analytical thought emerged from what can be called

---

* Written in preparation for "An Examination of the
Experience of Immigration: A Movement from A Familiar to
a Strange Frame of Reference," Eleoussa Polyzoi, Doctoral
Dissertation, University of Toronto, 1982.

a hypothetico-deductive framework. It was a framework in which I was socialized from my undergraduate years in Psychology at the University of Toronto. This was and still is a very classically oriented department as reflected in both the types of courses offered and in the type of research produced. Right from the introductory course in psychology, I learned that the definition of psychology was the "science of behavior." I learned that what psychology emphasized was normative behavior and that the prediction and control of behavior were psychology's prime objectives. By the end of five or six courses, I was learning quite well to see and interpret the world around me in terms of dependent and independent variables. Although I didn't realize it then, my undergraduate years in Psychology at the University of Toronto served as an effective socialization experience.

In terms of research, I learned that there was only one method to follow in conducting research regardless of what question you studied, and if you didn't follow this, your credibility as a "good" psychologist was questioned.

This traditional separation of method and content was difficult for me to move out of at first. I remember approaching one of the members of my thesis committee, when I was first thinking about embarking on a thesis in the area of the immigrant experience, and expressing my disillusionment with the literature on the immigrant with its almost total emphasis on the concept of "assimilation." At that time, my efforts were focussed on searching for a new methodology--one that would more adequately account for the immigrant's experience. The committee member's response--"Well, I don't have a method to offer"--puzzled me at first. In traditional psychology, where method dictates content rather than content forming method, I learned that this ordering sometimes led to "missing the phenomenon altogether," but at that time I couldn't understand that content and method should evolve concurrently.

Two years ago I began working for the Multicultural History Society of Ontario as a field researcher. Through my work I was able to interview a number of immigrants who made the trek to the New World in the '20s, '30s, and '40s. My contact with these relatively older immigrants and the vivid re-creation of the early events of their lives served as a constant source of both fascination and illumination for me. I was finally able to collect holistic data, uncompartmentalized into modal indices of assimilation and unfettered by sequential stages of adjustment imposed "top down" by social theorists.

It was this experience which prompted me to search for a question suitable for a doctoral dissertation.

The original goal of my study was to determine and articulate, through discussion, analyzing, and reporting of the immigrant's life-world, what it is like for him or her to be an immigrant. But I knew I had to impose some workable parameters on such a huge area. I thus decided to focus my inquiry on the experience of "becoming" an immigrant.

In the past few months, I've been working both on conducting interviews and on approaching an interpretive analysis of these interviews. Because my interest was in exploring the life-world of the immigrant from a new perspective, different from that of the traditional "assimilation" theorists, I began very early to gravitate toward the phenomenological literature in search of answers. After carefully reviewing some of this literature on phenomenology, I was particularly attracted to Glaser and Strauss's method of grounded theory for developing theory from qualitative data.

Phase #1

My first attempt at an interpretive analysis of my interviews, as a result, reflected a strict adherence to Glaser and Strauss. Going over each interview meticulously, I came up with a comprehensive list of categories (or concepts) and properties which reflected the main areas of the immigrants' descriptions as related to me through a series of unstructured interviews. Some of the categories I came up with, for example, were as follows: Leaving the Homeland, First Impressions after Arrival, Difficulties Experienced as an Immigrant, and Strategies Used to Overcome Difficulties.

Phase #2

But I was dissatisfied with this compilation of categories. They were too embedded in what I believed to be a superficial level of the immigrant's experiencing with referents that were either situational, chronological, geographical, or simply factual. I came to recognize

95

that I was failing to see the immigrant's experience from his/her own personal referents. I was not "peeling off enough layers" of interpretation, as it were. I had often heard, too, the word "problem" associated with immigrants in the literature. I knew I had to remove this filter. In this second phase of thought, I came to learn that "leaving the homeland" was not as important a category as a "heightened sense of bonding with the homeland" which was felt just before immigration; "first impressions upon arrival" was not as important a category as a "feeling of suspension" during the process of coming to Canada; "strategies used to overcome difficulties" was not as important a category as a "need to regain this lost frame of reference" and so on.

Phase #3

Recently, in my attempt to draw out further these new concepts across interviews, I found myself drawing too much on the interview data and again feeling dissatisfied with the lack of depth of my interpretation of the immigrant's experience. I felt that not enough analysis of the underlying meaning behind the immigrant's description was present in my work. My writing failed to make the immigrants' descriptions explicit--that is, failed to locate what stood behind their expressions. (This is the fundamental principle of a phenomenological work, which I am only now coming to grips with.) A second component of my dissatisfaction dealt with the degree to which "I" as "researcher" should be part of analysis. I came to realize that by omitting a record of my thought process in the selection of concepts, in essence I was leaving the reader at a loss as to how I came up with these concepts. As a result, in my fourth phase of thinking, I tried to incorporate these two analytical practices: that is, more effectively getting at the underlying meaning of the immigrants' statements in my analytical thought as well as providing a more complete record of my thought process as I did this.

Phase #4

In this phase, I allowed more of myself to enter the analysis (without, however, being intrusive). I allowed myself to be selective of concepts which I myself wished to focus on without being overly concerned with analyzing the entire interview. I was able to "bring forward" concepts which I chose to explore without feeling pressured to see them present in all my interviews. In analyzing each concept, however, I continued to ground them in my interview data--to provide ample evidence for their emergence in at least one of my interviews and in the immigrant's own words. I found, too, that by always "naming" the concept, usually by using the immigrant's own expressions, I was able to keep the concept present and focused in my writing of it.

As you will see in the two concepts which I have already begun to explore, and which I have "named" "I Can't Feel in English" and "People Caught in Time," I have tried to select concepts on the basis of their being at the core of the overall experience of the immigrant as well as being linked somehow to my personal biography (meaning my own background or history that I bring to the analysis). In this way, then, I am not forced to deny my presence or "influence," if you will, in the selection and writing of the concepts, but rather I acknowledge my presence as a natural component of my analytical interpretation. My personal biography, however--how I personally account for the choices both in the selection of the concepts and in their explication--may or may not be explicit to me as reflected either in the writing of or in the thinking of the concepts chosen.

This change in orientation of my thinking, then, is reflected in my fourth phase of analysis. By the end of the dissertation, I hope to have looked at, analytically interpreted, and expanded on most of the important concepts which speak to the immigrant's experience around the time of immigration. Although it may appear at present that these concepts are being examined in isolation, the connecting lines joining these concepts I hope will become clearer to me as I proceed in my investigation. I see the long-term aim of my thesis, however, as approaching a reasonably unified conceptual framework of the immigrant's experience from a more holistic, experientially based image of the immigrant.

Below are the two concepts which I have begun to develop, "I Can't Feel in English" and "People Caught in Time." They are included here as an illustration of my present phase, which I call "approaching the phenomenological."

"I CAN'T FEEL IN ENGLISH"

In reflecting on my first interview (Maria), I was

97

struck by the following statement expressing the participant's frustration with the English language.

"When I think . . . when I study in English and I
want to feel what I'm learning, I translate in Greek
because I can't feel in English."

Initially, I didn't see the significance of this
statement beyond its surface meaning. I interpreted it
as a frustration stemming from a lack of knowledge in
the English language. But then I realized how important
and powerful a statement it was in terms of what it
revealed about the character of language. What I found
most intriguing was the phrase "I can't feel in English."

What Maria connotes by this statement is that the
emotive quality of language is missing in English when
she attempts to read or think in this language. Language
in any case is a very important extension of Maria's
self-expression. As Maria learned words in the course
of linguistic development, a very important emotional
link became established between the words and the environment within which they were learned.

For all of us, every word possesses an aura of
emotional values which cannot be easily expressed in
words. Every element of speech acquires a primary con-
notative function and a special and personal secondary
meaning derived from the context or social environment
within which it is employed and receives a special color
from the actual occasion in which it is used.

To the immigrant, this means that her first language
carries with it a unique emotive quality which the new
language clearly lacks simply because of an absence of
this link between experience in the new country and the
use of the first language.

Personal meaning, then, is derived not only from
the communicative quality of speech but so too from its
emotive aspects. The former without the latter makes
language a very technical exercise resulting in the immigrant's necessary distancing of herself from the language.

Hence Maria's need to translate back from English
into Greek to recapture the "feeling" and then proceed
back to English.

"PEOPLE CAUGHT IN TIME"

Although my focus thus far has been on exploring
the early phase of the immigrant's life-world, in my
thinking I always seem to come back to the experience of
the immigrant returning to the homeland in terms of how
this illuminates or informs the former. In a sense it
is like the completed "other half" of the cycle.

This repatriation experience was highlighted for me
by another participant (Dina) who first came to Canada
at the age of ten. Fifteen years later she describes her
return trip to Greece in the following manner:

"Here in Canada, I kept thinking that those people
back there, they stood like, they were sort of caught in
time. Like they just stood as I remembered them. Because I could not conceive of them changing . . . I just
remembered them as they were."

When Dina first immigrated to Canda, she experienced
a "discontinuity of experience." Once she moved to
Canada, life at home was no longer accessible in
immediacy to her in exactly the same form. Although the
cultural pattern of her home group continued its historical development in an unbroken fashion, she was no longer
part of it. In Canada, Dina's only recourse to the homeland was through her memories of the past. And these, in
a necessary fashion, had stopped in time for her. She
"could not conceive of them changing." She "just
remembered them as they were."

But it was not only people that had become fossil-
ized in Dina's memory. The dimensions of size, distance,
and time were also very salient components of this
fossilization process.

"When I went back, distances . . . like before, when
I was young, they seemed so long and so far apart, you
know. And when I went back, the village looked so
small . . . It was just incredible. I guess it was
because I was small and the place looked big. And now,
I felt like I could just go all over the place in just
five or ten minutes. And the house looked very small
and the rooms looked ooohh very very small!"

Only when Dina was confronted with the difference
between Greece as she remembered it and Greece in
reality as she now perceived it on her return trip, did

she realize the incongruency of these two images. The immediate source of these changes lies in Dina herself, who left her homeland as a child and returned as an adult.

Reference

Glaser, Barney G. and Strauss, Anselm A. The Discovery of Grounded Theory: Strategies for Qualitative Research. Aldine: Chicago, 1967.

A PROPOSAL FOR AN INTERPRETIVE ANALYSIS

Ann Dean

*The organization of the conventional research proposal
is unsuited for an interpretive research which emphasizes the discovery of meaning, its sources, and shared
understandings, and the potential for creating new
"existences." A conventional proposal is intended to
plan a program of research which establishes the assumptions and boundaries within which inquiry is undertaken.
But as Dean notes, inquiry is dependent on the progression of experiences and, subsequently, the progression
of newly formed understandings. Thus, a proposal for
interpretive inquiry which is existential is not marked
as a beginning point with an end in view. Rather, it is
a place to pause in reflection for an inquiry already
begun by virtue of having yielded to what stubbornly and
unknowingly claims one's attention. Thus it must be
noted that proposals of different persons will have
their own unique forms. Dean's is only one representation.*

It is difficult to introduce the starting point for a
topic of inquiry. All research topics and formats are
dependent upon the experiences of the researcher and
the type of understanding which is sought. In essence,
the direction of this research is toward an understanding of autism. The basis for that understanding arises
from the interpretive focus of phenomenology. However,
within a phenomenological investigation a topic is not
pre-selected, but rather it presents itself to the
researcher and not just once but countless times so
that the topic constantly changes and transforms. These
changes are the result of the analytical movement of the
research which is dependent upon the affiliation between
the researcher and the inquiry. In identifying the
position of the researcher within phenomenological
research, Mishler (1979) noted that "the perspective of
the observer is intertwined with the phenomenon." (p.10).
It seems initially important, then, to examine and

---

* Written in preparation for "An Interpretive Approach
Towards Autism," Ann Dean, M.A. Thesis, University of
Toronto, forthcoming.

attempt to unveil the process by which autism emerged for me as a focus of interest in terms of my association with autism.

The decision to investigate autism as a direction for research is a relatively recent one. However, as a topic of inquiry, autism gained significance from within my own biography, and consequently already had a history for me before this research transpired. In a sense it became topical as a result of a variety of experiences which I had with autistic children. It seems essential to return to those experiences in order to examine the process by which autism has come to gain significance for me once again. Yet before I do so it is important to mention briefly the position that any author is placed in when introducing the biographical features behind a topic.

In admitting to the biographical component of an investigation, the researcher must not only admit to his/her own experience and understanding and provide a translation of those experiences, but also in doing so must recognize that he/she is giving an account of others. In offering this account the researcher has gone beyond him/herself, and it is here that any uncertainty must be met and challenged. Furthermore, it is in this encounter with uncertainty that the research is able to develop and move forward. It was the uncertainty behind my understanding of my past experiences with autistic children which contributed to the selection of the topic as well as the decision to turn to phenomenology as a basis for addressing the uncertainty.

In order to begin to examine my past experiences, I returned to several observational reports. Included in one of the reports was the following description:

In one corner of the room a child rocked silently, turning the pages of an old magazine methodically back and forth. She appeared locked in a world of silence as she neither looked at nor spoke to anyone. Intermittently, she would stop turning the pages and at these moments she would frantically grasp her left wrist with her right hand and throw her hand into the space above her left shoulder. Her piercing screams which followed echoed throughout the suddenly narrow confines of the room. Eventually she collapsed forward banging her forehead rhythmically against her

clenched fists which were pressed tightly upon
the floor.

At the time of the observation it was easy to see this
behavior as autistic. In terms of diagnostics, I could
see the rocking, the repetitious movement, the
screaming, the head banging as a way of confirming the
disturbance. These symptoms from a clinical perspective
automatically totalized into autism. In terms of
assessment, the symptoms did not require any explanation.
In this sense the clinical understanding can be identified as being the "taken-for-granted" (Schutz, 1967,
p.74). The "taken-for-granted," Schutz wrote, "is
always that particular level of experience which presents itself as not in need of further analysis."

Yet to see autism in this way (as a collection of
behaviors) did not leave me with an understanding. In
a sense it left only a possibility of "seeing" autism
without "knowing" it. Other than being able to identify its symptoms as they were displayed, I did not
know anything else. The only meaning which I could
attribute to the child's behavior was based upon the
knowledge which I shared with others, who could only
be seen as being "outside" of the child's experience.
To be "outside" was a part of the "taken-for-granted."
The barrier between the child and the shared knowledge
about that child was also a part of this understanding.
It was this realization which suddenly placed what was
"taken-for-granted" into question. And as Schutz (1967)
suggested, "a change of attention can transform something that is taken for granted into something problematical" (p.74).

Consequently, what was lacking before was a recognition of what exists between the autistic child and
myself. My notes, rather than being seen as a description of an autistic child, can at this point be seen
as an attempt to articulate what exists between us.
And what existed between us at that time was a barrier
of silence, which should not be dismissed as the symptoms of autism but rather recognized as a part of the
relationship between myself and the child. For me, this
barrier demands an explanation, both as it existed as
a "symptom" and as something which I was witness to.
Clinicians might accept the "barrier of silence" as a
symptom, as the illness, as the disturbance. For them
it may not require further interpretation. For me the

103

barrier of silence is endless. It is not a silence which is "fallen into," but rather it is a silence which exists and which always has existed. It is a silence which can prevent us from searching for the possibility of a resolution of that barrier.

There exists a tension in this understanding which must be addressed. It is a tension between having knowledge from the "outside" versus the recognition of what possibly exists in "between." This tension is what will come to be called the dialectic of "between" versus "outside" knowledge. And it is this dialectic which I see as the starting point for this research and in which I locate my initial commitment to research.

It is in the recognition of this dialectic that autism as a "topic" for investigation once again became a significant area for investigation. Yet I do not mean to imply that this study will revolve completely around this dialectic and the understanding that has been reached so far. Rather, this is to be taken only as a starting point for an investigation and interpretation of autism which will undergo numerous changes and "shifts of attention."

There has been an attempt made so far to recover how autism presented itself as a direction of inquiry and, more explicitly, in locating a starting point for research as a concern with what exists between the child and other. It would seem, then, that in order to explore further the notion of what can "exist between" and in order to unfold further the difficulties located within that interaction, the best place to initiate this research is to explore that interaction between the autistic child and his/her therapist. However, before continuing with such a proposal, it seems worthwhile to review some of the basic notions behind the interpretive focus of existential phenomenology.

In essence the focus of the review will be based upon the work of R.D. Laing and A. Esterson. Both of these authors have initiated a way of coming to understand how existential phenomenology can lead to a better understanding of psychosis. And it is based upon this understanding that a proposal will be based for an investigation into autism.

For both Laing and Esterson, as well as for many

other writers, existential phenomenology is a process of coming to an understanding rather than a research methodology. According to Laing, a person can be defined in terms of experience ("as a centre of orientation of the objective universe") and in terms of behavior ("as the origin of actions") (1967, p.20). Essentially he argues, "one will never find persons by studying persons as though they were objects . . . a person is the me, or you, he or she, whereby an object is experienced." All people, according to Laing, must refer to their own experience, as "beings-in-the-world," and it is this experience which becomes the focus of existential phenomenology.

For Laing, then, there is no dualism in his conceptualization in terms of a "co-existence of two different essences" (p.21). Rather, there is a dialectical sense to his view of man and his world, in that man cannot exist without his world nor can his world exist without him. Phenomenology is the study of "inter-experience" where the "other person's behavior is an experience of mine and where my behavior is the experience of the other" (p.16). Additionally, Laing suggests that "all men are invisible to each other as we cannot experience the other's experience but rather "I can experience you only as experiencing" (emphasis added). In any experience, then, it is the relation between persons which is central to our understanding, and people are related to one and other through their "experience" and "behavior."

The existential element in dialectical knowledge according to Esterson (1970) can be located in the process of relations and interexperience (p.190): that is, how I come to know the "other" is through myself. Consequently, "in this relation each implicitly constitutes himself a person confirming and confirmed by the other" (p.188).

It can be seen that the focus for Laing and Esterson is a concern with the patients' way of "being with" them. (They both worked in psychiatric settings.) Essentially this process is a movement away from the clinical perspective. It is based upon inferences about a patient's thoughts and feelings, but inferences, as Laing suggests (1965), "based upon my understanding of what exists between us" (p.31). The point is that we perpetually place interpretations on the behavior of others, even in the "absence of reciprocity" where "we feel that there is no one there who is responding to

105

our approaches" (p.31).

Autism as an area of investigation within the confines of psychiatric work does not have a lengthy documented history. It was only at the beginning of the twentieth century that psychiatry first labeled the "disorder" in children. In order to distinguish autistic children from other "disturbed" children, researchers and therapists soon developed a checklist of symptoms against which they would compare the child in question. The checklist remains as a diagnostic tool for those who work in the field. This conventional or more clinical approach has been modified, elaborated, and essentially retained as a widely used method by which to identify, compare cases of, and treat what has come to be known as early infantile autism. What it means to be autistic, then, is typically answered from the authoritative position of psychiatry and psychology. From that realm of understanding, some forms of research would resist regarding autistic behavior as meaningful (outside of its diagnostic implications), as it also is those behaviors which define the autism. And if the behavior checklist is the method which is utilized to identify and diagnose then it would be impossible to see the autistic child outside of those parameters. For this reason then, the present research will be based upon a phenomenological understanding, which, as Foucault pointed out, "rejects an a priori distinction between normal and pathological" (p.55).

However, the conventional (the "taken-for-granted") way of understanding is not disposed of, but rather will become a significant part of the study. Laing (1965) has suggested that psychosis as "psychiatric jargon" "is a social or biological failure of adjustment" and that "sanity or psychosis is tested by the degree of conjunction or disjunction between two persons where the one is sane by common consent" (p.36). What is interesting for me in both Laing and Esterson's work is that it is this "sense of failure" (which can only be known in contrast with the sense of success in ourselves) which becomes the starting point for understanding. In a way, by admitting to the difference, we cannot help but commit outselves to the "suffering" of another. With autism, the difference is visible by way of the "symptoms of the disease"--symptoms which totalize into autism. As Laing has suggested:

106

> To see signs of a "disease" is not to see it
> neutrally. . . . We cannot help but see the
> person in one way or other and place our con-
> structions or interpretations on "his" behavior
> as soon as we are in relationship with him.
> (1965, p.31)

What seems important is to see these signs, these
symptoms, as a part of a clinical understanding which
exists and which must become an essential part of my
research. This necessity became evident in some other
observation notes:

> One of X's ritualistic behaviors includes
> pouring water back and forth from one container
> to another. Although X has been labeled re-
> tarded as well as autistic, I can see several
> features in this behavior which would possibly
> deny such a diagnosis. First of all, X never
> selects a container which is too small for the
> amount of water she has in the original.
> Secondly,the pouring process suggests that X
> has an understanding of a "transformational
> process" which should not occur for another
> year. Also, the fact that X pours the water
> back into the original container suggests
> that she senses the existence of an inverse
> relationship. . .

Although the clinical understanding is the understanding which usually denies any other possibility of
meaning, here it has added to that possibility. The
existence of the clinical knowledge calls into question
the diagnosis of mental retardation. Here is an
initial step in seeing how the "taken-for-granted" can
become problematic. Esterson similarly uses the psychoanalytic to come to another understanding of the same
phenomena. Although Esterson was not interested in
only a psychoanalytic understanding, he utilized that
understanding as a basis for "shifting attention." It
is for this reason, then, that this "taken-for-granted"
must be understood as an integral part of the research.
It is essential to see the "taken-for-granted" and to
come to know it better, as it will always stand in
between myself and the possibility of locating another
meaning. Therefore, what I bring to the research must
also become a part of the study. As Esterson commented
with regard to schizophrenia:

107

The attempt [to treat schizophrenics as persons]
is . . . unlikely to succeed if the psychiatrist
is unwilling to become reflectively aware of how
he contributes to the other's suffering through
his clinical way of relating. He must see how
he participates in, and contributes to, the
social situation that induces and evokes . . .
He must see himself and his clinical relation
as part of the field for study. (1970, p.192)

As already discussed, the distinction between the
clinical understanding and the possibility of that
understanding formulates in essence the tension which
allows one to question the type of knowledge which the
"taken-for-granted" offers. It is this notion of
tension which provides the basis for dialectical
reasoning, and it is this reasoning which formulates
the basis for understanding in phenomenology.

The type of knowledge sought in the present
research is dialectical. Unlike natural science,
dialectical principles allow for constant change and
the unexpected (Esterson, 1970, p.198). There are
three consecutive moments behind dialectical knowledge.
According to Esterson, they can be explained as follows:

In the first moment, the observer's pattern
of experiencing himself and the system is
disrupted, in and through his becoming aware
of elements in the situation not congruent
with his existing totalization of the system
and of his relation to it. In the second he
negates this synthesis. In the third, he
retotalizes the situation, reconciling the
former gestalt with the contradicting elements
in a wider view. (1967, p.199)

It is these ruptures or breaks Esterson refers to which
formulate the basis for analysis.

Although the literature reviewed here was essentially the work of Laing and Esterson, I do not imply
that this research will be a carbon copy of theirs.
Unlike in the work done by these authors in the area
of schizophrenia, the interest here is neither to find
the origins of autism nor to discover a way of developing a new therapeutic model. Rather, the focus is on
the possibility of meaning. Since it is the relation

between persons which formulates the basis for understanding, it is this relation which will be the direction of the investigation here. The starting point of the research will be to examine the relationship between the autistic child and his/her therapist. In order to achieve any sort of understanding of the interaction, it must be made meaningful. Therefore, in essence, in this study I want to search for the possibility of meaning, to be found in the relationship between child and therapist.

Within the interest proposed here, the difference between the child and the therapist is visible from the beginning and is a distinction which must be understood initially. It is only through coming to recognize and understand that which separates that we can see the potential of the "inter-human." Undoubtedly, the question of "inter-human" and the concept of dialogue will emerge in the research as a major conceptual issue. For the moment, however, the issue turns the discussion back to the issue of dialectics, for the difference between treating an individual as "subject" versus "object" has ramifications for the possibility of a dialectical understanding.

> Sometimes on sunny days, X will push the largest table in the room in front of one of the narrow windows. He then places a truck on top of the table and proceeds to push the truck back and forth from one edge of the table to the other edge with great precision. It was the precision which I initially watched, and so it was only after watching X perform this activity several times that I realized that he never looks at the truck, once it is in position, but rather he seems to be watching the movement of the truck's shadow on the wall . . .

Once again I have a sense of "seeing" without "knowing." "X" understands what it is that he is doing, and I can see what he is doing without knowing what it is. I am unable to "make sense" of the activity from the position of the child; rather, I can only understand from my position, from my conceptualization.

The dialectic which emerges here is a tension which has previously been identified, by others, as the self-other dialectic (Silvers, 1981). The source of any dialectic arises from a break in understanding. The

109

source of the dialectic, which I identify here as the "self-other," can be located in the ambiguity of meaning which exists between the child and myself. Initially this tension can be regarded in terms of that notion which was previously identified as a "sense of failure" (for the child) versus success (for myself), or the difference between autism and non-autism. However, it would seem that it is much more than that.

In one sense I could say that I understand "X's" behavior as being autistic (referring to the persevering movement of the truck); and yet, even at the time, that understanding was disrupted at the moment that I realized that "X" was doing something else. There was something to be found in "X's" actions (i.e., moving the table and the truck in order to see the shadow). Yet what must be realized is that in order for this event to be meaningful it is I who attribute meaning. It is at the moment I realize that I can only see without knowing that I am suddenly confronted with the limits of my own understanding. And it is in this confrontation that the possibility of movement (analytically) is apparent.

What is particularly informative about the tension, at this time, is the movement which it addresses with regard to a dialectical understanding. Dialectical reasoning is progressive reasoning, and although the analysis is not complete, some of its progression has been identified. The "totalization" as I saw it was disrupted, and that disruption (the tension) became the new focus for understanding. In essence, then, I must return to the way I experienced what appeared before me and confront the limits of my understanding.

By treating the child in the above example as an object, I was unable to move past the notion of autism. It took several attempts at watching the child's activity before any sort of break in understanding could occur. But more important, it was not until I came to begin to see the limits of my own understanding, in relationship to the child as subject, that dialectical reasoning could progress. In order to see one's own understanding, it is essential to step away from the research itself. That is, the limitation did not become apparent during the observation but rather occurred at the moment where my own presence was realized as problematic. It is also at this moment of

110

recognition that my presence in the research is attained.

Since within the area of phenomenology one cannot set
the groundwork for the research (i.e., plan, methodology)
then the first purpose here was to somehow offer the
reader a brief example of what the research might look
like. This example was based upon a previous understanding, and it was within this understanding that the
commitment for the present endeavor was located. What
remains to be touched on are several details which are
necessary to develop this understanding.

For the clarity of the research there must be some
way of identifying a meaning for the term "autistic."
Consequently, an autistic child will be one who is
identified as autistic by the individuals who are
working with that child. There will be no attempt to
re-evaluate the child; nor will there be an attempt to
re-define autism from the clinical perspective. In
essence, the aim of the reserach will not be to develop
a better clinical understanding of autism; nor will it
be to address the effectiveness or ineffectiveness of
the therapist. Rather, the direction of interest here
is to investigate the interaction between the child and
the therapist. The investigation is to be based on
observational work, and the preference here would be to
observe in the most inconspicuous way possible, so as
not to disrupt the interaction in any way and not to
interfere with the routines of the center involved.

The investigation is to be based on observational
work. In terms of methodological concerns, the research
can be seen as being divided into two major parts. In
the first part, observational notes based upon video-
tapes of therapeutic interactions will be generated. In
the second part, these observations will then be utilized
as a basis for analyzing the shareability and negotiabi-
lity of understanding which exists between the therapist
and the child.

There is a Toronto agency for autistic children
which has expressed an interest in the research and is
willing to release videotaped sessions of therapist-
child interactions. The agency made these tapes last
year for research and training purposes of their own.

It cannot be overemphasized that the focus of the
research is toward developing an understanding of a

111

difficult interaction. What I am interested in are sessions of time spent between a therapist and a child, and what occurs during those moments.

Finally I wish to address the question of how the research might assist those who work with autistic children. In an analytical sense, existential phenomenology points not only toward the possibility of meaning which an event has in its natural setting but also toward what might be standing in the way of that understanding. Its focus is toward "everyday life," and in this sense some of the observations in the research might be of interest to those individuals who spend time with autistic children.

References

Buber, M. The Knowledge of Man. New York: Harper and Row, 1975.

Douglas, J. D. "Understanding Everyday Life." In Understanding Everyday Life. Chicago: Adline Publishing Co., 1970.

Esterson, A. Leaves of Spring. London: Tavistock, 1970.

Foucault, M. Mental Illness and Psychology. New York: Harper and Row, 1976 (English translation).

Laing, R. D. The Divided Self. Harmondsworth: Penguin, 1965 (originally published 1959).

_____. The Politics of Experience and the Bird of Paradise. Harmondsworth: Penguin, 1967.

Mishler, E. G. "Meaning in Context: Is There Any Other Kind?" Harvard Educational Review (Feb. 1979), 49(1), p.1-19.

Schutz, A. The Phenomenology of the Social World. Evanston, Ill.: Northwestern University Press, 1967. (originally published 1932).

Silvers, R. J. Analytic Notes, unpublished manuscript, October 1981.

_____. "Understanding Phenomenological Inquiry." In Darroch, V. and Silvers, R. Biography and Discourse:

The Knowledge of Interpretive Inquiry. Working
Manuscript, OISE, Toronto, 1980.

Walker, J. "Embodiment and Self-Knowledge," Dialogue
(1969-70), p.44-67.

THE PROPOSAL AS PROCESS

Jack VandenBorn

While the previous proposal found its source and expression in affinity with the principles of dialectical knowledge, VandenBorn's proposal demonstrates its origin and its possibility within the wide context of life as it is lived in its daily variations and with its biographical commitments. VandenBorn, in his proposal, shows the re-seeing of his question as it transforms itself over considerable time. However, this proposal is especially valuable because it also exemplifies how the writing of a proposal may precipitate the researcher toward new "interpretations" of what is behind the inquiry. We, for example, as readers might ask VandenBorn: is "playing" as a general category the same as the concept "intellectual playing"? Is the link of "play" between knowing and friendship a metaphorical link, or does it possess its full abstractness in its relationship with the two?

A topic for inquiry comes into being for the prospective researcher most constructively when a powerful but clouded portion of his or her lived experience generates a vague outline of coherence. Because there is a connection to important commitments in such experiences, the vague outline is necessarily invested with an attractive force, drawing the researcher nearer and nearer. Then, as the inquiry proceeds, the outline begins to show itself as a skeleton connecting to many other portions of experience. With the new clarity, the enriched topic can come to participate in communal life, adding possibilities and dimensionality.

In order to be subject to inquiry, a topic cannot be something wholly unfamiliar; it must be enclosed in a kind of pre-understanding, suggested by the words "vague outline" above. The inquiry aims to clarify this pre-understanding, to show its coherence, to discover its inter-connections to life and then to allow this transformation to participate in the life of the researcher's community. In fact, it is in the

---

* Written in preparation for an inquiry into "Classroom Playing for Friendship and Knowing," Jack VandenBorn, Doctoral Dissertation, University of Toronto, forthcoming.

participation that the best understanding comes to be realized.

The evolution of a topic begins with the welter of previous life, of courses taken, of readings, of discussion, of strong commitments, of intentions for the future. The demand for an inquiry, a dissertation, helps to push an embryonic topic outward. A first tentative description based on the pre-understanding helps to give the topic a conceptual fix. But it is a foggy concept. In the subsequent conceptual and exper- iential growth, the topic serves to generate boundaries marking off elements of thought and life as relevant or irrelevant. The boundaries are distant and obscure at first, but as the inquiry unfolds, the region in which the topic moves shrinks in size. Finally the concept of the topic gains definition with clear connections to or separations from other elements of thought.

Thus my topic of "playing" will not be carefully or theoretically defined at the outset. It must unveil itself, unfold over time. This is so even though I have a pre-understanding of playing, a fairly strong notion, in fact, and even though various theoretical definitions are available.[1] The beginning sense of play I have relates it to a lack of ultimacy, to things that are the utterly fundamental. Playing is an activity that seeks no further consequences but is serious in that it ab- sorbs attention fully. Playing with ideas is similar

---

1 For example, "Play is an activity or occupation executed within certain fixed limits of time and place, according to rules freely accepted but absolutely bin- ding, having its aim in itself and accompanied by a feeling of tension, joy and the consciousness that it is different from ordinary life." J Huizinga, Homo Ludens: A Study of the Play Element in Culture (Boston: Beacon Press, 1950/1938, p.28). Or from Jean Piaget we learn that play "occurs when assimilation is dissociated from accommodation but is not yet reintegrated in the forms of permanent equilibrium in which . . . the two will be complementary." Play, Dreams and Imitations in Childhood (London: Routledge & Kegan Paul, 1951, p.162). Here Piaget has play be an activity that is at the assimilative pole of behavior, i.e., on the interpretive side, not the adjustment or fitting-into-reality side of behavior.

in that the ideas are not granted some high-level status
of Truth. The planned inquiry, however, aims at per-
mitting the topic to shift and slide under the discussion and involvement of a small group of some ten adolescent students with whom I hope to play in several
ways. The topic must find its resting place at the end
of the interactions.

In this proposal I wish to give an account of the
commitments and the growth of understanding that has
brought about a push for an inquiry regarding playing.
I shall offer theoretical grounds for the proposed style
of research and then indicate the general procedure for
conducting the inquiry. These accounts will be followed
with an example of a small inquiry I have already conducted. The concluding section will offer a brief
analysis of how the exemplified research could be
improved by adding a third voice of reflection.

Background

At its key points, my life has been surrounded with a
circle of Christianity tracing its lineage through the
Netherlands to the Reformation impact of John Calvin.
The Calvinism of John Calvin has not been unaffected by
the nearly 450 years of history since its appearance.
As well, my version of the worldview contained by the
concept of Calvinism may well be at variance with more
standard formulations of contemporary Calvinism as
might be met in Toronto, Edmonton, or Grand Rapids, for
example. But my version is not so far from the center
as to warrant my dismissal of the label.

The main element in my notion of life's directions
is that this earth, all the things above the earth and
all the things in the earth, is presented to human beings
in order to make the human experience the richest experience possible. All of it is here so that the human
worlds we create and inhabit may be an enduring delight,
a profoundly contented shalom. Reaching for such worlds
asks for comprehensive understandings, masterly insights,
authentic commitment, and abiding peace, but also a
playful recognition that whatever culture or civilization is produced is only one of many possible. Yet
it is not in the realm of philosophy or ethics that
experience is at its most elevated status; rather, it
is in the relationships, the friendships forged with
other persons, in the connectedness of communal bonds
that the human experience attains its apogee. It is in

117

the overlapping human worlds where love is, and that is
where the mystical center of Christianity, Christ, is.
It is that setting of love where playfulness can be
present abundantly. And so it is to a gamboling
togetherness that my deepest commitments go.

My Calvinism also recognizes shortfalls and hind-
rances restricting the heights to which such love can
reach. They are called sins. A lifetime does not overcome them; neither does any scholarly achievement. The
errors of understanding, intention, or trust falling
under the rubric of sin slice away the top layers of
friendship's best. But my Calvinism also permits me
to say that in the end none of this matters. The worlds
we construct and the experiences we produce are all
merely possibilities--none have timeless status, even
though their existence is never lost. Each biography
leaves its sedimentations. Still they are washed over
and away.

An important conclusion to this briefly stated
perspective is that friendship and knowing stand next
to each other: friendships make of knowing what it is,
and knowing shapes the version of our friendship. I
shall attempt to trace briefly the growth of understanding that permits my coming to this statement.

I had been a school teacher for nearly fifteen
years when in the spring of 1980 our family made the
final decision to leave Edmonton and spend a year in
Grand Rapids, afterwards extended to include a year or
more in Toronto. There in Grand Rapids I would be
able to study and think carefully about life, scholarship, and philosophy in the surroundings of a Calvinist
institution.

For the nine prior years I had been involved with
teaching in a special program for gifted students in
the age range of about nine to thirteen mainly. The
usual practice had eight or ten students come to me for
half-day periods once a week. It was not so much the
case that I was to teach knowledge or skills to the
students, although that happened, as I was to push them
into creative and thoughtful expression of ideas on a
variety of concerns. I took myself to be a person
squeezing spongy students, pushing out rivulets of
research, writing, and dialogue. The classes resembled
graduate seminars in several ways. Students encouraged
each other in formulating ideas and projects within the
confines of some fairly broad topic which had been

chosen by the group after the merits or demerits of several topics had been intimately argued. The group was engaged in preparing a publication thereafter, a publication which was distributed to school libraries and homes.

During these years my thought about students was usually in terms of creativity, intelligence, and productivity, with all of this motivated from within the warm intimacy of our class. Friendship, knowing, and playing were there but not in any interpenetrating format. While important elements of my conceptions were oriented to individualistic modes, the educational movement of classes was clearly not that. I was not setting up young geniuses to bend a recalcitrant barrier their way; no, it was a joint enterprise in which we were involved--a task force, we called ourselves.

We arrived in Grant Rapids, and a variety of courses in theology, philosophy, psychology, and history absorbed my studies. As I think back on the question driving me on, it seems that it was the nature of persons I wished to grasp, a theory of consciousness that I would possess. It was about intelligence, mind, and commitment that I wanted insights, this within the confines, the perspective, of Christianity. It was a beginning in the human studies for me.

The tradition of phenomenological thought absorbed me most convincingly. Edmund Husserl and Martin Heidegger, along with Herman Dooyeweerd, a Dutch Calvinist and philosopher,[2] sedimented another kind of metaphysical underlay in my understanding. I rejected the positivist world that seemed simply to inject an array of indubitable facts into my thought and, instead, I came to accept that we constitute our own world largely, each of us does. This may be a substantive philosophical transformation, probably worthy of elucidation, but I shall not tell it, as it is not especially unique.

---

2 Herman Dooyeweerd was a close reader of Husserl but diverged from his thought at many points. See his A New Critique of Theoretical Thought (Philadelphia: Presbyterian and Reformed Publishing, 1969/1936). But I also learned to appreciate the lucidity of the Calvinist Nicholas Wolterstorff.

The 1981/82 study term at the Ontario Institute for Studies in Education allowed me to absorb the pulsebeat of phenomenological psychology more directly. It was there that I came to collect the existential reality of my understandings, however halting they may yet be, into a more coherent scheme. Reading the English philosophers David W. Hamlyn and Michael Polanyi was also helpful in constructing a skeleton theory of consciousness, a theory which seems capable of holding together playing, friendship, and knowing.[3] My theory has, of course, not yet got the clarity or power of some dazzling, metaphoric artesian spring.

My picture has consciousness as always conceptually layered. That is, when we are conscious of something, we are consious of it conceptually, in terms of concepts. When I see a tree, I see it in terms of the concept of a tree. The light rays that energize my eyes are organized conceptually, because otherwise I should only receive energy of light rays as a stone does. Instead, I see a tree; the stone warms slightly. Concepts are not some timeless sort of entities, although some concepts do reach across vast stretches of history. It must be so, because otherwise the writings composed several thousand years ago would be hopelessly incomprehensible. Since it is possible to come to interpretations of such writings, there must be some similarity to the concepts then and now. But concepts can also be fleeting, once-only entities serving only to organize some momentary perception. Then that perception is gone.

More important, though, is the notion that concepts evolve both historically and within a person and community. They change, they connect, they fade, they come to clarity. It is the influence of our human associates that finds concepts especially malleable. A discussion with an acquaintance can not only raise up some matter to prominence but result in a distinctive formulation of the concept. I marvel at the extent my thinking is affected by what others near me indicate, especially about matters that have not yet hardened into clear distinctiveness. Thus the delight I had in a tasty dinner diminishes when someone points out that the

---

3 D. W. Hamlyn, Experience and the Growth of Understanding (London: Routledge & Kegan Paul, 1978), and M. Polanyi and H. Prosch, Meaning (Chicago: University of Chicago Press, 1975).

persimmon unfortunately has a remaining touch of astringency, a fact which had not come to my attention previously. My conception of the dinner has thus acquired another aspect making the overall conception less favorable. Similarly, matters that once were well defined can fall into confusion because of commentaries that cast doubt on their validity. This is in fact what happened to my conception of truth during the past couple of years. Much of this conceptual modification occurs beneath the level of awareness-- "subsidiarily," as Michael Polanyi might say. It is only with a retrospective or reflective analysis of one's thought that such conceptual movement can be documented.

But it was the discussion of concepts by David Hamlyn that allowed me to understand the role of friends and community in conceptual development more precisely.[4] He indicates that much of traditional epistemology has presented persons as "solitary centers of consciousness" whose most fundamental problem was the construction of a world, a world that included other persons as just one more item amid the rest. However, says Hamlyn, the construction of a world, the constituting of it in consciousness, is directly connected to the "sharing of common interests and concerns." The practical upbringing of children is a particularly important element in the development. In other words, the kind of world a child (or an adult, for that matter) conceptually arranges is dependent on the way the world is constituted by the people surrounding him or her.

Hamlyn explains this position by suggesting that having a concept of X means to know what it is for something to be X. A particular kind of knowledge is presupposed in having concepts. While it is not wholly clear just what this kind of knowledge may be, he does state that it is a knowledge invested in the common understanding of a community as that is lived on a daily basis. It derives from the stuff of everyday life, the unreflected-upon agreements that, for example, have us all accept a smile as an indication of pleasure or contentment. Now, I hestitate to use the word "knowledge" for such common understandings, preferring to retain that word for a layer above the conceptual, that which

---

4 Ibid., especially Chapter 6, "Concepts and Their Conditions."

the conceptual brings about. Neither do I wish to narrow the notion of having a concept to the Xs Hamlyn would seem to require, although he does not state a range for the Xs. I think concepts are had of a broad variety of phenomena and events, not just of something being an X. When I look at the back yard I see it with the concept of a back yard. But this concept can be broken down into a collection of concepts which I can also have of, say, the lawn, the garage, the shrubs on the border, and so on. Similarly, I can have a concept of my whole life, which becomes a large entity.

The concept of concepts must clearly be a difficult matter to conclude. I do conclude that the way we constitute our experience, our perception and our understanding, our intentions and our memories, has an exceedingly wide range of possibilities, this because the conceptual layer is not necessarily of any one sort. It is fashioned from the ontic stuff of everyday life in alliance with the people who form the circle of our acquaintances. I must hasten to add that this circle does not construct the conceptual basis of experience mechanically, in some ineluctable process. The procedure is steeped in interpretation. It is mainly through confirming or disconfirming actions or statements that the conceptual underlay is gently pushed in a particular direction.

I want also to point to the role of our bodies in everyday life. We dwell in the agreement of communal bonds that cocoon us because it is through our bodies that we are present to our associates and the world we construct. Our body, writes the Catholic Adrian Van Kaam, is the "spontaneous, unpremediated entrance into the dense reality which permeates and surrounds me."[5] This is not at all to say that any concepts we have are derived from biochemical changes in our brains or elsewhere, but only that it is with our bodies that concepts and knowledge is held. We are, each of us, inescapably embodied selves. Michael Polanyi puts it well: "Though rooted in the body, the mind is free in its actions from bodily determinations."[6]

---

5 The Existential Foundations of Psychology (Pittsburgh: Duquesne University Press, 1966, p.16.

6 Meaning, p.51.

But persons can, of course, only communicate understanding through bodily behavior. The common framework
in which a community lives is given expression in movement, in gestures, in facial expression--that is, in
body language as well as in conventional language.
These communications are the means by which affir-
mations or discomfirmations are offered in respect to
the conceptualization of experience. Much of the expression and interpretation of the understanding takes place
below awareness. For example, where a tradition of
respect for elders is shown in the posture customarily
adopted in their presence, youngsters acquire the attitude quite unaware that they are adopting anything at
all arbitrary.

Much of the communal tradition as it is expressed
in behavior will remain beneath the surface, so to
speak, because it is not easily susceptible to articulation. Indeed, there is no call to bring it into
awareness. Embodied knowledge of this sort, contributing to the organization of experience, cannot all
be examined in any case. It cannot be looked <u>at</u> because
it is <u>with</u> it that we look. In Polanyi's word<u>s</u>, embodied knowledge is subsidiary knowledge: "All knowing
is action in that it is our urge to understand and
control our experience which causes us to rely on some
parts of it subsidiarily in order to attend to our main
objective focally."[7]

My present notion of consciousness has it as always
consciousness of something in the world which has been
constituted. And the consciousness of the something is
the concept we have. Beyond this, there is a large
place for the behavioral expression of understanding and
its interpretation; there is a large opening for conceptual arbitrariness and a place for the strong influence of friends and associates in making the concepts
just what they are. The way in which experience may
be organized must then be highly variable. We see it
that way, in ourselves, in specific traditions and
through history. Changes are not instant, not the
quick conversion usually. Yet it is possible to document the changing understanding of some matter or other.
Indeed, it is an excellent scholarship that manages to
chart the changing concept of this or that across an
era.

---

7 Ibid., p.42.

The second half of my earlier conclusion--that
knowing shapes friendship--is more easily given a
beginning form. It seems to me that friendship develops when two persons develop an important common
interest, an activity or concern to which each contributes. A common interest can only be common when it
is conceived of, thought about, in a similar way.
There must be an overlap of understanding regarding
the interest, for otherwise the respective contribu-
tions to it are unintelligible. In their joint activities, the two beginning acquaintances can come to
trust each other, to hold high regard for each other,
and to become friends. But it is an initial commonness
in knowing that permits the subsequent friendship. He
or she we cannot understand is not able to be our
friend.

The previous pages were intended to show how I
came to connect friendship and knowing. I also want
to introduce the idea of playing, especially intellectual playing as in playing with an idea, as another
element in the connection. Perhaps it will be the
shuttlecock that bounces between the two former items.
Playing arose as a "topic" for inquiry from two sources--
the search for a dissertation topic and discussions in
class. I can perhaps add, at this point, that the understanding contained in these pages is subject to change
because of the light offered by further study, but more
important, because of proposed inquiry with students.
The pages have been built up from concepts and, as noted,
they are subject to transformation.

My first sense of a possible inquiry worthy of a
dissertation was fashioned early in 1982 from the word
"reflection." Just what was the intellectual activity
designated by this word? What were the ontological and
epistemological aspects involved with it? Those seemed
to be at least two of my questions. John Locke had
reflection to be "the perceptions of the operations of
our mind within us, as it is employed about the ideas
it has got."[8] Locke assumed that reflective thought did
not disturb or affect the ideas that entered the mind
through the senses. Subsequent philosophical thought

---

8 An Essay Concerning Human Understanding (New York:
Dover Publications, 1959, p.123).

124

has come to show that this assumption was in fact just that and, as such, even doubtful. For me reflection also had to be something more than just an internal mirror, viewing the ideas in motion through their own energy.

Jean Piaget explained reflection as "the act by which we unify our various tendencies and beliefs," much as dialogue within a community can serve to even out the various conceptions of some concern.[9] This definition makes reflection a more energetic activity than mere observation. Phenomenological thought seemed to have a different version of reflection yet, perhaps several different versions. One made reflection to be the unearthing of mind that brought the subsidiary world of assumptions into awareness, as in critical reflection. Another possibility likened reflection to retrospection. It returns lived experience, brings it back to awareness for examination, but recognizes that the returning process is itself an unconscious selective process. The selective process is worthy of consideration and inquiry, being even more interesting than the examination of the lived experiences perhaps.

It was some version of these latter notions that drew my interest. I wished to better understand reflection and I wanted to know if adolescent students did any reflection. I believed that a sound comprehension of the process could be helpful to the community that claims my loyalty, because our Christianity too has an urge to self-examination, a push to know oneself, to test the spirits at work. It was on some similar though less explicit basis that a first dissertation proposal was fashioned.

During this same period classes in one course presented an introduction to interpretive inquiry. The introduction was heavily weighted with the role such inquiry would serve in the future. There was an ultimacy about the projected pattern of events that needed to be undone by a more appropriate style of research and life. My reaction was, yes, these matters are worthy of attention, but it was not our task to shoulder a responsibility for unfolding all of the future. Such a responsibility is presumptuous and entirely beyond any of us. Instead, I believed we

---

9 Judgement and Reasoning in the Child (Totawa, N.J.: Littlefield, Adams & Co., 1976/1928, p.204).

should "play" with our understandings, taking them
seriously to the reality of our everyday existence and
basic commitments. We should offer ourselves to our
community fully but recognize that we are not prospective saviors of the future.

It was in this position that intellectual playing
crossed over and replaced reflection as a center from
which an inquiry could flow. And, working with another
class now in Toronto, a different "push" came from an
interview with one of my grade 8 students.

James is one of the 17 students that I teach in
the mornings. A competent student, a pleasant boy,
James is a student who I thought took the ideas presented in the science and history courses as just one
more theory among various possible theories. I felt
confident about the matter, because on those occasions
in which the classroom instruction had focused on
various theories, as on correct action by Christians
in war, James had been one of the students who most
explicitly seemed to recognize the acceptability of
more than just one right answer. In other words, I
thought James could play with various theories and
recognize that he did so. I still think so. But when
the conversation I had with him moved from playing to
playing with an idea, James could only reply, "No, I
don't think I do that much." Yet I believe he does do
it. And I think that many grade 8 students, perhaps
grade 7 students as well, are capable of recognizing
that they in effect play intellectual games with that
which they learn, knowing that the ideas have no final
standing. So playing by adolescent children has become
an unknown to me, something about which I would know
more.

Thus I came to see a connection between playing
and reflection. Reflection points out that the concepts and assumptions with which we organize our
experience constitute only one among many possible
sets. We can play with theories or understandings
because we recognize that there are always various con-
tenders, none having ultimate status. But my Calvinism
does not permit consciousness to reside in a completely
shoreless ocean of relativity. There is at least one
basic assumption that is beyond intellectual play, and
that is the matter of belief in God. However much
human thought is involved in this belief, I am convinced
that ultimately it is an act of God whether someone

126

believes in God or not. The injection of this belief into the structure of consciousness is not without its effect. But given this one item at least, we can play for all we are worth.

The Inquiry

I think the best vantage point from which I can look in on playing is the teaching situation with which I am most familiar, one with which I have been involved for nearly ten years. This is with a group of eight or ten adolescents, students from grades 7 or 8, perhaps 9. Older students may be more desirable, because they are, according to Jean Piaget, more capable of constructing hypothetical worlds and recognizing that the earth that clusters around them is but an instantiation of one possible world. Piaget's view, however, is not entirely convincing, because grade 7 students have shown me that they can appreciate more than one theory to account for some event, a physical event at any rate. A theory is not a world but the embryonic world of other possibilities is. So it seems wise to have somewhat of a mix of grade levels represented in the group. It would also inform the group itself that playing with ideas asks for a multiplicity of stances.

The group at best would meet for one hour three times a week. It may be necessary, because of school timetables, to have five sessions of forty minutes. I would teach history, Canadian history, to the group, for several reasons. I have taught such a course for the first time this past year, and it retains a freshness, a captivating character. More important, history is about people, and as such it supplies material about the way others have constituted their worlds. Because it is Canadian history, these people are not so far away in place and time as to make identification with their understanding difficult. We should be able to enter their thought through an interpretation of the records and materials that have been deposited. So the study in history provides a link to the conceptualizations of experience that others have constructed. In other words, history is a good subject from which to point out alternative understandings.

My sense of the instruction would be to proceed with many of the usual elements of a history curriculum. There would be a basic textbook and supplementary

127

reading materials. We would look at films and travel to local historical exhibits. We would examine replicas or actual artifacts, making interpretations about their human makers. The entire effort would be aimed at capturing the everyday character of the particular people under consideration, getting at the common understanding that prevailed among them. We would recognize that there were individual variations of that common understanding, variations according to traditions alive within the community, variations deriving from differing expectations or biography, variations due to differences in daily living. Thus we would attempt to grasp something of the larger intellectual currents pressuring individuals and groups, putting their thought and person into tension or conflict.

A few examples may be helpful. In the cold winter of 1605 the "Order of Good Cheer," a weekly banquet, was initiated by Samuel de Champlain in Port Royal and changed the way of life for the struggling settlers. The French of Acadia between 1713 and 1755 were asked to take an oath of allegiance to the English throne; but they feared being drafted into the governor's militia, who might end up in battle with their friends and cousins across the St. Lawrence River. The various attitudes Christians have adopted toward war could be considered with respect to the War of 1812, for example. Or we could simulate debates on various issues: slavery and separation in the United States of the early 1860s, Confederation in the British colonies in 1866 and 1867, the appropriate response of the Ottawa parliament to Louis Riel's requests in 1885. In all these adventures I would push outward the notion of many understandings, the many points of view that are available to mankind. And in the classroom we would adopt some of them for a time for the sake of playing with them, trying them on like a suit of new clothes. We would play games of pretend that we are . . . What would we do? What considerations would be involved with our actions? What would be tugging at our hearts asking us to do this or to do that? What would be in our dreams and daydreams?

My role would be that of both the teacher and the researcher. The students would have a similar double role, as students and as researchers. Their entry into the second role would develop more slowly than mine, perhaps a month or two after the beginning of the project. The purpose of our inquiry would be to exhibit and understand our intellectual play through documenting

128

the continuing transformation of our friendship and
knowledge. At this point I am concerned for the documentation of altering friendships. Will young students
be able to cope with the intensity of such self-confron-
tations? Children feel free to speak about their
friends, the way they are with them, the games they
play, and so on. But putting this on paper, opening
it to analysis, may be too strong. At any rate, I
would lead the way, trusting the strength of my commitments to keep away from any examination that would
place students in untenable positions with respect to
their classmates. My firm desire is toward an enrich-
ment of experience, an enlargement of our understanding,
love in friendship, and joy in our sessions. It may
mean that the explication of the existential pressures
involved in our class relationships needs to be kept in
the background.

Immediately with the onset of the project I would
begin to write short papers, perhaps a few pages, after
every class meeting. These papers would both document
the developments of the sessions and seek to let the
topic of playing reveal itself. They would, as I now
envision it, be similar to the "Invitation to Play" paper
of the next section--that is, an accumulation of experience as recovered by me and a multi-level analysis of
both the recovery and the recovered done in an existential-phenomenological mode. Gradually, I would ask
students to join me in the self-exploration, in the
study of our topic. It may be by way of a private
journal shared with me, perhaps not.

An important aspect of my writing is that it is
intended for reading by the students, at least in large
part. It is to be an injection into the class, contributing to the material of study. My reflections on the
sessions, while reporting something of the events as a
diary might, aim to re-enter the experiences which are
their origin, asking about the principles that direct
the recovery of those aspects of the originating experience and driving forward to enlighten and transform our
group with the reward of playfulness, friendship, and
knowledge hovering just above. In order to do that
well I would need to use a preteritive language,[10] words
that link together like a doughnut, an outward form with
an empty center. The reader fills this emptiness.

---

10 Preteritive languaging has been discussed by Vivian
Darroch in "Notes for a Language for Existential Pheno-
menology," Reflections: Essays in Phenomenology. Vol.3,
No. 1, 1982, p.34-48.

But the writing cannot be for the students alone. It must reach beyond them into the academic community, especially as that community is represented by a dissertation committee. Just as the short pages aim to tie deep bonds between our class and teacher, so the dissertation, a compilation and extension of the short papers, must seek to give a profound understanding of a possibility for the way a group might be, to reveal the nature and dynamic of the transactions between people, and to do this by presenting the subsidiaries of everyday life--an archaeology--as directly as possible. But the dissertation ought not remain as just presentation, to be shucked away lightly. If it is written well, preteritively well, it will provide the scholar with the opportunity to re-comprehend his or her own ego, to reflect deeply and thus appropriate anew the effort to exist. "The eschatology of consciousness," writes Paul Ricoeur, "is always a creative repetition of its own archaeology."[11] The reader is invited, through the writing, to refashion his or her self to become empty, but then to refill the self, richer in contentment and playfulness. The writing cannot be a tract, a how-to book for better living; no, it is to be a preteritive exhibition.

To a degree the justification for the inquiry proposed in this paper is already embedded in and scattered through the previous pages. These pages expose steps, intellectual steps in understanding, taken on the way to the words that lie here. Even in writing the words, understanding has grown and adapted itself to pressures that had not been anticipated.

Psychological research takes many forms. Certainly one form has it as a development of understanding, a documentation of the shifts in the way experience has been conceptually ordered. In such research the reader is invited to accompany the inquirer on a journey which, if well told, also becomes a journey for the reader. The destinations, however, are identical only as metaphor. Thus the inquirer styles him or her self as a representative person, someone like all others and in whom others can see themselves, even if it be only darkly. As a theorist on a journey toward a beguiling upsurge in the center of history, the inquirer must

---

11 The Conflict of Interpretations (Evanston, Ill.: Northwestern University Press, 1974, p.324).

be conscientiously watchful, seeing truly and deeply.
But there is also a returning, a homecoming, which is a
hermeneutical task.[12]   Interpretation is needed to make
a plenitude, a sensible sketch or illustration of the
sounds and sights encountered. A reflective recovery
of the journey is demanded. An explication of principles governing the recovery, an accounting of the
pressures that welled up suddenly to arrest the flow of
words and the tingling edge of an originative insight,
are also part of the hermeneutic that would open to the
reader an understanding of the intentionalities now cap-
tive within the inquirer. From these the reader may
establish her or his own destination, one consonant with
her or his own life world.

Psychology is a study of persons (psyche, soul,
self) and their interrelationships and transactions with
other persons. It is a penetration into the order and
dynamic of consciousness in its communal webbings. The
inquirer cannot just enter this intersubjective netting
pretending that the weight of his or her presence has
not been placed into the fabric and tension of the
strands. To be human means inescapably to-be-in-the-
world, even when an inquirer for psychology. This need
not be a threat to the coherence of the community,
because the inquirer comes to raise up awareness and
understanding and to increase the wealth of the inter-
connections as they are constituted. "Know thyself,"
said Socrates. To be an effective inquirer, one must
swallow the adage. The coherence perceived will depend
on it; the linkings forged between inquirer and community will depend on it; the interpretations made will
flow from it--all of this even though the task of self-
examination must necessarily be endless. The knowing of
self can grow in height and depth, in eschatology and
archaeology.

Recently, I have learned something of letting my
self be present to inquiry, to recognize the biography
of this self, to analyze it and allow the results to be
there when actively engaged in a topic, thus transforming my understanding of experience, including the
past as it is now present, the present as it is alive,

12 A. Giorgi, C. Fischer, & E. Murray (eds.), Duquesne
Studies in Phenomenological Psychology, Vol.3 (Pittsburgh, Duquesne University Press, 1975, p.239).

and the future as it is within the now, the future as an
intentionality of the present. This is what I take to
be the existential component of research. Not that it
means a wholly uncensored display of self: narcissism or
egocentrism cannot be justified. Psychological research
must avoid an immature self-presentation directed merely
to a claim for recognition rather than enhancement and
comprehension. But the existential component also includes the pressure toward specific conceptualizations
as these are exhibited and affirmed by communication of
friends and others near by. In other words, the
inquirer is not hermetically locked into the attention
bestowed by an "individual" biography. For me it means
an urgent presence of friends, of a Christian community
in a Calvinist tradition, and of charged academic associates. These persons are never wholly absent at any
time in the inquiry.

Phenomenology has long stood for a return to the
foundations of all knowledge. A phenomenological
inquiry rejects obvious categories for purposes of
description, preferring to grasp lived experience more
directly. Such a grasping is, of course, problematical,
because lived experience is not a thing, not like a tree
or a physical event. Lived experience contains its own
presuppositions; hence Paul Ricoeur's call for both
archaeology and eschatology. A relentless reflection is
demanded, a reflection that never ceases to push outward
one set of subsidiary concepts while allowing another to
take its place. Another set has to take the place, for
otherwise our experience would degenerate to a stony
silence of emptiness. Phenomenology does not eschew presuppositions; it only asks that they be examined.

Nor can phenomenology then reduce persons to objects. A full subjectivity must always be assigned to
all participants in an inquiry. Thus the inquirer
becomes responsible for many subjectivities in the
research, not only an inquiring self. Each subjectivity
becomes a human text that presses out from itself
symbols and structures linking it to the communal web-
bing, this expression always done in reflexive relation
to those symbols and structures absorbed from the community. It is on this complex of coherence that the
inquirer practices the hermeneutical task which is the
existential-phenomenological inquiry.

The result cannot be a timeless formula of truth
beset by mathematizable categories. No, it is the

record of a human truth as it is unfolded and lived;
thus it is a personal knowledge whose only claim is that
of a possibility, a possibility that others may wish to
claim metaphorically for their own selves.

Invitation to Play

I wrote, earlier this term, about making interpretive
inquiry fun. It was a reasponse to the brooding clouds
hanging over my informal seminar paper on interpretive
inquiry. "The serious task of interpretive inquiry," I
wrote, "was right, but it needs a light, not quite
frivolous context." This was the contention. And I
still think the idea of a "playful researcher" has much
to commend itself. The present paper, however, wants to
turn the topic a little; it aims to inquire interpretively into playing because the present student of interpretive inquiry wished to make the student enterprise
more serious than might reasonably have been anticipated
from his initial, fluttering comments. The flippancies
were anchored to substantive grounds inside.

A First Step: Note moments of play
in the ontological stuff of daily life.

Jacquelyn (our daughter of fourteen) and I, we play,
sometimes, on the way to the bus stop early in the
morning. Suddenly it happens that our pedestrian walk
finds a left leg that fails to move forward past the
right. We move with whole and half-steps alternating,
clownishly. Lance (a son and brother three years
younger) joins in. Or it may be that we are running
for the bus already visibly on its way to meet us and .
. . our knees reach higher than they ought. Heads are
thrown back. We are a marching band on maneuver, at a
too fast pace. It lasts for fifty yards. We smile with
an inside, knowing smile, if we catch each other's eyes.
"Crazy walking" the kids call it. The bus comes . . .
the subway . . . we lose ourselves in the Globe and Mail,
sixty of which we have delivered an hour earlier.

     Lance plays hockey, street hockey. He has acquired
the language of hockey and refreshes himself daily with
the escapades of Laurie Boschman, a Wayne Gretzky, a
thousand hockey cards, Globe and Mail sports. I turn to
the front page, catch the "Morning Smile," scan the head-
lines, read a paragraph, perhaps two. The editorial
page comes along soon and there I sometimes find a
gently cynical editor poking at the pretentious bombast

of some bureaucrat malfunctioning. And we point out
Gerry Trudeau's "Herman" cartoon to each other, someone
always oblivious to his or her own immense oddity.
Jacquelyn reads some of the same, although her eyes
fasten on clothing designs, not completely disdainful.

The train is thick with passengers, but each stop
thins out the density, like young carrot rows in June.
Until Finch station, the end of the line. We must
occasionally play hockey on our departure. I lead
since I'm bigger. A bodycheck, gentle yet resolute.
Sometimes Jacquelyn leads, checking to the side the
too eager commuters who would not let us escape. Even
Lance (he is smaller) catches the capricious flavor of
running the morning gauntlet. We smile if we catch
each other's eye. Technology's marvels can make a
momentary game.

We are away from the subterranean monster and we
go to our separate destinies as schools enter our hori-
zons, both inner and outer. My world fills with others.
Mathematics and history open doors from which ooze
lessons and questions, textbooks and notes, discourse
and structures. A student mentions an upcoming geo-
graphy class, on Australia. "Australia!" I am aghast,
subtly mocking. "It's a hundred thousand miles away.
When would you go there? Why in the world do you study
that?"

History comes. "In July of 1838 Lord Durham
arrived in Quebec. Durham was like our James: a
piercing eye shone out from his gaze; sparkling clothes
fell from his frame; a resonant voice beat off the
flatterers; and a commanding presence flooded his sur-
round. Why would the Colonial Secretary have sent
Durham on the Canadian mission?"

"Maybe he was a relative."
"He was competent, a good governor, a powerful per-
sonality."
"The Secretary wanted to be rid of him, send him
into the bush."
"The last answer, that's the one."

Recess comes. "At 10:40 I want all of you, grade
8, to be outside or softly constructive in the classroom." There is an edge of raw firmness in my voice--
"I don't like it when you get mad ," says Ed. Humor-
less. But outside, a change. Bryan and Peggy hang on

134

my arm. "You can't get away from us," they laugh, too uproariously. Carla comes, linking arms: "How are you, eh?" The 10:40 rule dissolves and there is a hollowness, an opening for others in which to play. But the hollowness is not quite empty: there is a border shifting around inside, a border not to be overstepped. We, at least most of us, know the border and we smile at the stricture, but smiling heedfully.

School is over and the trains carry me to academia. Is there play there? Sometimes, not so often. Wednesday afternoons, seminar afternoons, permit laughter. An exaggeration, a warmth of silliness, a joke about tardiness, an intentional misinterpretation invites all of us to a momentary playfulness. The topics are heavily weighted; the air in which they rest is not. These moments push aside the hurriedness, the far purposes of graduate education. They are playfulness.

And it happens that a conquest over an obtuse conceptual structure is made. The author's words, previously opaque, become translucent, perhaps by reason of a key word switching from one notion to another or because of the heart of an experiment becoming suddenly apparent. It is not the slow accretion of a complex structure piece by piece into mastery of which I speak; rather, it is the startled surprise of receiving a revelation. After that another sort of play begins. The concepts become my possession. I can be possessed by them. Writing with them and about them is possible. Metaphors can be made, hiding them but not so darkly. It is intellectual play, a playing with something that has the smile of conviction. There is an unconstrainedness, an openness to doing what you will with objective knowledge no longer distant or reverent in its objectivity. It's mine to do with as I will.

Then the academic world fades into the background, darkly absent. I make the last steps to my home. Avlyn and our children are there. The dog wags an enthusiastic welcome, but we don't play now. There is more a calm sea of contentment, of quietness, of peace-- not always but often. Playing is for times before evening serenity.

A Second Step: It has been my words that have defined playing for me and for others. For the others, the words may be different. I'll need to talk with them.

I had wanted to speak with Jacquelyn the other evening,

but I hestitated and did not. Even now I am wary about talking about "crazy walking." The moments seem fragile. The tender bond that joins our antics appears to be destructible through discussion. How can this be? The fear is that "crazy walking" may come to be understood as a routine, a contrived routine. Contrived and routine, an exercise, and then, even worse, it will be suspected as a cover for something that wants to be hidden. Is this what our delight may come to? If it is a cover, what may be underneath? Will I have to account to my daughter and son for that of which I do not have any knowledge? Some absurd Freudian complex?

On the other hand, it seems possible to make playing even richer, a more abundant time now and then, a project we invest with more of ourselves. Speaking of it cannot damage the design we all have for delight. And Lance, what will he make of our talk about "crazy walking". In the antics, he is more the follower. Can he, through dialogue, not become something more in our playing?

The writing of these words, these pages, has made of "crazy walking" something other than it has been. The writing was preceded, of course, by the recovery of playful moments, and then, already, the notion of "crazy walking" received a transformation. But this account, more propositionalized, has given the authenticity of the actions, their spontaneity, the kind of cold shroud. There is a sadness, a loss. Perhaps dialogue with my children can bring back to life what has fallen asleep.

I shall also ask James, a grade 8 student, for an interview. I think he plays in ways not unfamiliar to me, with intellectual matters but also otherwise. But with his interview, I am less unsure. The classroom humor has been more public, more accessible. Perhaps it will be possible for us both to make more of playfulness even if it is already beyond us both.

Today, ten days later, Lance and I talked about playing. Playing, he had it, was that kind of thing done at recess time or on Saturday, "a kind of goofing around with a hockey stick or a ball glove." And playing is done with friends, other persons roughly your own age. These were Lance's first thoughts, a working definition of play. It is an understanding that puts clear boundaries around that which can be called play; it puts walls around the concept that we will carry with us for the next while. Inside the walls, so far, there are mainly activities that resemble organized sports like hockey and baseball.

(But I must guard against this writing becoming the words of an expert external to the conversation, the words of someone removed and outside the flow of trans-formative power within the writing. Even the interview had too much of me questioning and Lance answering. This page is for us both, after all.)

In the interview I spoke of we three--Jacquelyn, Lance, and I--sometimes playing when running for the bus in the morning. "Oh, yeah," Lance agreed. The accep-tance allowed for some shifting around of the definition of play within its walls. The door to further talk was opened. This kind of playing around makes us laugh. "It looks pretty funny," said Lance. Nobody else sees the playing though; nobody except the three of us. And if other people were looking, we probably would not run crazily. The clownish walking gives us something com-pletely our own, something no one else can possess. It ties us together that way, at least for those few min-utes. No one will ever know about our antics unless one of us tells. I think that the one will be me. But it will still be like a secret between friends, because not many people will read this paper.

Then we talked about acting silly for our friends, "like being a character," in Lance's words. It is not something done for someone whom we have just met, some-one who may become a friend of ours. Acting silly at that point would not make a very good impression, and the friendship might not develop. But acting like a clown is done by persons already friends. There it shows that you don't always have to be serious, that play is for friends and between friends.

The next day. We started, Jacquelyn and I, in trying to gather a description of playing. Playing the piano and playing with friends were two quick categories. We talked about playing with friends. A first thought made this to be a kind of sport, kicking a can, playing base-ball, perhaps tennis. Earlier in the day of our con-versation, Jacquelyn had gone shopping with a friend. Was this playing too? Not quite. Because, well "Playing is when you exert yourself." Shopping with a friend, spending time with her, is not really doing anything.

I did not really understand "not doing anything," because shopping does involve doing something--walking around, talking, looking, trying on. "I know, but you're not . . . Yeah. When you're playing with dolls . . . It's kind of weird." The game concept and the exertion concept of playing began to fail. But it was Jacquelyn who was struggling with the notion, not me. I had gone through the definition struggle with Lance a day earlier. But, still, the door to the concept was open. What would "playing" mean for us in this discussion?

I asked about playing at school. No, not much there. There isn't time for it really. Was telling a joke, making someone laugh, would that be called playing? "Playing . . . yeah . . . I don't know. It's weird. 'Playing' is weird to define."

"Do we--you, Lance, and I," I asked, "do we ever do any playing?" And I mentioned the "crazy walking" we sometimes do on the way to the bus.

"Oh, yeah! It's acting dumb sort of. I guess that's playing. You make a fool of yourself. Yes, I like it. I think it's fun." I thought, though, it wasn't so much making the fool, since no one sees us. And even if someone did see us, someone driving by in a car, for example, Jacquelyn added that that it wouldn't matter "because you're never going to see those guys again anyway."

The conversation had opened to several directions. The understanding of playing had hopped over the physical-game wall and had come to be connected to delight, laughter, antics as well as friendship. For me, playing isn't only like a game. I summarized: "It's just where you do something for the fun of it. But with someone usually. It can be acting dumb but it doesn't have to be acting dumb . . . I think playing has got more to do with being friends."

This theme of friendship, communion, sociality, mutuality lays deep claim to my thought. It takes up attention often, injecting itself in many locations. It has come to infect the very center of my notions of belief, knowledge, and theory, constructions that have been considered the most individual of all human enterprises. "The idea of the autonomous and responsible individual," writes Newton Stallknecht, "characterizes our civilization, and its reflection in religion, social policy, and the arts is often considered an index of our cultural maturity."[13] Not only our noetic structure but the very center of Western civilization is presumably premised on an outflow of individuality. I cannot agree. Beliefs, knowledge, theory, religion, politics, art are much more the combined constructions of persons in community. They are the consequences of intersubjective bridges, like conversations, constituted by the speech of two or more individuals. Conversation rests on neighborliness, even if agonized. So it is with the conceptual undergirding for knowledge, art, theory, and the rest. And for playing.

Jacquelyn joined playing to enjoyment. Although there are various things done for enjoyment--eating, for example--yes, playing is a way of being happy, laughing, and things like that. I suggested it is "where you just put all the big jobs you have to do aside, the big jobs like being a student or teacher or whatever." Jacquelyn added: "You just act like a little kid again, who doesn't have a care in the world." The cares don't just disappear, of course, but they don't occupy your mind and body, not right then. That's the way it was today, shopping. "I didn't think about anything at home. The only thing I was concerned about was the prices." Shopping, it turns out, is playing too.

I recommended that studying can be another version of playing. "I sometimes try and learn things, from a book or so, but kind of playfully, because it doesn't matter to me. I would like to know it, especially things about history, for example. But I'm not going to teach history, not very much anyway. I would just like to know it, that's all. Not know it for anything else." Jacquelyn added: "Just because it's interesting," which I turned around--"I'm interested in it." We become interested in a topic and we play with it, in reading, in discussion. And what happens in the exchanges "does not get hooked up with important stuff, whatever important stuff is."

In writing the "important stuff" paragraph, the

---

13 Marjorie Grene (ed.) <u>Toward a Unity of Knowledge,</u> (New York: International Universities Press, 1969, p.9).

thin veil of ambiguity around the main idea came into attention. Just what are things that can be important to a person? How do they come to be important? How can a person tell what is important? How do commitments grow or unfold? Hegel and Freud, according to Paul Ricoeur, have made us all suspicious about statements of commitment consciously and intentionally spoken. A posited connection between our efforts and some eschatological reality is apt to be nothing but a faint vainglory. Similarly, but from underneath, the statements may represent little but the twisted rationalization of an ego delicately balancing the tortured forces of an id and superego. Consciousness is self-deceptive by definition, said Jean-Paul Sartre. But is it?

"Is being a student important to you?" I asked. "Yes, sort of," came the response. "It occupies the whole of my time in school and I have no choice about going to school. And it's important because you learn things you have to know for later on. If you don't, you can't get a good job." A good job, of course, is not something plainly defined, but after a minute or two--"A good job is the job that you like, that you enjoy doing, not for money or anything like that. My friend, Connie, has a job like that . . . at a daycare center. She really, really likes it."

I asked if Connie played at the job. "I don't know. Playing always seems like you're going to . . . I don't know. 'Playing' is such a weird word." "Now." "Yeah." "It wasn't before." "No, not until you thought about it."

This last exchange brought Michael Polanyi to mind. He writes about the difference between subsidiary awareness and focal awareness. There is always an unspecifiable group of clues or concepts through which we attend to that on which we focus. The subsidiaries are tools for the focus. And if we focus on a word, talk about a word, as Jacquelyn and I did with "playing," it takes on an emptiness, a weirdness. In order to have the word function normally once again, it needs to slide back to subsidiary usage, as in a sentence where the word is used to give expression to something other than the concept of playing.

A good job, however, seemed in the end to have something to do with playing and with friends. We did not explore this path any further, though. It is only me who has a job after all, not Jacquelyn. I think it is a good job, most of the time.

I asked Lance and Jacquelyn to read the words I wrote. Lance read carefully. "Pretty good," he judged with a kind of uninterpretable look on his face. I made something of it, though, a kind of "yes, that is what we talked about and it all makes sense but . . . I don't quite get it. It's about us, isn't it?" But we did not discuss the gestural message. Jacquelyn also read her pages. Also a "pretty good." Nor did she know quite what to do after finishing the reading. She uttered an awkward but friendly "thank you" as she left the room. The text, I thought she said, had been faithful, honorable, pleasant with respect to our conversation. Was it also helpful, transformatively edifying? Or would the largesse be evident only later, some early morning?

It was over noon-hour lunch bags that James and I connected ourselves to playing. The definitional beginning first placed playing next to friends, a more open placement. But playing was also very definite--either one played or did something else. I pushed the conversation to intellectual play, playing with ideas. I mentioned the notion of learning some information, such as the procession of events following Lord Durham in 1838 or a technique or algorithm in mathematics. The information can be learned while still not taken very seriously, not invested with some high version of truth. "The ideas may be fine, but they have a layer of glass under them," I said. The information is just something we can use as we see fit. And I suggested that James, in fact, viewed and accepted the items of the school curriculum in that way.

"I read it from your face, James." The expressions there tell me that the things you learn in history and mathematics, well, are fine, that they are worth conscientious effort, but that they are not worth a high level of energy or investment.

But James did not find himself in my speech. "No," he said, "I don't think I do that very much." A conversational door closed; my steam ran out.

We turned to the playing James does with his friend

141

John. Playing is just doing some things together, making a joke, trying to get a laugh, doing whatever comes up. The talk allowed me to write the following:

There is an unconstrainedness, an unpredictability to playing. To be playful involves adopting a certain style of being, one that keeps consequences out of view, one that places a range of judgments about conventionality aside, one that keeps, however, a special interest for the playmates. The aims are to generate laughter and pleasure in being close together, to venture the unexpected, the exciting, that which is different. The friendship between persons is given a flesh of joviality on the bones of a relationship.

Playing, moreover, takes up all of attention. There is not a reserve, a looking aside, a halfheartedness to the activity. The wholesale presentation of attention to the other, this being-there-for-the-other, permits a confiding in each other. The exhibition of these secrets of confidence to others places the friendship in jeopardy. The presentation of a trust-built confidence to an outsider is in fact an act of destruction. It is ratting, especially if the presentation displays what could be construed as a weakness.

We spoke further. I told of a kind of playing with life, with a whole future. Our family had moved to Grand Rapids from Edmonton last year, and this year we had come to Toronto. No one told us to go. It was our family, mainly my wife and I, who decided. And we recognized that the choice we made was only one of several possibilities and that any of the other possibilities would also have been acceptable. Our decisions would not make the world go one way or the other. That is God's business. I'll play my best shot where I happen to live.

And James spoke about becoming a baker. Maybe a minister. We laughed about a piece I had written in a newsletter, a piece picturing James in 1994, mounting the pulpit of his first church, decked out after the model of Lord Durham.

Playing denies the tyranny of future-making. When playing, the choice of possible futures, that two minutes away or five years away, is pushed aside. Playing is not done in order to construct any particular future. Yet, the playing does construct a present order of

142

events, an order that does not evaporate without leaving sediments. The impact is seen to be relevant primarily to the relationship, the nature of the relationship, that will characterize your friendship with your playmate.

I encouraged James to talk more. His words had already opened the way to several paragraphs--the unplannedness of play, the full absorption of attention. "You got any more?" I asked. Now, we had talked, just previously, about the different kinds of play I did with grade 7s as compared to grade 8s.

James: [A hesitant laugh.] You said that . . . but then your . . . uh . . . still, the kind of planning when you talk to the grade 7s. You still kind of plan you might like to make a joke. You still have to plan that . . . I don't know . . . that you . . . that you can't really enthuse them to laugh or . . . because you know that they will carry on. So . . . you can't really plan that . . . uh . . . so that you . . . you have to . . . like to tell a different joke to a different person, you have to . . . like . . . it might just come up at the right time. But you still have to . . . like you can't . . . you have to tell kind of . . . say a different joke to Rochelle than to John.

Me: Yes, that's right.

James: Rochelle won't laugh at the same thing as John will.

Me: Yet I'd like her to laugh too.

James: Yeah.

Me: So you have to . . . That's neat, hey. So what you're saying, you've got to . . . The playing you do is different for the person you're playing with. You play differently with John than with Ed.

James: Oh, yeah, sure. I'm always rowdier with John.

Me: How come? You don't plan that.

James: I know. It's different people make me feel different ways, I think.

Me: I think that's right. Because when I am with

143

grade 8 or grade 7 . . . I talk quite differently with you than I do with Ed, or with anybody else. That's interesting. We don't really know we do it; we don't think about that, do we? I don't.

James: No.

Me: You just are a certain way with each . . . So I play differently with my children than, say, Bryan and Peggy who hang on my arm outside--which is allright. But I would feel funny if you did that. I don't know what I'd do. [Laughter.] Somehow there must be something in the air almost that allows us to act differently. See, James, how helpful you've been!

James: I should write something in the paper.

Me: Yeah. The Globe and Mail. We play differently with different people.

James: We can even split that up more. If we play with somebody we respect, you still respect that person. But still you play differently than you play with your grandmother or your mother. You respect both--they're both older than you. But you play differently with each. Or, even differently with your mother than with your dad.

Me: Or, maybe, differently at different times . . . James, these are jewels that you've given me here. That's why this has been worthwhile. Do you have any famous last words, yet?

James: The end.

Another Voice

The "Invitation to Play" paper was written about a month before the Background and Inquiry sections of this proposal. On reading the paper for purposes of this section, I found it difficult to locate its structure. Plainly, there is a temporal aspect to the piece, a forward movement through time. A self-survey takes place one day, discussions with Lance and Jacquelyn follow, writing and analysis, occur, and so on. Yet the sequence elaborated in the paper was not identical with the actual sequence. In other words, the written presentation is not a daily journal. The changes in the indicated sequence of events must have been prompted by

some concern different from time, a concern which I
think has been a commitment to simplicity and clarity.
The inclusion of all manner of involvements that came
to my attention during the three or four weeks taken to
prepare the pages were eliminated, and similarly the
convolutions of sequence flowing from these involvements
were refashioned in the interest of clarity. Thus the
paper is not stream-of-consciousness exposition.
Rather it is a reflective recovery of events with a
view toward yielding the record of a transformation of
understanding and subsequent experience. So there is
a planfulness within the writing, a planfulness beyond
that contained in an existing, intentional self.

Another aspect of the writing is its resistance to
speaking in terms of abstract universals. There is a
rawness to the presentation of "crazy walking," for
example. The characterization is not an instantiation
of some general category of three people on their way
to the bus stop. There is no hinting toward potential
mathematical measures or formulations of the experience.
Instead, there is a push toward a conception for the
uniqueness of the lived experience, a once-only-concept.
Yet the crazy walking is there as a possibility for
others. It would demand a refashioning of the steps
and mood, because otherwise the surprise and humor of
the event would vanish. The repetition would become an
exercise, a trial. The written presentation of the
experience appears to contain the implicit demand for a
reformulation when taken as a possibility for others.
So it is a preteritive exhibition.

Involved with this second aspect is the full-bodied
presentation of a self in the midst of the topic. There
is no conspiracy to keep my person outside the inquiry,
presenting some diaphanous, ideational self instead.
While this existential presence is available, there is
a concern for transgression of narcissism's border. It
was the strength of the topic's boundaries, it seems to
me, that kept narcissism at bay. Another side to the
existential self-presentation was accomplished through
the use of dialogue taken directly from taped interviews.
Dialogue tends to resist the slots of abstract categories, especially the sort of dialogue implicitly containing an authentic openness for the other to say something to you, for the other to know that your understandings be modified. This openness was not always
there for me in the interviews, especially when the conversations dwelt on definitional concerns for playing.

My pre-undersatnding loomed too large at these points,
it occupied too much of the region. The paper shows it.

Beyond these points, a comment can be given with
respect to the more analytical elements. They occur
in the gaps opened up by the descriptions of the events
or dialogue. It was while I wrote about the experiences
or while I transcribed the dialogue that the more sub-
dued philosphical, analytical utterances pushed their
way onto the paper. They seemed to make the other
parts more intelligible, more coherent, more archaeo-
logical. They made more explicit that which I thought
while reflecting upon the events that were at hand.
They provided a justification for the conceptions of
the experience just given.

At one point I had decided that a few pages of
conclusions should follow the interview with James. Yet
when the moment for beginning came, I wondered what to
say. The reader was to be invited to play, to transform
his or her own understanding, and a set of conclusions
was just what was not needed. Another force, however,
was the playful ending James set up with his stating the
words "the end."

But I believe a dissertation could be improved
with more planfulness than that displayed in the paper.
I will use Darroch and Silvers's three voices of reflective discourse for "interpretive human studies," that
is, for existential-phenomenological inquiries.

The first voice makes the usual understanding of
human experience problematic. It refuses to accept the
customary classifications and instead reaches through
the encrustations and stereotypes for the dynamic
fueling of the event. It is to the phenomena themselves
that the first voice is summoned, to the central energi-
zation of lived experiences. This voice shows experience to be an effusion of a self enmeshed in a world,
pressurized by intentionalities organized from above
and below, bending to the winds of neighborly influence,
caught up in with endowment from the past while still
being beckoned through an opening which can rupture
the continuity of time. It shows being-in-the-world as
a nakedness, an appearance shorn of categorical fig
leaves. The familiar becomes estranged under the power
of this voice and it can be seen anew. I judge that my
sample paper sings this bass voice with a moderate
resonancy.

146

The second voice is characterized by a "lostness."
It continues harmoniously from the problematization of
the ordinary to a full suspension of the taken-for-
granted. I interpret this tenor voice to be a setting-
off of experience against a nothingness out of which it
is an upsurge. Why is there this upsurge rather than
emptiness? What in the historical sedimentations hidden
away by the sheen of the present has conspired to push
outward this event, the one I have just grasped? The
lostness refers to a topography. There is a region of
twilight in the splashes of darkness and light. A
reverence is contained in the muted notes. I judge
that this voice has been heard but infrequently in my
"Play" paper. The analytical segments point to the
roots of understandings but do not well define the
placement among other interests. There are analyses
that account for that which showed itself to me as it
did. A more thorough probing would examine others
involved in the events more closely as well, with the
result that the contours of the experience would stand
in sharper relief.

The final voice, a contralto voice, speaks gently
but with the throbbing impulse of life. It shows forth
a lived meaning as it unfolds itself and penetrates the
history of the inquirer's associates. The transformations of understanding and experience are documented as
they flood into the density of speech and event. But
this voice also has a higher range, one not yet in my
power. It is more hermeneutical, more metaphorical.
It unleashes prospects for being, it renders interpretations into a variegated manifold. The inquirer himself is reduced to an empty sample, a demonstration out
of which new life flows. The inquirer dies under the
spell of the song only to be reborn after a time. So
the reader as well. I judge this range to have been
largely absent from my sample paper. To possess this
range I shall need to listen more closely to others.
Experience cannot stop at the end of a typing event.

FINDING THE FOCUS OF STUDY

Karen Holtzblatt

*In Holtzblatt's discussion here she describes the pro-
cess by which she arrives at recognizing what is at the
centre of her inquiry. She traces her thought from her
entering concern through her attempts to conceptually
define her inquiry for her participants, through her
attempts to describe her inquiry to herself (and to her
readers), and through her attempts to understand the
directions of her thought as it became influenced by
her collection of what appeared to be diverse experiences which resisted focus. We can see here how clarifying the beginning dialectics leads to a way of organizing a representation of a study.*

In trying to identify my unarticulated agenda behind my
interest in women's friendships, I recognized that I
paid more attention to the participants when they
talked with intensity and feeling about certain friendship contacts. I knew that my phenomenon was present
when I tried to understand the words that the participants used in describing these "feeling" friendship
experiences. Words such as "connection," "distance,"
"support," "clicking," and "closeness" were a major
part of what the participants and I sought to explicate
together. But to what focus did these words point?

In discussing the difficulty of defining my focus
with my thesis adviser, I was asked, "What do you want
to speak about in reference to women's friendship?
Where does your energy lie?" In recording my response
to this question, I wrote:

I was surprised that I had an answer to that question.
I said that I could not speak for others, but for myself
the most important thing about friendship was the transcendence of existential aloneness and isolation through
profound connection with a woman. In such an interaction, I experience myself as being known and understood

---

* From "A Study of Women's Friendship Relationships:
Involvement and the Psychological Sense of Community,"
Karen Holtzblatt, Doctoral Dissertation, University of
Toronto, 1982.

and not alone in my experience of the world. I emphasized "with a woman," for I believe that there is a specialness in the way a woman can touch. But I said that this is my significance, not necessarily the significance of friendship for the participants, although I guessed that something like transcendence was important for all the women. My adviser suggested that I try to understand the other women's experiences grounded in my own significance.

But I could not speak of the women's experiences from the vantage point of transcendence alone, I found. For transcendence emphasizes the negative. That is, when I say transcendence of aloneness, I become centered in looking for aloneness. But transcendence implies no longer feeling alone. Much of what is found in friendship experience is the positive, the after-having-transcended experience. The participants are not necessarily expressing feelings of aloneness, or even feeling aloneness, when they talk of their times with good special friends. If aloneness is the negative polarity, what is the positive?

The positive, I thought was found in my basic beginning concepts, which I explored with the women: community, connection, transcendence, and the bond. I know existential aloneness is a key. It is our knowledge and sometimes experience that we are ultimately alone in our subjective experiencing, that no one else can completely know, maybe even partially know, what our thoughts and feelings are. When we walk in the world, only we know our experiencing of our lives; no one can know what it is to be living my life. Existential aloneness places us apart from others, separates us from others. If we experience this so-called reality, we would describe ourselves as feeling isolated, cut off, alienated, locked inside ourselves. Yet many of us do not feel this way. As one participant said, "I do not feel alone in the world."

This is the statement with which I began. We may say that the significance of friendship, in part at least, is that when we have friends we do not feel alone in the world. I keep responding to how the participants and I are not feeling alone in the world and I try to understand this. Why do we not feel alone? What do we feel instead? I have come to see that the positive experience associated with aloneness is the experience of connectedness with others. One significance of

friendship is the way it contributes to the women's
sense of connectedness with others. I claim that this
experience of connectedness takes on its significance
against the backdrop of existential aloneness. We might
say that one consequence of transcendence is the experience of connectedness.

So I may state now that the core concept with which
I will approach the data is the two-sided experience of
connectedness and aloneness.

Here is my first articulation of my focus on women's
friendships. What excited me about the women's friendship experiences were interactions after which the women
experienced themselves as being known and understood and
not alone in the world. In my own life I was very aware
of my feelings after conversations with good women
friends when I felt the total joy of being understood
and not on my own in my life. What I recognize first,
here, is that for me aloneness is a fundamental backdrop
to understanding friendship and to my focus on friendship. Yet in articulating the importance of aloneness
for me in understanding friendship, I was directed to
the continual references to aloneness that the participants made when speaking of friendship. Friendship
becomes a phenomenon to be appreciated in one's life in
its juxtaposition with experiences of aloneness.

For me, friendship became an issue when I moved to
a new city and had no friends. In reflecting on this,
I wrote that my husband and I "found ourselves feeling
very alone, isolated, and much like we did not belong in
Canada, Toronto, or to our graduate department." But at
the same time, I began to speak to my female friends in
long-distance conversations about women's issues. In my
resulting joy and relief at the identity of our concerns
and perceptions, I recognized how alone I had been with
these issues in my life before and how alone I currently
was with these issues in Toronto.

Similarly, the other participants spoke of their
aloneness and friendships simultaneously. Debra told me
in our pre-discussion meeting that she was very interested in friendship because two years ago all of her
closest friends left in the same year. She said that
she experienced a tremendous void in her life. She
recognized that "something was missing" when these
people were no longer dropping in to see her. Missy
spoke about the importance of friends to her in order
"to have some adult to share things with," for Missy's

151

husband works nights and she works days. Shana was very
lonely and frustrated in her life, for she had no one to
speak with about her life's work of theology. Julie
emphasized the value of her closest friend's ability to
listen and help appropriately during a time when Julie
felt isolated with the knowledge of her child's handicap. Cathy spoke of how she was "really all alone"
after her closest friends, with whom she worked, were
all transferred to another town. Now she reflected on
the special qualities of those relationships and how she
could create something similar with current friends.
Joan and Janet both became aware of the importance of
their female friendships when they separated from their
husbands. Sally said of her friends, "These women fill
up my life," at a time when she was the only woman in
an all-male firm; she now lived with her parents instead
of working and living with her friends, as she had previously done. Ann, a widow living alone, spoke of her
worries about what would become of her when she could no
longer care for herself. Yet, following this thought,
she said, "But I know that there will always be interesting people happening, even in a home . . . no, I am
not alone in the world."

All of the women spoke of friendship from within
the context of aloneness in their lives in one form or
another. Friendship became a phenomenon for us as it
counteracted the negative experiences of aloneness or
as we became aware of it from the aloneness that resul-
ted from the loss of friends. Yet, although aloneness
gives friendship a particular meaning, I did not speak
to the women about their experienced aloneness. Aloneness as an experience simply points to and highlights
the meaningfulness of friendship for the women. Against
the backdrop of aloneness, the women and I have come to
recognize the positive dimensions of friendship. It was
to the expression of this positive dimension of friendship that I was attending in our discussions.

I was looking to understand those friendship experiences that were associated with statements such as
Ann's, "I am not alone in the world." I was looking to
give expression to those positive friendship feelings of
connectedness, as opposed to the negative feelings of
disconnectedness. I was asking what friendship experiences allow us to transcend our aloneness and to feel
connected to the world and each other. Even with this
articulation of focus, aloneness, and connectedness, I
did not yet speak of loneliness and community.

With the focus on aloneness and connectedness, I
set up a discussion with Janet, a woman whom I thought
would have an intuitive grasp of what I meant by
connectedness. I stated to her in advance that I wanted
to focus the discussion on those times when she experienced aloneness and connectedness in friendship. Out
of my discussion with her, Janet raised for me the
implicit meaning of the word aloneness that I was using.
Although I began my focus with an orientation toward
existential aloneness, Janet pointed me toward the
relevant dimension of existential aloneness. We agreed
that this aloneness referred to our internal experience
of being an individual person with unique sets of intrapsychic experiences which set us apart from others and
which could not be directly experienced by others.
Whether or not this state may be completely transcended
is certainly debatable. Yet when I spoke of aloneness
I was not simply referring to this recognition of the
fundamental alone state of each individual. Nor am I
speaking of "self-imposed aloneness," where we remain
physically or experientially alone by choice. Aloneness,
since it may have multiple meanings, is not really the
backdrop of connectedness. Rather, loneliness is the
backdrop. In speaking of loneliness, Janet said that she
has "a feeling of separateness, or not connection," and
she will make appointments to see friends "because it's
obvious to me that at a particular time in my life I am
feeling a need for connection." Loneliness is being
alone when aloneness is not desired. Yet when I spoke
of existential aloneness, I recognized that I was not
speaking only of the physical presence of the friends.
Rather we may be physically present with others and
still experience loneliness because our intrapsychic
experiences are not perceived, received, or understood
by others. For men, then, aloneness refers to loneliness. The meaning of loneliness, at least at the
inception of the study, was more than not having people
present in our lives; it pointed to an experiential
dimension of loneliness that friendships can transcend.

In my choice of Janet as a participant, and in my
shift in the definition of focus resulting from our
discussions, we can see again the process of inquiry.
I entered my discussion with Janet with an intuitive
grasp of the meaning of my compound phenomenon of
"aloneness and connectedness." In seeking to define
this focus further and to gather data pertinent to it,
I entered into dialogue with her about my current conceptual understandings and queries. Through that

dialogue I came to recognize my own meaning of the word
aloneness as I was seeing it in this study. I also
uncovered different meanings of the word aloneness which
were pertinent to her. Yet in my future discussions
with women I did not pursue these other two meanings, for
they were not theoretically relevant to my still implicit
focal concern. Thus, even when Janet points to a different phenomenon and thereby participates in the interpretive process, my focal concern directs which data
will be considered pertinent. The distinctions between
the aloneness phenomena were made by Janet. The phenomenon I pursued was still part of what was significant
for Janet in friendship. I did not dismiss Janet's
experiences as not fitting because I could find no overlap between my entering interests and her experiences or
interpretation. I pursued that part of her experiences
that was relevant for her and my research. However, this
clearly gives me only a partial understanding of Janet's
experience.

In looking for the overlap between my interest and
the women's experience, I am able to delineate what I
speak about and to ensure that, in thus focusing, I am
still considering that which is relevant for women's
friendship. My responsiveness to the women and the data
serves to shape my focus even as my focus shapes what
data I consider relevant. With each discussion with each
participant I leave with a somewhat different focus and
orientation. No two discussions are alike either in
content or in the directing focal interests I hold. An
idea derived from one participant will be present in my
awareness in talking with the next participant. Ideas
thus become modified both as I reflect on the data I
already have and as I use them with the next participant.
As this process continues, the discussions with my last
participants become more focused than the broad, very
open discussions I had with my first participants. With
Janet I was only interested in certain aspects of her
experience which will bear on my developing theory of
women's friendship.

Thus the data collection process cannot truly be
separated from the data analysis process. Insofar as
the women and I are constantly altering my interpretations and forming new ones, the understandings that
will emerge from this study are being developed even as
I gather the data relevant to these interpretations. My
talk with the women becomes theoretically directed while

154

I am expanding the theoretical perspective to include more of the women's friendship experiences.

Each new participant adds to and simultaneously challenges the previously existing understandings. Moreover, as I seek to respond to and incorporate each woman's experience into my undersatnding, I am forced to change and expand my understandings and challenge my entering assumptions. Insofar as I am able to define these assumptions, I am able to expand, and reject if necessary, my entering conceptualizations; as well, I am able to define more accurately the area of women's friendship I seek to speak about. The turning point for the study and the recognition of focus came as I tried to incorporate the experiences of some of the women into my implicit understandings of closeness and connectedness.

In talking to Janet I realized that loneliness was the relevant backdrop of my phenomenon. All of the women and I spoke of some form of loneliness in conjunction with the meaningfulness of friendship. But Janet in part defined loneliness as "a need for connection." What did she, and what do I, mean by this term? Janet said, "The meaningfulness of my life is enhanced by my love and caring for friends and theirs for me." I asked her if "friends contribute to the meaningfulness in life because . . . of the sense of connectedness." She responded, "Meaningfulness would be synonymous with connectedness, in its broadest sense." Janet is telling us that for her to have meaning in her life is to be connected. As in Ann's statement, "I am not alone in the world," I recognized in Janet's observation my implicit focal phenomenon. Yet when I asked if connectedness contributed to the meaningfulness of life, was I referring to the same connectedness as Janet?

My initial response to this word called up for me the moments of connection or closeness that I experienced when speaking with my women friends on the phone or in person about meaningful intimate topics. Connectedness occurred when I was understood by the friend and so I transcended that sense of experiential loneliness. For me connectedness was bound up in a certain form of relationship--the confidant relationship. In addition, connectedness referred to that fleeting feeling of profound contact with the other which is reminiscent of Buber's "I-Thou" relationships.

155

Janet described to me certain friendship contacts in which she experienced connectedness. These friendship contacts, although not always one-to-one talking, such as the evening when her friend came over to sit with her after oral surgery, still were not fundamentally different. Although Janet did not speak to her friend about her pain, her friend was still supportive and understanding in a non-verbal way.

But when I spoke to Ann, Cathy, Julie, and Shana, I could not find any evidence of this form of connectedness. Ann, whom I recognized as pointing to my phenomenon in her statement "I am not alone in the world," also said, "I don't have any close-close friendship. I don't think you are going to find very deep friendship; I can't see that I give time to it. You've stumped me all the way along as I thought about it because I knew I hadn't any great friendships to report." How could I reconcile a focus of connectedness found in Ann's statement of not being alone in the world with her lack of the confidant relationships in which I found connectedness?

But Ann was not the only participant who lacked confidant relationships as I understood them. I probed Cathy relentlessly about her friendships, searching for how she dealt with problems and what she shared with her friends. "I go off by myself," she said. "I think you are looking for something that is not there." In speaking with Shana, I was surprised at her attitude that she should not burden her friends with her problems. For her, closeness did not emerge within this context.

Here again we can recognize the dialogical nature of the inquiry. My entering hypotheses were structuring the content of my talk with the participants. I believed that confidant relationships were pertinent to my phenomenon and so searched for data on them. Yet even as we can recognize my myopic vision of the phenomenon at this point, we can also recognize the strength of the participants. These women, whose relationships could not fit my working model, did not create appropriate friendship contacts for me. They constantly indicated to me the misapplication of my assumptions, reminding me that their experience did not fit my model of relationships. Clearly, the women could have allowed me to reinterpret their experiences for them. But in emphasizing the active role of the participants in this study and in sharing my ongoing interpretations speci-

156

fically to receive the participants' responses, I believe that I opened the way for these women to challenge and redefine my way of thinking when it did not suit their experience. By their continuous challenging of my conceptualizations I was forced to be continuously responsive to the data lest I dismiss a clearly relevant portion of the women's experiences.

As I was probing for connectedness in the confidant relationship, I realized, through my discussions with the women, that I was preoccupied with one idea of connectedness manifest in one way of spending time with friends. As I focused on what was absent from these women's lives, I was missing what was present in their friendships. For even as I wondered at this lack in their relationships, I recognized that the friendships they described did exemplify connectedness and closeness. It was Ann who spoke of not being alone in the world; Cathy spoke of connection and clicking as descriptors of her relationships, providing me with my first focus conceptualizations. Shana also spontaneously spoke of connection and clicking. Thus, insofar as these relationships manifest connectedness, they were part of my phenomenon even if they did not manifest the "close-close" intimacy that may be present in a confidant relationship. I was thus compelled to articulate the nature of this connectedness. In trying first to understand the difference between the experiences in the confidant relationship and in other forms of friendship, I compared Ann's description of a week with her friend Wanda, in which I felt that connectedness was manifest, to my own description of a weekend with one of my closest friends, Beth.

In speaking of her vacation period, Ann states:

It was so easy to share jobs, talk of who'd do what and who'd go to town and who'd buy what, who'd treat that day to dinner. We always had to go to the races because her father had been a little addicted to horses. And then Wanda was interested, and Bob. So we tested them. I mean, it was such a variety of interests. And then reading and thinking always about people in foreign parts because that's really where her heart was. . . . This is the everyday thing we did while I was at that cottage. Oh, go to town, of course, and enjoy the horses, do the buying and small jobs, and fishing in the trout creeks around and bringing home fresh fish and digging for clams.

Following is an excerpt from my account of my
weekend with Beth:

Usually on these weekends there is some time for
catching up--alone talk--Beth and I. We sat out in the
back yard, lying in the sun and catching up on one and
a half years. How could we? There was no problem
bringing her into my life now. Here I am now, my
concerns and worries, the high points and hopes and
blahs. Beth spoke too. There was no moment of hesitation, no worry of the other's opinion. Indeed, no
thought like that at all. We just talk and share, some
tears maybe, encouragement; no perfect understanding
but close; not always listening, wandering minds and
back again. Warmth. Later we were entertaining the
baby in his pool. Somehow we were talking again, I
telling her of my past and growing up. All the feelings
present, I then back in the past, felt her wrapped into
my story, I felt her presence by me in my life that was
past. Suddenly I said, "Why am I telling you my life
story anyway?" "Because I asked," she said. "I wanted
to know."

At first one might perceive these two experiences
as very similar. They are both extended overnight
stays with friends. We were both vacationing and intent
on relaxing. We both did things together. But if one
looks at my description of my time with Beth, one can
see that what I chose to compare was an encounter where
Beth and I are mainly focused on each other. Even my
thoughts at the time, as I recall them focused on being
with Beth. I was aware of our spending this kind of
time together. My friend was primary in my consciousness. The settings of our friendship encounters, the
back yard, could be changed or removed, but the experience of this time would for me be still basically the
same. Beth and I in face-to-face dialogue are essential
to the creation of my friendship experience. The emphasis in this friendship encounter is on the dominant
experience of one friend to the other. I was mainly
aware of both my friend and my immediate relating to her.
The feeling of connectedness of me to Beth and Beth to
me dominates my experience.

Stopping now to look at Ann's friendship description,
I immediately realize that my focus on the other will not
characterize Ann's experience of her vacation with Wanda.
When Ann speaks of these friendship contacts, she
emphasizes the setting and activities that she engaged in

158

while with her friend, "sharing jobs . . . enjoying the
horses . . . buying . . . fishing in the trout creeks."
Unlike in my experience with Beth, the persons, the
settings, and the activities are integrally linked.
The setting for this friendship contact could not be
changed or removed without also changing the nature of
the friendship experience for Ann. Also, the people
cannot be substituted with others. Nor can the people
be eliminated altogether, leaving Ann relating to nature.
Wanda, Bob, Ann, the setting and activities all come
together in Ann's experience to create that particular
friendship contact. Ann points to this when she says:

. . . she's such a good friend in the outdoors when
cares are gone and there isn't anything to think about
in this little lovely setting . . . that's the kind of
thing that I love and that she obviously loves. I think
that's when I knew her best, when we lived together . . .
it was sort of getting down to basics and liking it
together. . . . We just loved being there together and
doing those things.

"Liking it together" is a key phrase here. Ann liked
the activity, the setting, but she liked it "together."
Ann did not say only that she liked to fish, or that she
liked being with Wanda. Rather, Ann linked the activities with the people. Ann says, "and the brother was
part of it, too, because he knew the streams." Ann
could not describe her friendship contact, as I could,
without really including the men present. On my weekend
both my own and Beth's husbands were with us most of the
time and we did do things together.

The persons, the activities, and the setting are
linked in Ann's experience. Indeed, when I pressed Ann
to separate her contact with Wanda the person from the
whole of the friendship experience, she did not know
what I wanted. I asked how she felt about the people
during the vacation. First Ann spoke of the people they
got to know in the nearby village. Then she spoke of
Wanda in general. She spoke of other times that she had
visited that area as contributing to her friendship
experience. Finally, after a series of questions, I
directed her to her experience of Wanda at the cottage.
Her experience of Wanda, unlike my experience of Beth,
was not a natural part of that friendship experience.
Whereas after my weekend with Beth, I would be prone to
speak of relating to my friend and knowing her better,
Ann would have no such inclination and would speak of

the activities she experienced and came to know with her friend. Ann does not experience her friendship independently of the activities they shared.

Ann says of her friendship, "We are good friends when we are together What I now realize, as Ann implicitly did, is that her friendship feelings of closeness and connectedness emerge out of the two friends sharing a particular activity or experience. Thus the closeness of the friendship occurs during the time of that activity. The closeness is not to the friend in the form of the intimate affection that Beth and I have for each other, although certainly this too can occur.

During our discussions, I classified Ann's friendship contacts as "enjoying life together." Ann readily confirmed this interpretation. In this phrase, I recognized that in her friendship contacts Ann is simultaneously connected to the friend and to the activity. The friend, the activity, and the setting are experienced as a whole to which Ann is in relation. The person, activity, and setting form a unitary experience. Ann states, "We all spread out along the streams and shrieked when we got something." Each person did not fish alone and meet later on. During the fishing itself, Ann implies that she was aware of sharing this experience with her friend standing downstream. Both the catching of the fish and the shrieking were integral parts of the experience. Ann thus experiences a dual connection to her friend and to the activity. But the connection to the friend emerged out of sharing that activity and "liking it together," not through a direct link between the friends in dialogue.

Thus through comparing these two experiences, which intuitively represent connectedness to me, I am able to uncover two forms of connectedness in two forms of friendship contact. I begin here to distinguish the feeling of closeness or connectedness associated with a focus on the friend from a feeling of closeness or connectedness associated with the interactive compound of person and activity.

These distinctions are the rudiments of the more developed understanding that I reached in distinguishing between "incorporation" and "creating life" developed in later parts of the thesis. Here the distinction is between a direct involvement in the life of the friend

160

and a mutual involvement in a life emerging from the
friend's mutual interests. It was only with the recognition developed here (that activity-oriented friendship
contacts are also a manifestation of connectedness) that
I was able to look away from the confidant relationships
and experiences and become aware of the true nature of
my focus.

With my interpretation of Ann's vacation experience
I realized that connectedness is manifest not only
between friends when relating through face-to-face conversation. Ann not only was connected to her friend but
was simultaneously involved in a particular activity.
Connectedness was manifest when friends engaged in
activities together. I thus began to articulate ways
that connectedness was manifest.

In describing my phenomenon as connectedness, I was
drawn to describing and making sense of discrete times
with a friend during which time a peak emotional
experience that I labeled connectedness occurred. I
have stated that my entering idea of connectedness
"called up for me the moments of connection or closeness
that I experienced when speaking with my women friends .
. . about meaningful intimate topics." With the recognition of connectedness in Ann's experience I have
expanded my understanding beyond discussion of intimate
topics. But I have continued to focus on the idea of
"moments of closeness." When I asked Janet to speak of
connectedness and aloneness, I asked her to describe
times when she felt connected to friends. As I requested,
she described isolated incidents during which times she
felt connected to friends.

Even as I sought to articulate the nature of these
peak momentary experiences in friendship, I realized that
I was not capturing my phenomenon. I spoke continuously
of a dissatisfaction with this concentration on peak
moments in friendship. On the one hand, I realized that
these special moments between friends did not describe
the majority of Ann's, the other women participants', nor
my own friendship contacts. But more important, I recognized my phenomenon as reflected most directly in the
women's statements, "I am not alone in the world," "These
women fill up my life," and "These women are central to
my life." In these sentences the women spoke of their
world and life. They pointed to an experience associated
with friendship that affected the whole of their life,
not just moments of it.

It was at this stage in my thought about friendship
that I wrote the account of my weekend with Beth. I
knew that my phenomenon was somehow reflected in the
whole of that experience. I was trying to capture the
encounter's salient aspects for myself. Yet in my
original comparison of my experiences with Ann's, I
used only one paragraph of that account. I could focus
only on how my friendship experience was different from
Ann's. With my dissatisfaction and my more open understanding of connectedness I returned to my account to
try to re-see what was present for me in friendship.
In the more elaborate account of that weekend experience
I saw that the confidant interaction was only a very
small part of the time I spent with Beth. In reviewing
the whole account, I read each paragraph and asked
myself what I was trying to convey. In the margins of
my story, paragraph after paragraph, I wrote "acceptance
into life." I saw how Beth had accepted me into and
made me a part of the ongoing flow of her life. I saw
that not only was I connected to Beth in my closeness
but I was also connected to Beth's life. I participated
in her life. Connectedness then had to do with how we
participate in the lives of our friends.

With this realization, I saw the relationship
between my experiences and that of all of the other
participants. Ann talked about the way life was shared
at the cottage. Cathy talked of friends who disrupted
her life. Missy spoke of her friends as sisters who
came into her home like family. I began to see connectedness in the relationship between women's lives.
Moments of closeness occur within the context of lives
that are connected. To feel connected to others as part
of the flow of our lives is a characteristic of relationships, not moments, between people. In recognizing the
connectedness of the women's lives, I was immediately
brought to my articulated focus. The connectedness I
wish to speak about is not the feeling of closeness or
connection experienced during special moments between
persons. Rather, connectedness speaks to the way women
experience themselves as a part of each other's lives.
It is in this understanding of connectedness that I find
reflected the psychological sense of community. Better
than connectedness, the term "the psychological sense
of community" points to those characteristics and
experiences of life that could lead one to say "I am not
alone in the world." Thus this work will address the
relationships between women's friendship experiences and
the psychological sense of community.

162

In my search for a way to speak of friendship in terms other than moments, we can see more clearly how my intuitive sense of my phenomenon directed the development of focus. Though I found myself drawn to these special times in friendship, I recognized that they did not reflect the whole of the phenomenon I wished to speak about. Even though my final focus and understandings will also not reflect the totality of women's friendships, they should at least reflect the whole of what I wanted to speak about.

Overall in this discussion of the evolution of focus we can see that though I began my work with an idea of the relevance of the psychological sense of community, it was only as I came to put meaning to those words as they related to my data and to my intuitive sense of the phenomenon that I came to see that community was my phenomenon. With this focus on community I had located an understanding that would allow me to enter into dialogue with the data without being pulled off on tangents, without being swayed into a total description of the women's experience. Before I had articulated this focus, I would enter the data and stray from my purpose, and would produce no coherent understandings. It is only with an awareness of focus that I am able to choose data that are connected conceptually and that can be built into an elaborated understanding. Yet, even though I can now name community as my focus, the meaning of community in the context of friendship is still unclear. Clarification of this meaning is the purpose of my subsequent dialogue with the data.

Upon realizing that participation in life is a relevant aspect of friendship experience that is related to community, I immediately recalled that Ann, Debra, Cathy, and I all spoke of friends in terms of living together. I therefore turned to the phrase "we lived together" as a beginning point in clarifying the friendship experience as it relates to community. Indeed, this phrase and its articulation becomes the focus of understanding the friendship and community experience as a whole.

Once again, the articulation of the friendship and community concepts, which emerge from an understanding of the descriptor "we lived together," is directed by my intuitive understanding of these concepts which have been shaped by the women's friendship experiences. One may ask how I chose to first speak of living together.

163

I can respond only that it was my first thought upon
realizing the relevance of participation in life.
Clearly, I was directed to this understanding by some
relationship between the experiences surrounding living
together and their ability to give meaning to women's
friendship experiences relevant to community. I am
suggesting that the process of understanding is fundamentally intuitive rather than conscious, rational, and
logical. I cannot deduce my understandings; I discover
them as I dialogue and respond to the data, moving with
the purpose, if not the clarity, that my focus provides
me.

Reference

Buber, Martin. I and Thou. Charles Scribner's Sons:
     New York, 1970.

A TRANSFORMATION OF UNDERSTANDING

Margret Hovanec

*In a reflective account of her interview with a patient,
Hovanec pursues a disturbing and bewildering comment.
The patient's expression of fear of a medical drug is
beyond Hovanec's initial understanding. (Hovanec is a
former nurse.) Hovanec attempts to locate the patient's
meaning in an analysis which requires (1) a consistent
responsiveness to the patient's descriptions and explanations, (2) a recognition of a self-other dialectic
between the researcher and the patient (i.e., the person
studied), and (3) an existential account of the researcher's interpretive practices in order for her to attend
consciously to the sources of her initial conventional
understandings. Hovanec's analysis of an understanding
of a patient's fear offers an example of how she has
been able to go beyond what is known by herself and
beyond what is said to her by the patient.*

When I first heard a woman say that she was afraid,
"afraid of gold," her treatment, and that is "scared
her," I was surprised and bewildered because I knew
that the course of her rheumatoid arthritis to date
indicated that gold would be the treatment of choice in
her case. I knew also that the gold treatment had been
discussed with her by her doctor and that she had consented to it and begun treatment with it. My bewilder-
ment, in some way, reflects the idea that I felt she
had not resolved being frightened with her physician
and had engaged in a treatment without being sure of
it within herself. She did not seem to be accepting
the treatment and assisting in her treatment. The tone
of her voice, as well as certain passages in her interview, pointed to her non-acceptance. She seemed to
have a knowledge of the disease in her body, an experience of rheumatoid arthritis, that had not been acknowledged or taken into account with her treatment.

I wonder now why I was surprised. Was my surprise
because I knew this woman had always been well and

---

* From "The Experience of Rheumatoid Arthritis," Margret
Hovanec, Doctoral Dissertation, University of Toronto,
1981.

active and now I perceived in my presence in the interview that she was expressing what to me seemed to be
her obvious need to immediately get rid of her disease?
After all, she had said she "hated being sick," that
she could not "totally accept it." The vaguely con-
cessional, pleading tone in her voice, which I also
recorded in my journal, seemed to indicate that somehow
she wanted to engage someone in knowing of her fear. I
also felt she might see it as my responsibility or place
to either reassure, explain, or encourage her in her
treatment. I had perceived myself in this position many
times as a nurse, and I believe my response was inherent
in what I had learned of justifying medical treatment to
other patients at the direction of physicians. So I
located what I experienced within myself as this need
to rise to the occasion to try to comfort her in some
way. In the tradition of allopathic medicine in which
I had been trained, this was an explicit responsibility.
I realized that in these feelings I was responding in
a way that I would have as a nurse. But, as a nurse, I
would have been able to reach into my armamentarium of
available solutions and would have tried to implement
some traditional comfort measure, some means of making
her treatment more plausible for her, some way of
reinforcing her present medical treatment. My dis-
comfort was more obvious to me without this backup. I
might also have wanted to define her problem as anxiety
rather than fear or my distress. We have anti-anxiety
medications. In some way also, I was uneasy because I
had a sense that fear is not a compatible emotion to be
used to describe treatment. I expected, I perceived,
there should be a reduction in fear in the presence of
a diagnosis and the beginning of treatment. I think
also that I had a sense of the woman drawing me into
feelings of hers that she has not expressed to others.
I wondered if she wanted me to be a kind of spokesman
to mediate between the forces that were about to give
her this treatment, or the people around her, for
instance, her family.

I know that these responses are something within
myself; yet I can ground them in the transcript. Something in me responds to someone confiding in me, and I
know that I automatically respond to that feeling by
trying to devise ways of helping rather than staying
with the feelings expressed to me. What do I make of
this feeling? Why is it given ascendancy? Perhaps
because it is part of both my autobiography and my
biography.

Staying with her feelings of being frightened and also overtaken with rheumatoid arthritis increases my sense of helplessness. I think my sense of helplessness can only be reduced by implementing something that has at least a component of being a comfort measure. From my past, there is a need to respond to pain and to try to alleviate that symptom and others. This inherent or learned problem-solving rather than feeling-staying response is part of myself. I know now that I fight against my helplessness. I did not know then that I thought I fought and always won that battle. This seems to be my greatest difficulty in listening to people with rheumatoic arthritis describe their experience.

What does all of this tell me about the experience of rheumatoid arthritis? It tells me that people are frightened and that they reach out. They reach out for alleviation of symptoms and for some kind of understanding. Also they might instill a sense of helplessness and anger in those around them who recognize that they cannot truly help them.

If I were to recall what my "angry nurse" responses were in reaction to, I believe that I would say they came in the presence of these helpless feelings. As an angry nurse, I could not have the luxury of attending to feelings, to attending to people by talking to them. My presence at the hospital bedside was that of implementer of treatment decided upon by a physician practitioner. My sense of helplessness emerged as I heard people talk of their fears, of their fears of treatment, of their fears of having rheumatoid arthritis. My sense of helplessness was augmented almost exponentially when I delivered treatment that did not have the desired disease-decreasing effects. I may not have had confidence in my methods (after all, I admit I did not question them), but I was identified as being on the side of powerful medical technology. And it did give me something to do.

I am uncomfortable with her because I feel that I must do something to change her feelings. But I sense now that I have been found out. I have been exposed as not believing in the utility of the sick role, or of current allopathic medical practice. I am forced to cope with the fact that she may suspect this. I recognize also that I am made aware by what is being said, by thinking of the rheumatoid arthritis in the sense that it has invaded this woman's body. That invasion

167

makes her fearful and makes her reach out for help from others. Somehow, this woman who placed enormous trust in her body sensations, who hated illness and fought against it, can no longer trust her sensations. She can no longer mobilize sufficient resources to counteract illness. She sought additional help, and that helper took over her fight. If I stay with the sense of invasion, I see that she is now invaded by another force--this counteracting force against her disease. No wonder we hear about the "battle" or the "war" against disease. Her body, in my imagining, becomes an occupied war zone with disease fighting against treatment, with doctor fighting disease. Does she seek me or seek others to raise the white flag, call a truce, and try to negotiate a settlement for her health?

When I check my journal notes, I notice that there have been other times when I have made statements about reacting to people's fears and not being able to do something about it. I felt that my search for information about the experiences with rheumatoid arthritis was somehow a rather selfish one, one that would not be met by my working to resolve an individual's fears as I would have once as a nurse. I sensed myself as somehow violating her presence in areas that could be regarded as intrusive by her. She was vulnerable.

If I were to stay with her words and recognize my response of being bewildered and surprised, seeing myself as rendered helpless and somehow taken back by what she was saying, I can facilitate being surprised by her response and allow my surprise to evolve into a kind of curiosity about dimensions of her fear. I saw this movement in myself, in that I had to remove myself consciously from focusing on my reactions in the interview to returning again to her presence and words in the interview for the source of this sense of fear in her experiencing of rheumatoid arthritis.

This movement led me to focus on the stated object of her fear, the gold. I know that we both know gold is presently a common treatment for rheumatoid arthritis. I know gold is myochrysine, a clear, sterile, injectable liquid containing gold salts. But how does she know gold such that she is made afraid? What is it about gold that makes her voice change noticeable when she even uses the word "gold"? How has the ordinary become strange to her? I wonder how she

imagines gold? Before I knew of gold suspended in a
medium and made injectable as a medical treatment, I
knew of it as a precious metal. I knew of it as expensive, inert, solid, and yellow. Any of these characteristics would be seen as distressful, depending on
one's circumstances. I wondered if she saw gold as a
metal as in her wedding ring--solid, physical, hard,
and likely expensive. Imagining such a metal injected
into one's body could be rather frightening. I remember, as a radiographer, seeing films of pelvises of old
men, immigrants to Canada in the early 30s, who had
been injected with bismuth salt as an early treatment
of syphillis. Years later, irregular masses were still
visible and palpable in their bodies. I wondered
silently if she might have had such an image of gold
depositing in her body. This nugget-like image of a
foreign substance encased within my body would be
frightening to me. Did she share this kind of image?
I have some difficulty imagining the gnarled shapes of
nuggets along with what she might have seen as the
potentially gnarled state of her bones. This really
could have been just our differences in imagining, our
differences in our autobiographies and biographies. If
she did not see the gold as a solid because she realized
it could not be injected in that form, I wondered if
perhaps she saw it as more of a gold dust--small, shiny,
flaky particles suspended in a liquid that on entering
her body would find their way to affected joints, cover
and lubricate them with a protective film that would
retard any further disease damage.

I did not know but what her source of fear was that
someone had explained to her that no one knew by what
mechanism gold worked in the body. I know, at this
level, that I consciously held back on giving her this
information, knowing that this, if new information, could
confuse her. It is still a source of my surprise that I
must locate. I am surprised that I have never addressed
myself to this before. I have always known that the
mechanism of gold is unknown. I have also known that
there are very serious side effects. I am surprised
that I have not questioned the aggressiveness and
wonderful magicness--almost archaicness--of gold and
the enormous side effects that even I was prepared to
sanction in its use as a treatment. I also know that it
was not my responsibility to transgress into the manage-
ment of her disease. I wondered if this meant my not
listening or my not looking for alternatives with her.

It is when I know that I suspend my specialized knowledge of the area that I become very anxious about dealing with patients, with this woman. I began to sense that I was focusing more on my withholding of information than seeking more information from her about her fears. I know how dependent I am on information for my own use, on information that I have learned and used previously to solve problems with people I regard as patients. I realize this becomes more and more obvious to me within the hospital situation or with people with physical mechanical difficulties. Perhaps it is not only the hsopital setting but the potential helping situation that makes me ill-at-ease when other people itemize their problems. I cannot seem to separate problem and experience. I do not put myself on the same level with the patient. I lose my generous position despite my avowed helpfulness.

I cannot depend on this woman using the words as I understand them, so I must attend carefully to how she uses them. What has also happened here is that I have changed in how I regard gold. I began with the objective meaning of the word "gold" and tried to move through it to discover a subjective meaning. I have tried to imagine what she could have had in mind when she spoke of "gold." I reflected on the vagueness and uncertainty I heard in her voice when I heard her speak of the gold as treatment. I must always interpret, with her, her subjective meaning. There is also something vague and uncertain about gold. Objectively, gold as a treatment does not have a certain or specific outcome, nor does it have a known mechanism for working. That gold as a treatment for this woman is vague and uncertain seems to be transmitted to her and, later, to me. So here, maybe, the objective as well as the subjective vagueness that frightens her is known between us on a level that we cannot express other than in reflection.

In a suspension of my now non-specialized knowledge and experience, and in the active imagining of how someone might see gold, is the only way that I have formed a new way of understanding her fear of it. It was seeing gold as gold, a physical substance, as it is commonly seen, that made me think how she might feel if her body were invaded and injected by that physical substance. Given this familiar thing, gold as a physical solid, a specialized knowledge made the ordinary become strange and threatening. At one stage, she had voluntarily ingested medicine, mostly aspirin, to help her

overcome the symptoms of rheumatoid arthritis. Now
someone had dictated that even this control be taken
from her, and he had replaced this active control over
her ingestion of medicine with her passive depersona-
lized submission to the injection of a physical substance. It was now another act of invasion and a
physical presence that she had to submit to. Her
familiar, pleasing, active body had been intruded upon
by a force, rheumatoid arthritis, an unbidden, elusive,
resilient force. On the diagnosis of that disease,
the physician had taken it as his responsibility to
attack the disease. That attack had been made in the
presence of her body. Her body held within it the
presence of rheumatoid arthritis and her physician
was determined to reduce or eradicate it, at least to
control it. Her body had now become the battlefield
of a disease and a physician. Her role was passive.
Again she was a victim. I think that in some way I have
a sense of her helplessness now. My self-sense of
helplessness is that I may not help her in any disease-
reducing way, and her state of helplessness is that she
cannot help herself. Yet I have heard the same woman
say that she feels that the solution of this all is
"mind over body." I have heard her say, "It's mind
over matter. If I could convince my mind, I've always
said you can heal yourself. You really can. I really
believe that you can heal yourself with your mind. This
mind over matter business. I really believe that your
mind can take over and no matter what you have, I really
believe that you can cure it . . . inside somewhere, you
have the ability to keep yourself healthy and do it, but
I do not think that I have figured out how to work it
yet."

This woman told me that she senses that within herself she can cure herself but cannot adequately mobilize
that force. Others have expressed the same thoughts.
The others I interviewed also tried to mobilize their
natural resources against the disease by believing their
attitudes altered the effects of treatment. It is the
hesitation in not knowing how to mobilize one's own self
of body, one's own knowledge of body, that eventually
forces one to "accept" the disease and seek cooperation
for the eradication of it. Despite the often reluctant
acceptance of it, a cooperative effort between individual and physician is sought. There appears, however,
to be a time at which cooperation is abandoned because
of the severity of symptoms, and full control over treatment is given to the physician, who is regarded as the

171

keeper of the supreme knowledge. When an individual begins to sense that her body is not providing her with accurate cues to the disease, then her resolve becomes weakened; then she might become a patient and might accept the sick role. When a physician, from lab reports or X-rays, is able to tell the patient how she is really feeling, will be feeling, then the patient relinquishes her sense of knowing her body. The total dependency on the doctor and his method now replaces her long-kept dependency on her own body and own reaction. It is not surprising that a patient would build up a mistrust of a physician's methods, harboring it under the marveling at present-day technology. One woman expressed this dilemma to me in this way: "Maybe another way to put it is that I'm sort of in disguise. I'm feeling good but underneath I'm not really that good."

I thought that the individuals I interviewed gave me information that I have no experience about. I feel that they have given me information that I cannot really imagine. In some ways, I cannot process all this information. Their information is like a physical substance I cannot assimilate or accommodate. I wonder if the disease and the gold, in its physicalness as a treatment, might be something like this. It increases helplessness, lack of control, a sense of being under the influence of somebody or something else; and it increases mistrust of one's own experiences. But now I have a sense that disease and treatment are unbidden, unwanted, intrusive, invasive forces. They are all retardants to autonomy.

DISCOURSE IN A SEARCH FOR
A COMMUNICATIVE RELATIONSHIP

Ronald J. Silvers

*In this paper, Silvers's discussion depends upon self-
conscious attention to three voices in his discourse:
one voice which uncovers a movement of understanding; a
second voice which speaks to "discover" what was said
by the first; and a third voice which seeks a dialogical
meaning of the text. His accounting for his reflection
as it proceeds is episodic and conveys a quality of incompleteness. Yet the value of Silvers's paper is in
showing just this: reflective discourse must necessarily be characterized by continuous incompleteness in a
movement toward a knowledge which is edifying and which
transforms the relationship of the researcher to the
text he studies. This is so because the domain of
interpretations is "beyond" persons and their utterances.
It begins within the rupture of discourse as the original materials of study (dialogues and presences) are
transformed again and again as the researcher not only
observes what he researches, but creates it. In his
paper, Silvers is at once the receiver of a message and
an author of the same message in pursuit of a communicative relationship with a text.*

This paper is written within the context of interpretive
inquiry and from a perspective within existential phenomenology. My interest is to show with specificity in
what ways a social phenomenon (a video text) holds both
immediate and potentially new meanings through conceptual elaboration, what "selection" of interpretive
features this requires, and what kinds of processes of
reflective thought can thus be established for both
existing meanings and for the constituting of new
meanings of a text. The topic of my study is the
understanding of children's discourse. But of equal
importance to the focus of this work is my attempt to
establish a communicative relationship with the text of
a child's conversation.

Reflective Discourse

The process of reflective thought, foundational to
existential phenomenology, is present in the language
of the human sciences as reflective discourse. For the
discourse of a study to be reflective, it must show

173

within its interpretations, analyses, and conceptualizations biographical-ideational sources that make it possible as it proceeds--it must be auto-referential in constantly showing its own grounds. Speaking or writing in reflective discourse is self-conscious and dialectical. The speaker or writer is self-aware about what is being said or written, and so discourse is directed not only to a topic; reflective discourse is also about the discourse of what has and is being produced in the conversation or text.

Thus, here I begin by noting my attempt to organize the presenting of the study in a manner that preserves the way in which research is conducted. In this paper I will attempt to show the movement of my analysis and my handling of video material as a progression of inquiry and as a praxis of research in the search for a communicative relationship. To offer such movements, to offer to you how interpretations are made and remade, how video material is methodically addressed and re-addressed, I find that I need to extricate the practices of my inquiry from the conduct of my research. I must look within my logic-in-use to create a reconstructed logic of that conduct. That is, it is necessary constantly to attempt descriptions and conceptualizations of what I am doing in order to account for my previous interpretations and to inform my future analysis. This is a practice of retrospective accountability calling upon my thinking to be reflective; this self-reflection is a bending back upon and a recovery of that which has been chosen, described, interpreted, claimed, conceptualized, or evaluated, but which remains implicit without self-reflection. Within the conduct of inquiry, reflective discourse preserves the way in which research can show, within its own movement, the sources of what is being offered.

As a project in existential phenomenology, I am attempting here a form of knowing committed to achieving an interpretive synthesis of the apparently autonomous worlds of children and adults. My paramount interest in this study is an understanding of children's talk. That interest is informed by my conceptualization that my understanding of children's talk is an adult's interpretation encased within the boundaries of an adult's sphere of meaning. Whether in the domain of common sense or in the field of research, in conversation the child becomes an "other" to the "self" of the adult. This interest in children's talk and its accompanying

provision of independent spheres of meaning is directed
not by or to the conventions and rules of children's
discourse but to the silences of their conversation--
silences which descend within the breaks or ruptures of
understanding between the child and the adult. It is
within these silences and it is through reflective
thought that we recover the limits of adult understandings, and it is in the recovery of these limits--again
in reflection--that we clear the ground for new meanings
that may yield a dialogue between children and adults.
Thus, the phenomenon of children's talk and the search
for conversational meaning are themselves circumscribed
by reflective thought and dialectically achievable
within reflective discourse as a process of the inquiry.
This study offers not knowledge about the worlds of
children and adult independent of a universe of self-
reflection, but a way in which actual knowledge-of-
children (=knowledge of any other) comes about of
necessity in a context of reflective inquiry.

I find that reflective discourse within my work
requires three voices for interpretations: a first
voice, uncovering my movements of understanding within
children's talk; a second voice, recovering the way I
locate, identify, and construct my interpretations of
these understandings; and a third voice, which carries
me beyond my initial understandings and beyond my reco-
verings of such interpretations to new communicative
understandings of children's talk which open this possibility of dialogue.

The first voice is that of sense-making commonly
applied to daily lives as we account for what those
events contain and what they mean. Thus, in my
research I use an ordinary practice to provide what I
encounter as I engage video recordings of interviews
of children; as such, the first voice appears to be a
narrative of these tapes and a constituting of their
meaning. I have not intended them as descriptions of
the interviews but as a telling of what I experience and
find in the discourse of the interviews as this telling
is an accounting of my own engagement of the playback
of those recordings.

The second voice arises in an effort to "discover"
the meaning within the first. Only in reflecting upon
and articulating the implicit of the first voice can
reflective discourse as paired voices fulfill analytically the task and stance of meaning within another's

175

discourse. The second articulation recovers the interpretation of the first voice, and in doing so, this
second voice may itself subsequently be attended to for
its own tacit meanings, as those implicit understandings
effaced in pre-reflective consciousness. Thus, the
second voice speaks in an effort to articulate the
grounds of an interpretation of children's talk, an
interpretation previously expressed by the first voice,
or else articulates tacit pre-reflective understandings
within my conceptualizing of my own interpretations.

The effort of the second voice is to take what I
have already offered in my own discourse--in my own
analysis of a former first or previous second voice--
and arrive at further clarity of meaning by reflectively recovering what was contained in what I had said.
In this way the paired voices of reflective discourse
turn back upon what appears to unfold in the text I
study, as I study it.

The first and second voices together clear the way
for moving beyond a culturally limited sphere of understanding, and permit the entrance of a third voice for
realizing the potential of dialogical meaning in an
interpretation of children's talk. The recovery of the
grounds of an initial understanding (found in the second
voice) releases the researcher from an enclosure of that
interpretation's tacit dimensions. What is released in
this recovery is the restrictive character of the interpretation of meaning through intentionality, where
intentionality shapes understanding through a movement
of attention to the consciousness (consciousness as
interiority or subjectivity) of the child as speaker.
Thus, the third voice looks not to the speaker's
motives or to what the speaker may be thinking as
referents for the meaning of the speaker's discourse.
The third voice examines the surface tension of the
words in a context of equal parties in dialogue; the
third voice speaks of what is carried dialogically
among partners in conversation.

While the first and second voices provide, phenomenologically, the scientific foundation of the human
sciences, the third voice underscores a commitment of
the humanities (what is human in the human sciences)--
a desire and potential for creating new understandings.
The first two voices are directed to the study of our
culture, while the third voice is an attempt to reform
and extend our culture in its relationship to other
cultures.

Moving Problematic

The relationship of the three voices--the interconnection between my first interpretations of children's
conversations and the reflective articulations of my
interpretive practices as a researcher which make those
understandings possible, along with the implications
of the latter for carrying me beyond my present existential dwelling place--is present in an always moving
problematic. This always moving problematic of study
is what I am constituting within these pages: questions
for inquiry which animate research and orient analysis.
This problematic is always what the research pursues,
but in that pursuit research and problematic recompose
as a movement within the analysis.

For this study, the problematic is initially
defined as a question of how and where I as an adult
may locate and understand children's talk found in the
context of interviews and initiated by adults as a
potential for dialogue between children and adults.
Immediate analytic and methodological questions attached
to this general problematic concern the form of interpretation I use in the study, the form of discourse
being studied, and the way in which research is conducted with video-recorded material. Thus, included are
several questions: What is meant by interpretation in
an "interpretive" study of interviews with children?
What phenomenon does the researcher examine in video
study and how are interpretations formed as well as
circumscribed by the video format? How are such events
described, and what is to be established in print form
as researcher interpretations of video recordings of
children's conversation? How does a reseracher effect
a grasp into the interpretive domain of children if that
domain is considered to be in a world separated from his
own sense-making?

Within my research these initial questions move
with the analysis and with the conceptualizations of
interpretations; that is, they evolve with the study.
No sooner is an utterance of a child identified for
its significance in pointing to the distinctive way in
which children make sense, than questions of interpretations are raised; no sooner is an interpretation of
that utterance formed, than questions of the grounds of
the interpretation are raised for conceptualizing the
interpretation with regard to the domain of the child;
no sooner are these concepts named and discussed, then

177

questions of my own interpretive sources must be considered. Hence, the movement of analysis through the study is interwoven with questions which that analysis prompts, and with later questions for the grounds of (the sources for) the analysis.[1]

Through my own reflective discourse and the reflective discourse of others, as a form of retrospective accountability, the work as a whole achieves an episodic reality. I present my findings in a succession of interpretations, attempting to build my understanding of children's talk from the moment of one interpretation to the next. I present more than one interpretation, not only to record the way in which interpretations developed and findings were achieved (hence, the attempt to preserve the structure of those interpretations), but also to show how such series of movements did permit inclusion of what I learned and formed conceptually into future analytic efforts.

This succession of interpretations as a series of analytic episodes formally circumvents hypothetic closure. Since the moving problematic provides for such an organization of study, an orientation to that movement results at each point in a partial understanding, the presentation of which within my research is formally "incomplete." Altering this feature of the work by distilling and recomposing principal insights through announced conceptual categories and repeated examples subverts understanding. I have preserved the course of the analy-

---

1 These questions are not only raised in the movement of my own thought, but are formed also from an organization of a research project in which other investigators discuss and critically examine interpretations, means of inquiry, conceptualizations, etc. My analysis and problematic is developed in the setting of a group of researchers who offer me their critical reflection of my formulations. By means of weekly meetings and from their analytical commentaries responding to my own analytical notes, I am able to move the analysis and the problematic forward. Here as recorded in these pages, the sources for the two voices of self-reflection are persons other than myself: Ann Dean, Don Dippo, Shawn Moore and William Walcott. Their analytic commentaries have accelerated the movement of the problematic, the depth of conceptualization, and the coherence of the study. Within my own remarks, I draw upon their analytical commentaries, identifying their presence within the stance of questions and concepts so offered.

tical notation and commentary in the halting, driving, straining movement they contained; what is preserved in the many interpretations and conceptualizations of two interviews is a record of my discoveries and formulations as a diary of the journey of research. This feature of the writing is particularly important, for the analytic notes and commentaries were attempts to find a conceptualization of children's talk without a prior, explicit conceptualization of the nature or structure of that talk; the study's concepts emanate from within the study.

This continuous incompletion of reflective discourse, I submit, requires a particular stance vis-à-vis certain formal expectations on the part of the reader: concern with the praxis of research, and patience within an unfolding of the knowing of the author. Just as there is no direct path to a discovering of the social world, there is no direct path in the telling of that world.

Analytic Focus

For the above reason the analysis is written as a narrative of the researcher's experience. The study addresses the basic questions of what is the practical life of research, what are its commitments and its moral choices, and how within this life do I, as a researcher, experience and relate to those I study? Most fundamentally, this study examines how the researcher is related to those studied--here, "the children of the interview"--as a particularly constituted population and context.

Is it odd to speak of a relation to those studied when the context in which the research is conducted is the viewing of a video monitor? In one sense I am studying people as they lived while conducting themselves within an interview. In that way I am studying those people just as they did what they did at that time, and just now as I "possess" a video recording of their interview. The images upon the screen, the sounds from the speakers, are those of young people and my response to them as such. But there is a "divergence" in the way in which I attend to this in the re-experiencing of the interviews. As history, as a document of a past event, I attend to the conversations in a manner other than I would if I were immediate to them. For this study is not analogous to field research interviews. My research is not at first hand as a part of the occasion of the interviews--even while I am in attendance upon the original recording. The context for the analysis is the eye and ear of video, and thus my experience of what it is that

I experience is circumscribed by that eye and ear. I may
bring forward other memories and other experiences to
what I find at the video monitor (even those of the
field experiences in the conducting and recording of the
interviews), but those are the tacit revelations which
play their part in the interpretation of the experience
of viewing the video presentation of the interviews. Previous experiences with children and the history of researching children as such cannot take authoritative or
privileged positions for my interpretation of these interviews. In other words, while the resultant knowledge
of children from the knowledge of such research cannot
be withdrawn from the context of experiencing the video
presentation of the interviews, so too they cannot re-
place the experience of viewing and listening to those
interviews on the monitor. My understanding of the discourse of children and my understanding of the possible
and distinctive ways in which children make sense of the
world are principally governed by what is immediate to
me in the video playback of the interview. I study the
playback of recorded interviews as I would study a text:
these recorded interviews are video text--a document for
interpretation by me, the viewer and listener.

From the immediate experience of the viewing of the
interviews as a foreground, I interpret what is at hand
from the background of the knowledge that I bring. Only
in viewing the foreground and background together can I
arrive at a conceptualization of an adult's understanding
of children. And only in showing the process of relating
background to foreground in the act of conceptualizations
can I responsibly account for this research.

The focus of analysis thus described sets up a
series of mirrors within research: we have first the
researcher's experience reflecting the act of his research in his interpretation of a video text; but
within this reflection we secondly find a reflection of
the phenomenon under study--the Piagetian clinical
interview.[2] Phrased differently, the researcher studies
how he studies research as he studies video texts of
Piagetian clinical interviews. This mirrored reflection

---

2 The works of Jean Piaget are theoretically central to
the developmental conception of children found in social
psychology. His "clinical interviews" were re-created
for this study. Jean Piaget, The Child's Conception of
The World.(Totawa, N.Y.: Littlefield, Adams & Co., 1969).

within the analytic focus is not an attempt to outline
features of Piagetian interviewing--although we come to
learn about it; nor is it an attempt to assess the
results of this form of interview. Rather, the
Piagetian interview is set up and attended to as a lived
world in an ordinary sense. Although the interview may
not be "natural" to the adult or to the child in what
they ordinarily experience in their daily routines, it
is in the researcher's experience an immediate, pre-
reflectively experienced world.

Narration of an Interview

In the study to follow, interpretations and analyses are
characteristically directed toward brief parts of the
video text: a relevant section of one to three minutes
of a conversation is thus described. While the selected
part is considered in the analysis without specific
reference to the whole in which it is contained, I
recognize that my understanding of that part is contained
within a totality of what these interviews are as an
organized occasion of interaction between child and
interviewer. To offer to you, the reader, an encompassing view of the video text of an interview as the
context within which you come to an understanding of a
unit of conversation, I present here a brief narration
of one interview, specific to this interview and not
exhaustive or representative of the interviews in general. Many of the interviews are painful to watch
because of the severe tension displayed by the children.
This interview does not contain that tension for the
child. The narration merely establishes what I find in
one of the video texts; moreover, the description is
only a sketch or outline of some aspects of the interaction:

> The interview appears to be held in a class-
> room. There are pictures in the background
> which seem to be attached to a blackboard.
> Centered on the screen an adult and child sit
> side-by-side facing the camera, but slightly
> angled toward each other. When they speak
> to each other they turn their heads and I see
> them mostly in profile. On the table in front
> of them are beakers and other glasses, smaller
> items which I cannot initially identify but
> which I later learn to be materials to be
> used in the questions.
>
> As the recording begins the adult and

child appear to be talking informally.
Both the adult (whom I later find is the
person asking the questions--the interviewer) and the child seem aware of the
camera; occasionally, they look directly
forward to the camera and back to each
other. Someone passes across the lens
of the camera and back again, which I take
to be a technician preparing the equipment.
This seems to be a time for preparing the
interview which has yet to begin--a behind-
the scene, as it were, such as found at a
television studio or the backstage of a
play.

The interviewer asks a person who is
off camera if she is ready yet. Finally
a voice replies that she is. The interviewer straightens herself in the chair and
the interview begins. "So your name is . . .
and how old are you?"

The questions appear to be arranged
in an ordered series: at times the interviewer leans to her left toward a sheet of
paper, and then begins with a new set of
questions. The questions then form into
sets: first, questions about the child's
friends, then about her family, then about
the ages of members of her family and herself.
Some of the sets blend one into the other;
but for others, the set shifts entirely. At
one point a large clear vessel of water is
moved forward between the child and interviewer and a series of questions regarding
the floating of objects is pursued. At
another time the beakers are used for
questions regarding comparative amounts of
liquid. A board and single marble are used
to ask questions about the equality of
distance between interviewer and child. A
lamp and cardboard shapes are employed for
questions about shadows. During the periods
of preparing materials for questions the
child sits quietly, watching the interviewer.

Occasionally the child looks forward
to the lens of the camera--and is thus looking

directly at me as I sit behind (in front of)
the screen. But mainly she looks at the
interviewer or off in the distance in a
shift of the eyes which I take to be a look
of thoughtfulness.

The comportment of the child varies
through the interview. At the beginning I
find quickness and excitement. At certain
points there is a slowing of pace within the
answers, and a movement in her seat which I
take to be nervousness. Interest and intensity of the interview varies with the sets
of questions and with time. The child's voice
rises and she becomes more animated with
questions which call for physical participation such as the floating of objects in a
tank of water or the manipulation of geo-
metrically shaped cards in front of a lighted
lamp for questions concerning shadows. There
is a slowing of movement, even a hesitation,
with abstract questions concerning the meaning
of social membership such as best friend or
brothers and sisters. As the interview pro-
gresses, the general rate of exchange of
questions and answers slows.

Finally, the interviewer says, "Well, I
guess that's all the questions I have." The
child stands to leave, at which the interviewer asks, "Would you like to see yourself
on television?" "Yeaa" replies the girl with
a smile, and the interview ends.

Amy's Conversation:
First Voice in Reflective Discourse

Conversation as Context

At the opening of the interview, Amy (the child)
appears relaxed in talking to Rona (the adult interviewer) and takes time in answering the questions; Rona
is also easygoing. But there is elsewhere an unease:
while both Amy and Rona seem relaxed, the conversation
between them appears stiff. I do not find an easy flow
of verbal reciprocity between what is asked by Rona and
what is answered by Amy. This difference between comportment of the participants and flow of their conversation causes me to return to the video text. I turn

again to the monitor to observe how they "feel" about
the interview as shown by their interactive relationship, and I find in my subsequent viewings that the ease
I first assumed about their participation is irregular:
the interview commences with an openness on each of their
parts, but, as it moves along, I notice that there is
twisting and turning by Amy in those moments when
questions are being asked by Rona. There is something
in Amy's gestures which tells me that these gestures
reflect more of a constraint within the interview than
a tension in being questioned (i.e., the interview may
be experienced as a test), or perhaps uneasiness with
being taped by camera. Whatever the circumstances or
experience is for Amy, her response appears irregular
to me. This irregularity and the general stiffness of
the discourse between Amy and Rona direct me to their
talk.

Though I am aware of the setting as an interview
conducted within a school classroom, this physical
frame appears on the screen as a distant background to
what is being said and what is being talked about. I
notice that it is not the physical location of the
classroom or even the eye of the camera which takes on
a status of importance. Paradoxically, it is the conversation itself which appears as the most important
background in catching and holding forth what is happening for the participants. The stiffness which I am
aware of provides a context for interpretively grasping
the meaning of Amy's answers.

I discover then in this initial observation that
conversation is both background and foreground: qualities of the talk are used in understanding what is said.
These qualities-as-background provide the context, or
"depth of field," in the study of the child's conversation, and, as observer, I note the way in which such
context informs me about and locates me "within" what
is significant in the child's talk. For even before I
begin to locate that which requires my interpretive
attention in a study of children's talk, even before I
can say what is analytically important about Amy's
answers, even before I identify a set of utterances
which hold a significance for study, it is the quality
of their converstaion which comes to my attention, and
thus constitutes an interpretive ground.

In the interview with Amy I first recognize this
context as stiffness. What, then, is this stiffness?

What is present--or perhaps I should ask, what is absent--in the interview? What provides for the quality of "constraint," the lack of ease and grace I observed in the discourse?

Such questions require a focusing upon the talk of the interview; but before addressing these questions, I recognize that the initial importance of the contextual quality of conversation as a background to the meaning of the utterances offers me, as observer, a way to center the study. For rather than undertaking an examination of the entire interview between Rona and Amy, which runs for 30 minutes, I concentrate instead upon that part of the interview in which I notice stiltedness in conversational exchange. The methodological import of the contextual quality of the child-interviewer conversation lies in that it is this that permits me to know what part of the interview I have selected as significant. I use the past tense to indicate that noticing stiltedness is a choosing of that which is important about this interview for study. The recognition of this choice is brought into practice by examining the first three minutes of the video text.

Locating the Meaning of Questions

Upon subsequent viewings of the tape I begin to recognize that what I have located as stilted or as a stiffness in the conversations appears as a lack of convergence between what is asked by Rona and what is answered by Amy. Stiffness is interpretively located as an absence of ease and flow, a halting quality between questions asked and answers given as those questions and answers are expressly presented by the two parties in the interview; interpretively, stiffness points to a lack of fit, or problem of discontinuity, between what is being asked and what is being answered.

When Rona asks, "What does it mean to have a best friend?" and "What does a best friend mean?", Amy responds by describing what best friends do together. The same type of exchange of questions and answers occurs with respect to the topic of brothers. Amy is asked, "What is a brother?" and "What does it mean to have a brother?" She answers that a brother, her brother, is someone who comes with you to the park and to other places. A brother is someone who accompanies you.

Analytically I begin to inquire about what Amy
185

means in this answer by asking what it is that she is
showing in this remark. What is being said about a
brother? Given that the answer is presented in response
to Rona's questions about "What is a brother?", I consider: What question is Amy addressing in her answer?
For, insofar as I identified the significance of this
exchange first in the contextual quality of the stiffness of the conversation, and inasmuch as that stiffness
appears to be the "signal" within the halting nature of
the way in which answers may appear to not address the
questions, when I look to the meaning of the child's
answer, I find that I must refer back to the question.
Yet in referring the answer to the question I look not
to the literal meaning of Rona's question but to my
understanding of the signal in Amy's understood meaning
of Rona's question.

While I could begin to think about the meaning of
Amy's remarks in both sets of questions (those asking
about "best friend" and those inquiring about "brothers")
as describing membership categories "best friend" and
"brother," and further, while I may consider the descriptive nature of her answers as references to the
selections inherent in what one does with a member of
each of the categories, I recognize that what is not
attended to is the general meaning of those memberships
in a structure of significant relationship. To say that
Amy concentrates on descriptions of the material nature
of her relationships to best friends and brothers is to
recognize a signal for the absence of the abstractness
of these categories. This is what Piaget notes in his
study of young children--an absence of abstract conceptual thinking and a concentration on the concrete. But
I wish to see further than the analytical contrast
within genetic epistemology as to what is absent in
Amy's remarks. I wish to find what she means within
the frame of her own domain of interpretation. And so,
if I take the realm of meaning within her remarks, they
show me that her answers about relations with others are
to be understood in terms of the "significance" of what
one does with others. She provides a meaning for relationships in doing rather than a meaning of relationships in a social structure--insofar as a social structure may inform us of the reciprocal nature of inter-
related positions and features which bind memberships
to each other. Amy offers me meanings of "best friend"
and "brother" as proximate features to her own life--
she informs me of these membership categories in the way
her best friends and her brother appear to her and what

186

she knows of those relationships in how they conduct themselves with her.

Yet, what does this answer offer the inquiry within the question? With this answer can I say that Amy has undertaken in this interview her own reasoning or her own theorizing (theorizing as a formulating of a possible world) in answering the questions? Can I say that there is in Amy's remarks a step of theorizing in going beyond the concrete to say what it is that is a best friend or a brother? Here I note that Amy offers a description, her proximate knowledge, but not that which for me would be able to stand as a signal knowing of the relationship to best friend and brother. It appears that there is an absence of theorizing that I anticipate and subsequently look for qua "signal." There appears to be no direct theorizing about signal-as-such on her part. Description appears to be an inadequate signal in the request of the question for theorizing. If the questions are a request for (in the perlocutionary meaning of questions) answers that exemplify theorizing, then we may see here the way in which Amy's answers miss the target of Rona's questions. Theorizing is not an outcome of the exchange. If I look to the meaning of Amy's answer as a response to the expectation, I find she is fulfilling an anticipation other than theorizing. She has not heard the expectation within Rona's question and appears to move out of a conversational relationship in the interview and into the realm of another signaled response.

Observer's Interest

I note that this discovery, the absence of theorizing in Amy's answers, is itself a "signaled" disclosure of the interest I bring to the analysis of children's conversation. Although I see this interest as one in which I share an analytical commitment with Piaget in his concerns with and in the pursuit of genetic epistemology, I did not commence this study with such an explicit concentration. My concern is to locate the expression of children, to provide for a way in which we may move into an openness in our understandings present within and apposite to their interpretive domain.

For the study, I conceived this openness as that conversational relationship in which I engage a video text of their interviews. But here in the analysis I find that what is salient in the talk that I find problematic is the unfulfilled expectation for theorizing.

I look within the talk of Amy for that which she engages
as a practice in her formulating within the very
research endeavor which rests reflectively upon my own
theorizing. I realize here that the signal for what is
absent in her talk is that which I expect my own analysis to rest upon--the act of theorizing. Thus, I note
that as an observer I seek within Amy's talk that which
I reflexively expect within my own words. I look toward
a mutual path, signaled by theorizing, between the words
of the child from the monitor and my own words as a
researcher of that video text. What I find within the
tacit confines of this first interpretation of the interview with Amy is that I search for a sign of a common
bond with Amy as an effort of my own discourse: conceiving discourse as a corporal presence (a socially
signaled presence) in which we may construct, as if on
cue from "theorizing," further as well as present
possible worlds.

Amy's Conversation: A Movement Toward a
Second Voice of Reflective Discourse

Toward Reinterpretation and Recovery

The return to interpretation is prompted by the need to
interpret the video text beyond that which has by this
point been made meaningful. To move beyond the meaningful is to raise questions about that which one has
understood in a way that creates a problematic of the
very conceptions that one has made. Here my conceiving
of the absence of theorizing becomes a topic addressed
by the comments by others.

We may address this topic by first asking about the
opportunity for and expectations of theorizing inherent
in the questions. To see the opportunity for theorizing
within the questions, we come to a particular type of
interpretation rendered in order to see the possibilities for Amy's theorizing. Of equal consequence in
raising questions about the absence of theorizing, we
may consider that Amy has an interest in the desire to
talk about things to which she bears a tangible relation. She appears to be attempting to give her own
presence in the interview situation significance. She
is striving to be an equal conversational participant.

How may I begin to consider Amy as an equal conversational participant in the interview? Was that not
my concern within my first interpretation: that I would

have to look to Amy's understanding of Rona's question
in order to understand the meaning of her answers? How
is it that I failed to establish this meaning? How had
I failed to consider Amy equally? I am moved to consider whether the interpretation I presented unreflec-
tively accepts the meanings of the question as givens.
It appears that even in the light of my attempt to establish the questions in the light of Amy's answers, as I
made sense of those answers, I unwittingly shifted and
began to assume a given meaning to which Amy was not
responding. Even as I attempted to see the interpretive
sense of the question for the child, I accepted an inherent meaning of the question for the child. Thus, the
problem raised for me is: how is the meaning of a
question established by me as I interpret Amy's answers?

Interpretive Sources for the Meaning of Questions

In returning to the video text I realize that although
I may hear the questions by Rona as requests for Amy to
provide answers that will satisfy what the questions
expect, I cannot take literally and consensually that
Rona's meanings as I understand them are obvious, literal, or even implicit meanings of the questions. The
fact that Amy responds, that there appears to be no
confusion in her voice and face (nor, it appears, for
Rona or myself), does not necessarily mean that what is
expected in one meaning of the question (its asking) is
understood and taken up as an expectation by Amy.
Because the conversation is not marked by the participants as ambiguous or unintelligible, I took the meaning
unproblematically. When I hear the question I consider
a horizon or direction to which the question moves. I
consider what will be offered by the child as a possible
answer within the realm of what is being asked. I
assume that any answer as a response is not itself sufficient in fulfilling the expectation behind the question; there has to be a meaningful fit between answer
and question. Thus, I begin my understanding of the
exchange between Amy and Rona by looking at the way the
question is satisfied. In this way the question has a
"force" in shaping my interpretation of the answer.
That force is the way in which the answer does or does
not satisfy the expectation of the question.

Such an interpretive stance of looking forward from
the question in an expectation of the answer results in
a direction of interpretation which precludes the possibility of considering the child as an equal conversa-

tionalist. But if I consider further my position as an observer of the video text, then my interpretive stance in considering Amy as an equal partner in the interpretation requires that I do not form the meaning of the question solely from Rona's utterance in the conversation. If I wish to understand the question I must realize that Rona's utterance of the question is meaningfully incomplete as a question embedded in interrogative discourse. I realize instead that all questions within the discourse of the interviews are incomplete for me as an observer of the video text until I hear an answer by the child. By saying this I mean more than the incompleteness of questions which receive no answers. Discursively, questions call for (invite) answers. What I mean here, however, is that a question is never fully spoken until an answer is given; that is, the meaning of an answer completes the meaning of a question. We cannot proceed to the answer from the question, but as I had intended earlier, we must reflect upon the meaning of the question from the vantage point of the answer. I must move my attention from the answer to what the question offers, for the horizon of opportunities offered by the question can only be understood through the answer.

Thus, in returning to the text we see that what we find is that the questions about what is a friend and what is the meaning of a brother are completed in the answers as in (1) expectation for a (2) request of a (3) description of what friends and brothers do. In a similar manner, I may interpret Amy's answer in terms of Rona's comment or question following Amy's answer. Rona does not respond to indicate that the expectations of her questions have not been met; she does not indicate an inappropriateness in Amy's answers. Just as I move from Amy's answer to Rona's question to find the meaning of that question, so too I move from Rona's response to Amy's answer to find the sense of that answer and, conversationally, the fit of each answer to each question.

If the procedure I have just described provides for the meaning of Amy's and Rona's participation in the interview, how is it that I first located a meaning to the questions beyond that which is interpretively justified? Even now I remain reflexively and dialogically ambivalent. Even with this interpretational schema I find that I still hold an understanding of the questions in which their expectations remain unfulfilled. Though I consider interpretively the conversation of Amy as an

190

equal partner in the interview, I recognize too that the interview has a direction for evaluating children's remarks independent of Amy, and whether or not that direction of purpose of evaluation is immediately available, it is impossible to dislocate myself from its immediate presence in the discourse of the interviews. It is this purpose that I seek to understand insofar as its meaning remains implicit in the talk of the child and interviewer. It is to the interpretation of future interviews that I look to recover this feature of the interview.

The Reality of the Video Text

In moving from the video recording of Amy to a recording of an interview with Bina, I am aware of a marked contrast between the two children as I engage in the video text. I say "engage," rather than "observe," because observing refers to a distance or disengagement between myself and that which I present in narration and analysis. As a researcher, my experience of the text, however, is not limited to a looking-toward Amy's or Bina's talk, nor to a concentrated concern with interpretation in a cognitive sphere; video text research contains features of the affective dimension of the ways in which I respond to the persons encoded in the images and sounds on the monitor. This emotive engagement is important existentially in the significance of how the talk of children informs me as to my own understandings as adult understandings.

The ever-present objective reality of the video text claims my emotive engagement to "person," rather than to my own ability to consider an interview as a case and a particular interview as a case of a child. Amy is hushed; her body always seems to settle with her soft utterance of an answer. Bina is staccato in her response to Rona: she is high-pitched, sharp, quick; flashes of smiles appear and disappear instantly. I cannot remove my feelings about these appearances, nor can I regard them, in the phenomenological tradition, as merely style. As video text these children as an Amy and as a Bina are here with me, not out there as research. The experience of the video, even in research, resists confinement to a suspended disinterest in the phenomenological epoche. As a research group, the five of us over the course of a year have spoken lovingly, painfully, exasperatingly, and suspiciously of different children. Thus, on the video screen and from the audio speakers, the children we engage are persons to us, and the mark of their personage affects what we respond to within their talk and within ourselves. When I speak of seeking a communicative relationship with children in a study of their conversations within a video text, I do so with a sense of my attachment to persons I see and listen to so often. The children stay with me insofar as questions which they raise in their negation of adult understandings are not laid to rest intellectually within a single "text." While the children I speak of are not persons to me in the sense that I have encountered "in person," nor social persons in the presence of interpersonal reciprocities which take place in direct communication, I cannot discount my relation to the persons who answer the interviewer. Nor can I remove the way in which my sentiments color my understandings of them. I note that what is of interest for the study is that which is biographically revealing about Amy. Her reference to her brother taking her to the park or to the library brings me into Amy's life. But this is not simply the narrative about that life; it is Amy's disclosure about a simple sharing between her brother and her which as a candid disclosure gives the person-of-Amy. Thus, I regard the disjuncture of her answers to Rona's questions which I formerly identified as stiffness, as only one source of my attention to that portion of Amy's interview. Attention, the very analytic source of this work (or what should be conceptualized fully as communicative attention to the child's conversation in the video text), is not only guided by an awareness that something has gone wrong in the interview (from the interview with Amy, initially found as stiffness and later recognized as a disjunction), but guided as well by the engagement of researcher to child as person.

While we may say that what is involved in researching a video text is not only the grasp of the researcher as an observer of the phenomena under study but also a grasp of the researcher as person in engagement with the person of that text, there is yet a third involvement which I should note at this point. As researcher, I am not only person and observer, but witness. For the retrieval system of video offers me an opportunity to examine the interview in a manner not possible in ordinary field research. In fieldwork with only my recorded notes I cannot bring back what it is that I have observed, as is possible with the electronic recording and playback system. Amy's and Bina's interviews are "fully" available to me, again and again; I view them not once,

but scores and possibly hundreds of times; I examine
parts of the interview in great detail; I watch the
interview frame by frame; I slow the tape; I edit the
tape to juxtapose different sections. These research
practices are ones which bring forms of attention to
examination that are different from those which I consider under the assumptions of observing; for observing
is in that which is studied there, as I study it; the
recurrence of observing permits me to attend to what was
preconsciously unavailable within any one observation.
Recurrence of examination offers me video detail of the
conversations as a microscope offers an optical detail
of living organisms.[3] This detail is, for me as a
researcher, in the form of a witnessing of the interview rather than as an observing of the interview; at
the point of watching a portion of Amy's interview
over and over I cease to observe as a simple watching,
and feel that I have accomplished the witnessing of an
event. A constant recurrence of the event affords a
taking in--as witnessing--that which is happening,
rather than an observing which reaches out to seek that
which is to be seen and heard. The constant examination
of the tapes places me as a researcher into a receptive
rather than a searching position. It is in such a sense
that I thus draw a distinction between examining as a
witness who receives and watching as an observer who
seeks.

Bina's Conversation: A
Beginning for a Third Voice

Recognizing the Stratification of Meanings in Questions

Bina begins and sustains her presence in the interview
in a lively manner, responding quickly to Rona's questions. She appears as a quick talker, and I find that
her answers closely follow Rona's queries. This quickness or sharp attentiveness seems to be characteristic
of her engagement in the interview, and I witness it as
a context for understanding her answers.

It is within this context that I am brought to the
problematic posed in my second interpretation of Amy's
interview. There I concluded that when I begin with a
concern with and an attention to the child's answers

---

3 Richard Frankel suggested to me the microscope analogy
of video study.

as those answers are part of a disjuncture to the interviewer's questions, I am brought to concentrate on what
the questions express in the child's answers. Much of
what I learned in the Amy interview is the sense of that
which was held implicit in the importance of my own
positioning as a researcher in search of the meanings of
children's talk. I face the child's answers in interviews for their interpretations only to find that those
interpretations require that I be repositioned to the
interviewer's questions. But in this second facing I
find that something remains unresolved: the disjuncture
remains for me as an awareness that, as yet, some
meanings of the questions are unaddressed by the child.
The problem which I am concerned with here is the temporal stance of the residue of meanings which I found
not to be attended to by Amy.

It is in the interview with Bina that I begin to
learn about this residue, this "other meaning" of the
questions, lost in the interview with Amy, but which I
held for myself.

At an early point in the interview I find that
Bina's responsiveness, her quickness and sharpness,
informs me about the presence of a dual meaning within
Rona's questions: Bina announces her recognition by
following her answer with a laugh and a smile. The
series of questions in which this display of recognition
takes place is on the topic of aging. Here, Rona first
asks Bina whether she has a brother or sister, and if
so, if Bina is older or younger than him/her; Bina
replies that she has a sister and that her sister is
younger than herself.

> Rona: She's younger, so who was born first, you
> or your sister?

> Bina: Me. (laughs)

Bina's laugh followed by her smile (and tilt of her
head) offers me an opportunity to see that Bina is explicitly responding to more in the question than what is
being expected in her answer. These gestures signal
Rona that Bina is aware of something within the question
which her gestures do not answer, but address topically;
these gestures are not within the movement of questions
and answers, but upon those questions and answers.

The same accompanying gestures are present in

Bina's answer that her mother is older than she is (responding to the question as to whether she is older or younger than her mother). Again, here she expresses amusement. The question for me is what does this amusement indicate? What is Bina aware of, and why would this awareness be registered in laughs and smiles?

If I examine the specific questions in which such gestures take place, I cannot find the reason for Bina's reaction, because it is not referenced in the question, nor in the puzzle it assumes, but in the way in which a question is seen to be a part of the interview. This is most readily seen in the question which asks whether Bina is younger or older than her sister. Taken only as this question, only in itself, then Bina may be seen to be answering a biographical question--a query about herself and her family. But the question cannot be taken to mean that, if Bina considers that she has already established her biography with Rona. She has already informed Rona that her sister is younger than she; therefore, the question of order of birth is redundant. If only taken as an unintentional redundancy, there would be no laugh, no smile, no recognition of that type. But here Bina reacts in such a way as to offer a sign that she sees more contained or implicit within these questions; there is more than what is obvious or explicit in what is being asked.

In the case of the query about her mother being younger or older, there is only one question, with features similar to the set of questions concerning her sister. Biography is not the concern, although what is being asked is presented in terms of her family. There is yet something else being expected. There is more to the question, and this more is submerged within what is immediately asked.

Where Bina cannot find the challenge of the question (i.e., where the question is all too obvious) to warrant that it should be asked, she begins to orient not only to what an answer can or should be, but what the question itself stands for. There are levels of meanings in the questions--the biographical ones about herself and her family--but the biographical details are not the interests in the questions. There is another level, another stratum of meaning, and it is there that the puzzle of the question lies: it is there that she may find the challenge within the question. Her amusement is one of discovering a disjuncture within

195

the interview and yet, immediately upon arriving at
this disjuncture, finding a repair to discontinuity in
the mapping of a stratified meaning of questions.

As I reflect back to Amy's interview, I realize
that what I was left with at the conclusion of the
second interpretation was a child's interpretation
which oriented to the biographical stratum of questions
(insofar as the questions about brothers can be taken
to be a request for information about one's family) but
which did not attend to or assume the existence of any
other level. I cannot say that there is a deeper or a
surface level, as appears to be the case for Bina. For
Amy, a deep meaning of the question and an explicit
meaning of the question are the same. For Bina, they
are not. For Amy, her understanding of what is asked
takes place within the realm of the biographical. But
for Bina, that realm is an instrumentally posited context in which to ask that which is of real concern.
She interprets questions posed by Rona as offering dual
meanings whereby the surface meaning (biographical)
holds the puzzle, but cannot be taken as the puzzle
itself; Bina realizes that she is being asked for more
than information and cannot merely return to the narrative of her family for what the question expects.

Since for her the questions cannot be taken literally and immediately, Bina becomes watchful of what
they mean. She begins to doubt the surface nature of
questions, and as the interview proceeds, this doubt
begins to be expressed in the tone of cautiousness
within her responses to Rona's queries. The beginning
of her answers to Rona are slowed; she hesitates
slightly, and in some cases qualifies her remarks with
"I'm not sure." Her earlier quickness and sharpness
appear somewhat blunted, as she appears to present her
answers with qualification rather than with quick
certainty. She seems in her cautiousness to monitor
what is being asked and expected, as well as what she
may offer as an answer.

Reflectively, the earlier recognition which I
interpreted in the gesture of amusement I now join to
a later one of caution. The two together point up the
salience of the questions of the interview: the issue
is, for Bina, what do they represent and what are they
designed to raise? Though in a much different type, in
the problem of how I come to interpret a child's talk, I
am brought again to the meanings of the questions.

196

Of significance here, which I arrive at reflectively, is that I must attend to the initial interpretive
problem of the adult's questions in order to understand
the child's response to those questions. I cannot
merely use preordained questions, or any prior talk
constructed by adults, as a point of departure for
understanding children: I must interpret what those
questions mean within the child's talk. But I take this
insight as not referring to the general nature of any
exchange between adult and child. Rather, I consider
the stratified meanings of questions together with this
interpretive principle: the answer completes the question by referring to what is embedded in these interviews.

The Adult's Interpretive Presence

Since the interviews are a specific form of discourse
between adults and children, within this form I encounter disjunctions of conversational meanings and an
ever-present concern with questioning. It is here in
Piaget's clinical interviews, designed to encourage the
reasoning (theorizing) of children, that I discover
breaks in understanding between children and myself and
between children and adults. The interviews appear to
stand in discord to their overt purpose--that of encouraging thoughtful responses from children--insofar as
questions are conceived; these questions do not open
up their talk, but either separate the children's talk
from the adult's, or separate the children from the
organization of meaning, questions becoming discursive
problems in themselves. Piaget's interest in reasoning
and my interest in theorizing are precluded by the very
means used to provide for their presence, the signaled
presence of reason and theory. The adult means of
posing such questions becomes a focal point for arriving at an understanding of children's understandings,
but these questions must themselves be understood in
their very posing. What must be considered here is the
adult's interpretive presence within questions. To
understand the adult's presence, to arrive at a communicative relationship between adult and child in which the
children are open to express how they understand what
they understand, in order to provide for an opportunity
in which the child's interpretive domain is made available to the adult, we must look at the way in which
adult engages child through a discourse of questions.

This brings us to consider not only the child's

meanings; in a broader context, the interviews themselves are to be understood as a form of discourse.
Before Amy's theorizing can be made sensible, discourse
itself must be recognized as a requisite state of
reciprocal topicality. Here, then, I begin to realize
that the initial positing of difference between children
and adults cannot be looked at through discourse. The
interview is not the avenue which I must travel in order
to reach to a disclosing or uncovering of a child's
special interpretation ground. I need to recognize the
circumstances (here the discourse) by which I experience
another person's talk (the child) to be special as a
talk beyond my own (the adult).

What appears to me here is that the encountering of
"episodes" within "interviews" indicates the range and
locus of my need to discover how I conceive myself as
an adult who occupies a world different from the world
of the child. When I encounter a disjunction in Amy's
answer to Rona's question, I take that difference to be
a sign of lived experiences and attendant interpretations. How then, is the conception of interpretive
difference established, and how is it operant within my
analysis of children's conversations?

Within the Rupture of Text Discourse: The
Presence of the Second Voice

Rupture as a Problem of Communicative Disjuncture

Looking back at Amy's interview, I discover that I commence analysis only when I find that something has gone
wrong with the interview. While the context of exchange
between Amy and Rona first informed me of this, and
while it is the person of Amy that I encounter most
strongly at this juncture of the interview, it is the
break or rupture of conversation that signals a beginning point for focusing my attention into an analysis.
Likewise, I see that this is the case for my interpretation of Bina's interview. Here the break is not
between the talk of the child and the talk of the interviewer, as in the case of Amy's interview, but a break
within the sequence of questions discovered by Bina
herself--as I find it in the video text.

Rupture appears in both cases as a communicative
disjuncture. Yet this break is not an error of speech,
not a misunderstanding which can be remedied by other
words or phrases. The rupture that I locate is within

198

the interview; it appears to be a part of the organization of the questions and answers, and thus its articulate structure.

This rupture appears to make the meaning of discourse problematic. That is to say, following the
rupture my interpretation did not locate meaning
within discourse and within the words of the children;
I did not look into the meanings of the terms brother,
friend, aging to find separate interpretations for
children and adults as two systems of reasoning and two
systems of language use; I did not consider linguistic
conventions. For there was in the rupture a release
from concentrating on the meaning of the what of any
question or answer to a concern with the meaning of how
questions interconnect and how answers relate to questions. The meaning that I sought in understanding Amy
was not within the content, nor yet the content of her
discourse, but an understanding of what interrupted the
flow of talk between herself and Rona and myself.

This analytic practice coincides with the commitment of this research: to achieve a communicative
relation with the child in which the child's distinctive
expressions may be heard as signal and responded to as
such. It is here in the rupture that this commitment
becomes initially relevant, for it is here that I discover the loss of being requisite to a being able to
hear the child. What is problematic in a rupture is
when the loss of understanding between adult and child
is signified as a failure of both to participate together in the organization of discourse. Rupture shows us
two organizations of discursive signalizations for interview in the case of Amy, two mutually exclusive organizations.

Presence as Interpretive Domain

The ways of organizing discourse signal different ways
of understanding; I reflectively grasp the experiential
recognition of this differencing as the presence of
child in Amy's answers, and the presence of adult in
Rona's questions. These presences are not personages;
they are not the presenting of people, as I found in
moving from one interview to another--presence, as I
speak of it here, is beyond person and personality.
What I mean by presence is an experience of a signaled
realm of understanding immediate to discourse: in
watching the interview and in listening to the exchange,

199

I experience Amy as presented to me not merely her
answers as particular comments, but a way of answering
that is different from the ways of adults. This
presenting is what I conceive to be at the source of
her understandings within her answers.

This presence, this way of making sense, appears
from a distant and strange world to my own sphere of
understanding. I experience it as going beyond any
particular thing that is being said, any particular
utterance, to a region which is signaled as coherent
and bounded.

This difference which enters into rupture-as-
presence, and which is related to an organization of
discourse, I conceptualize as a domain of interpreta-
tion--a term which I used in my first interpretation of
Amy's conversation. Here I wish to uncover the meaning
of that theme in my own discourse. By "domain," I
wish to indicate that the interpretations signal a
separate, independent sphere to my own. By "interpretation," I want to refer to the potential source of
understanding. And by speaking of interpretive domain
in this way I want to underscore that although what is
said is from a particular person, that which the talk
provides will signal that which is beyond that person
and utterance.

In conceptualizing domains of interpretation, I am
aware that they are interpretively recognized in everyday life. Although I offer the term as a second voice
in reflective discourse--that is, I conceptualize it
from my interpretations of the text by identifying that
which is distinctive and beyond my own sense-making as
an adult--I recognize that the practice of interpreting
a distinctive domain in the discourse of others emerges
reflexively from a first voice of reflective discourse.
This first voice is part of ordinary life: we find the
request for money on the street not simply an asking
for funds, but signaling the talk of a panhandler; the
question "Is there anything more?" at a restaurant is
not simply that question but the signal discourse of
one who serves--as a waiter at the conclusion of a
meal. The first voice, as an interpretive medium of
our world, is one in which we come to receive talk
beyond our own as a signal for a distinctive presence
which marks an occasion in which we find ourselves.
The identity of and response to a signaled interpretive domain is not the exclusive concern of researchers:

it is part of all lives. Here it is conceptualized
phenomenologically for analytic purposes.

The Appearance of Presence

There are moments within the interviews, because of
encountering such a domain of interpretation, in which
I engage the child. The child <u>enters</u> in the rupture of
Amy's discourse. But these ruptures provide for other
signed presences, even for multiple presences of the
same person within one interview. I find that although
at times I hear Bina and Amy as children, at other times
I find their presences signaled as ethnicity and gender.
The entire interview is not restricted to an occasion
in which the world of children is called into question.
While the purpose has been to interview children, the
discourse I encounter is not always children's discourse,
and therefore cannot be taken to be a signal sign for
the presence of children; only portions of the interview
provide for the child's presence; that or any other
presence is governed by signs for what is experienced
in discourse as I observe and witness the video text.
That is why I concentrate on small portions of the interview, perhaps from one to three minutes of a half-hour
recording.

I attend only to those parts of the interview in
which there is an intense presence of a child as a
distinctive domain of interpretation. This, in turn,
raises the question of how I may identify discourse as
distinctively children's talk. Given that what I encounter is within disjunction, and given that this break
offers me a way to recognize and theorize the signs for
an understanding beyond my own, how do I judge in that
difference the interpretive domain of a child rather
than an interruption of another type? I will attempt to
answer this question in the following section. Here in
this part I want to underscore the way in which observation and study of video texts provide signs for presences as independent domains of interpretation within
discourse. I want to emphasize the <u>significance of
presence</u> as an interpretive step within research by
describing other domains encountered in the interviews.

In conceptualizing presence in the preceding section I was reminded of parts of conversations in which
other realms of understanding broke through the organization of interviews. In these interviews I interpreted ethnicity, gender, and handicap. The descrip-

tions are from previous analytic notes. The ethnic presence is in an interview which I conducted:

> . . . I ask her name again, not having under-
> stood it at first. She turns to me and
> translates it as "Golden Flower." At once,
> as the researcher and again as the viewer
> of the monitor, the reason for my asking
> vanishes as I respond to the way she is named.
> Hearing her name "Golden Flower" (as an
> aesthetic calling) and that of another
> child's brother as "Tiny Bell" (as a play-
> ful calling), I am drawn to a potential of
> naming that is not within my immediate grasp
> of how I or others could name another or be
> so named. I cannot understand how such a
> name is chosen; I cannot see its possibi-
> lities. I am confronted by how Chinese
> name their children. The presence of her
> name is the signal for the presences of that
> society's names. The rupture of the interview
> is the naming of how one may be called.

Unusual for these interviews, gender and sexuality enter:

> She tells the researcher that she cannot
> reveal her name. "It's a secret," she
> replies, glancing downward with a smile.
> Here I recognize "coyness," as a signal for
> the presencing of a young girl to a man.
> She is but eight years old although I find
> her seductiveness fully authentic. This
> gesture of coyness stands at odds with the
> interview occasion. It cuts through the
> organization of questions and answers,
> transforming she who is interviewed and the
> interviewer.

But it is the entrance of a handicap which is most intense:

> "O.K., we are going to do something with
> pennies . . . And I'm going to put them out
> here," he says, shifting a long board on the
> table a few inches closer until it is centered
> between them. "O.K.?" She pulls her left
> shoulder forward and moves her face toward
> the empty place on the board where he is
> looking.

"What I'm going to do is put them in rows,"
he says, as he motions his hand across the
board. He glances toward her, but she does
not see his glance; she is intent on
watching the board. It is here that I
recognize the postural sign of a unity in
her intentness, the tilt of her head, and
the smooth motion of her body.

I am claimed by these movements and her gaze,
all of which give her one sighted eye a
place for its path of focus. And the interviewer, he follows, sways with the girl
unknowingly or unconcerned with the path
of sight, but in perfect rhythm with her
signal movement.

Each of these descriptions tells of an appearance
of a presence which stands at odds with the interview.
Each shows the rupture to introduce another interpretive domain--a realm which is finite, coherent, and
in sharp contrast to the preceding composure of the
interview. Ethnicity, gender and sexuality, and handicap are the signatures for presences other than those
of the child. I encounter within the video-recorded
interviews a plethora of such presences. Indeed, phenomenological study is a place where the researcher encounters interpretive domains other than his own. Inquiry in the human sciences is an engagement of domains
signaled outside one's own sensible world. In saying
this I immediately realize that the presence of differing domains requires not merely an understanding of
a discovered difference, but an analytic response in
finding a bridge of understanding in the signal articulations between separate domains.

There is no control or conceptual limitation, no
way of designating what presence will be encountered
by subsuming its signal value, there is no way of
ensuring the child's presence in a study of children,
for a particular presence is not fixed in pre-defined
concepts, nor by a design of analysis. Presence makes
its entrance in the breakdown of the study and is only
engaged in the openness of the experience of the
researcher to look beyond what he knows, understands,
recognizes, comprehends.

But where in this openness is the child? How is
one to interpret an entering interpretive domain as the

child's rather than one of ethnicity or handicap? What
are the features of my interpretive practice that constitute the child? To address these questions I return
to my earlier interpretations to discover the way in
which I pre-reflectively found a presence of child in
the discourse.

Recovering the Presence of the Child

If I look closely at my first interpretive encounter
of Amy's discourse, I find the entrance of child in
her answer about the meaning of brother. At that point,
Amy is not a pupil in a school, not a subject of a
Piagetian interview, not of Asian ancestry, not female,
but present to me as child.

The difference I experience in her answer turns me
away from the meaning of the utterance, turns me away
from what is at hand within the discourse--the topic of
the talk--to my own understanding of that talk. Finding
discourse problematic, I experience in that problem the
incompleteness of my own way of making sense.

Incompleteness I recognize as the sign for an
inadequacy or limit of my way of understanding. I
first encounter Amy's answer as an opaque comment; I
consider "What is this answer?" I experience Amy's
response to Rona not only as a rupture of their discourse (as that which is beyond their interactive
relationship) but as a rupture of discourse for me
which I engage; while the first rupture dwells within
the interview as encountered in the video text, a second
rupture is in my relationship to Amy's conversation. As
I cast myself forward in interpreting Amy's answer, I
meet the second rupture as a negation canceling the
sign-value of my interpretive domain in failing to be
able to find her meaning in my realm of sense-making.
Negation places in doubt the extension or devalues the
completness of my domain, as I act in order to include
that which I encounter. Here as a first step in interpretation (a first step in my recovery of a pre-reflective experience) I locate a negation which forms a
tensive relationship between my realm of understanding
and that which falls beyond it as I attempt to encounter that which I have previously read (and subsumed as
the signal of closure).

But in a tensive relationship I move forward again.
I move toward the disjuncture, and with the sense of

negation I shift the focus of absence from myself to the source of the discourse. Without Amy's attempt to redirect the talk in an explicit manner, without her explicit notification to Rona that she is changing the course of conversation, I interpret the disjuncture to be a feature of her inability to properly identify what is being expected in her answer. Thus, I reverse the sign value of negation from myself and my way of undersatnding, to Amy and her way of understanding. No longer do I ask myself what is she saying, but I interpretively judge, "She is not answering the question being asked." The second rupture is thereby repaired, for I understand through my signal-evaluation the disjuncture of meaning for myself. But the first rupture remains: there is a signed disparity between the question of an adult and an answer by a child: the tension of this disparity prompts my movement forward in interpretation.

The reversing of negation is the second step in engaging the discourse as a presence of a child. In this reversal I begin to assume an evaluative stance not for myself and for the finiteness of my own interpretive domain, but an evaluative stance in judging a domain of interpretation beyond the one I am located in. Negation, as I formulate it, is a concern with the signaled limits of understanding introducing an evaluative dimension. In addressing limits there is a questioning of what can and cannot be included in the realm of that sense-making: once I begin to conceive a negation for Amy, I introduce an assessment of the boundary of her interpretive domain. But this assessment does not satisfy the tension of the negation for Amy's interpretive domain as a child, yet exists independently in a signaled co-presence with my own domain as an adult.

I cast myself further into another step of interpretation. Seeing her domain as limited and my own as possessing a larger vista, I conceive Amy's presence to have signaled a limited horizon of understanding. She has signaled her confinement _in_ what she can understand within the conversation; she is limited from seeing the embedded perlocutionary meaning of the question.

It is here in the receiving of her discourse as revealing a limited horizon of understanding in comparison with my own that I take a third step in interpretation. This limited horizon I hold within my own vista.

That is to say, in my judgment of her answer and in a perspective of comparing interpretive domains there is an orientation to size: a larger, more encompassing domain of interpretation (that of the adult) contains within it a smaller, limited interpretation (that of the child). I can, therefore, see how what Amy says to be a mere (though non-operative) part of my own domain of interpretation. Here, then, is the presence of the child as I reflectively recover it from my initial experience. The child is self-referenced, and signaled thus a smaller part of my own world as a limited universe of discourse within my own potential universe. I encounter the presence of child as I discover the limitation of child's horizon subsumed within my own adult's horizon. The independent co-presence of domains is replaced by an interpretive form of subsuming the signal values of one domain into another. With the absence of the co-presence, negation and its tension are removed, and I am able to conclude an analytic recovery of pre-reflective understanding.

The Setting for and Presence
of the Third Voice

The Limits of Recovering Pre-Reflective Understandings

This interpretive account of the presence of child brings to light an important feature of my analysis. It offers an opportunity to see the potential as well as the limits of the signed understanding I have arrived at, and in so doing to recognize the limitation of the analysis itself. It allows me to realize what is open to our understandings through phenomenology and what may remain beyond its potential for our understanding of the meanings of others.

In reflecting upon my analysis I find that the formulation shows how discourse of child and discourse of adult exist in dissonance. I know the source of the dissonance in my adult interpretation of the child's limited horizon of understanding. I have an understanding of how rupture can occur. Yet what remains outstanding is the child's meaning. My interpretive practice of judging the child's domain by reference to the adult's domain leaves me without an understanding of what I have evaluated as limited. I have not arrived at the meaning of Amy's answer. Instead, I have replaced her meaning with an understanding of what is absent in her discourse. I have replaced an understanding of her meaning with an evaluation of her meaning.

When I look back to the original interpretations of
Amy's conversation I find that I initially wrote, "I
wish to find what she means within the frame of her own
domain of interpretation." How did I forget such a
desire? I began with the rupture of discourse which
showed me difference and which offered me an opportunity to search for her meaning. But when I encountered
signaled difference within the rupture I did not pursue
her meaning. Retrospectively, I see this movement away
from an interest in meaning as related to my initial
anticipation of the difference of children's culture.
The difference which I had anticipated before viewing
the video text of the interviews was a difference in
substance rather than a difference in form. I had
expected that children would offer in their discourse
an opportunity to see the world in a way different from
that of the adult. I conceived difference between
children and adults to be cultural insofar as there
were different systems with their own particular forms.
I expected to find different perspectives, different
conceptions, different cognitions. But in my viewing
of the video text of children's conversations, when I
find difference as a rupture of discourse, what I
encounter is not substantive at all, but how signal
talk is conducted. I encounter a difference in form.
Amy does not offer another conception to the membership
category of brother; she does not counter a conception
of brother as a family sibling with an alternative
abstract category. Instead, she talks about brother in
a way I am not prepared to hear as a sign-sensible
answer to the question.

I forgot my desire to find the distinctive sense-
making of the child when I could not follow the signal
articulations within its path of discourse. That is
how I lost my way in the first interpretation (thus
requiring a second interpretation), and that is how the
loss is again represented in my analysis of the child's
presence. In the first interpretation I became enmeshed
in the absence of her theorizing. It is absence which I
as an adult face in the problem of understanding children. It is the judgment-of-absence that removes for me
the signs for human potential to understand the child as
co-equal. The study of Amy's answer brings me to an
analytic question of why adults hear what is absent in
the discourse of the child. What is the source of this
interpretive practice? I must wait for other interviews,

other interpretations, and further analysis for that problem. Here I turn to my desire to understand Amy's answer. The memory of this desire returns me to the provision stated earlier that a (signal) question is never complete until a (sign-articulate) answer is given. But it is my commitment that I see Amy as a co-equal in conversation that brings me back to the text. What signal is it that Amy is answering within the question? This I have not answered, and therefore I return to find its realization as the most important part of, the sign within, the moving problematic.

Extension of the Text

In my interpretations of Amy's and Bina's conversations, I comment upon what they attend to, and what they see within the questions and movement of the interview. To speak of Bina recognizing a stratification of meaning for questions, and to show Amy addressing a uni-dimensional meaning of interview queries, suggests that I know what is predominant in the experience of the interview and the situated meaning of that experience. Even as I appear to assert a knowledge of these interpretations by observing and studying a video text of their conversations, I am not in the room with these children; nor do I have an opportunity to ask them about what I understand to be their experience. I have only the recorded interview. How then may I understand what is present for the children from such observation and study of recorded material?

To answer this question and the ones raised at the conclusion of the preceding section (analysis of Bina's conversation) I go not to phenomenological concepts, nor to an analytical design (i.e., a prescriptive methodology), but to the interpretations themselves as answer-mechanisms. I return to my own interpretations to find their articulate grounds. It is in the text of my interpretations that I seek analytically for such grounds for the researcher's interpretive conceptual practices.

This return, I realize, creates an extension upon that which I study. The original investigative material is the video recordings of children's conversations; these recordings are only the seat or beginning for that which is investigated. For, in my interpretations, in the meanings which I construct, I add to the presented

208

range of the studied text. Thus, extension is not restricted to theorizing the grounds of an interpretation as a function of limit, as I embark on such a project here; a dilation of interpretive range occurred earlier, when I returned to my initial interpretation of Amy's conversation (the first voice) for a recovery of the taken-for-granted at the beginning of the second voice, and this again extended when I studied what I had uncovered in Amy's discourse for an understanding of Bina's gestures. In this phenomenological practice the text grows as interpretations are made and grows again as the analysis is studied for further conceptualizations.

The extension transforms the original material insofar as I now view and listen to a recording not in the same way as in my initial viewings; while the text remains the same, the experience of the text is transformed. I am not merely the observer and witness of that which I research as a responsive inquirer, but a creator or designer of it; I am at once both the receiver of a message and an author of the same message.

Herein marks a paradoxical station for my research activity. To be true to my work, I must be open to respond as dilation to what is offered as the child's distinctive expression. But in that openness, I come upon my own constructive act of changing that which I study, by reordering the context from the field of video text to include my own interpretations and conceptualizations. The paradox informs me that even when my own discourse is not a topical commitment, that which I study, that which I dilate "upon," is my own understandings through the discourse of child and interviewer. I now recognize that my own interpretations are brought into the range of examination because of my relationship to that which I study. My relationship to the child's discourse thus necessarily creates a triadic interconnection between the child, the interviewer, and myself. I am included in the investigation by the action in which my own interpretations become part of the discourse which is relevant for bringing clarity to the meanings of the child's experience. To study the talk of the child (her answers), I must include not only the talk of the interviewer (her questions) but my own discourse (my interpretations and conceptualizations). I must be open not only to the presence of the child, not only to the presence of the interviewer, but to my own presence as "action." I must seek to see how my

209

own discourse enters into an activity of understanding the discourse of others.

Recomposing Meaning

As with my other formulations I return to the video text and to my previous interpretations. The answers which Amy offres to Rona's questions are contained in short utterances.

> Rona: What is a brother, Amy? [Pause]
>
> Amy: A brother is someone that aah, aah, comes with you sometimes.
>
> Rona: Comes with you? Where does he come with you?
>
> Amy: Sometimes when I go to the park he comes with me.
>
> Rona: Ahuh.
>
> Amy: And sometimes to the library.

When I look at these utterances, I find Amy's answers provide Rona with a biographical source of what brother is. It is to Amy's biography that we turn in learning about brother, and within that biography we find that a brother is in the practical, lived experience of going together. Amy's brother comes with her. That is the meaning of brother, but what meaning is this? How does it inform the question? What does it complete within the question?

Conceiving an answer as a fulfillment in conversation, we find the answer directs itself to what is needed in the question. Here this need is to find the practice of what brother and sister do as a biographical picture of the meaning of brother. Significantly, we cannot find the meaning of brother without seeing what a brother is in relation to a sister. The practical lived experience of brother is in its social relation to what is sister. Biographically, Amy gives the meaning of brother as a practice of going together, brother and sister.

Just as I found that the meanings of questions are stratified and that Amy cannot proceed on the basis of the surface or literal meaning of the question, so too

210

here I cannot hear Amy answer in a surface or literal
meaning. To say that the meaning of brother is the
practice of sister and brother going together as a lived
experience is not simply that as a concrete or material
interpretation of all that brothers are to their sisters.
By her offering the going-together and by her referring
to the library and the park we cannot say that that is
all that a brother means. Rather, we must see the
answer in conjunction with the question and with the
signal need of the question. I refer here to what an
answer attends to in the need of the question rather
than to what the hearer of the question may take as
the request of the question (the perlocutionary meaning).
In the latter case we have what the hearer may take as
the intention of the question--what the asker intends
through the question. But as a matter of need I find
Amy's answer orienting to what is needed in Rona's
question. This need is, in the arc of the answer to
the question, what must be supplied to the question for
the question to be informed by the answer.

Amy offers concrete descriptions of what she does
with her brother rather than abstract definitions for a
concept of brother. This may be taken to be what is
needed for this question. If we look at the nature of
the concrete, we can see that within it the answer
supplies signs of what is needed to come to a meaning
of the term brother. If we think of Amy's answer as a
practical course to follow, let us say--as an itinerary
to arrive at the meaning of the term brother (note here,
in the stratified sense, a deep meaning of the answer)--
then the answer forms a practical course of action for
meaning. We can think of this practical course as:
take the focus of going together, take the descriptions
of going to the park and to the library with my brother,
and here you will find the signals for the meaning of
"brother." The meaning of brother is to be found within
signs for the praxis of instruction of the answer as the
answer attends to the need of the question. This need,
I believe, is to be found in what the question and answer
are together in signaling form in the conversation. No
preceding basis for the question was established; to
answer the question, Amy begins with what is basic and
with what one would take to be the starting point for
arriving at the meaning of brother. I am not suggesting
in this interpretation that Amy conceives of a need to
start basically because of what Rona does not know. The
signaled need which Amy's answer addresses is in the
conversation and not within Rona or herself. The need
of the concrete and a praxis of instruction is in con-

211

versationally arriving at a meaning of brother without
any prior discussion of the meaning of brothers and
sisters. In shifting the interpretation in this way
I am pointing to what is "signal" in the discourse, but
not to what is in the consciousness of the questioner
(Rona) and the answerer (Amy). In arriving at a conception of the need of the question, I am moving from
a beginning-point that is attention to the exterior of
the utterances in conversation as parts of signed
interpretive domains, without interpretive reference
to the parties and what they think.

Rona does not follow the path of the praxis of
instruction. Although she asks Amy to provide her with
the places where Amy and her brother go together, once
Amy offers two descriptions, Rona does not pursue the
questioning and this topic of the interview. The cur-
tailment is unfortunate insofar as it cuts short the
narrative of what Amy's answers provide. For we can
see another part of the practice of attaining meaning
conversationally which is potential, but unfulfilled
in the exchange. Coming-with or going-together between
brother and sister is here what in the conversation may
take place between the question and the answer. Rona
may take up in another question or in a comment what
is potential for the meaning of brother from what is to
be found in Amy's answer. Thus, coming-with or going-
together is a praxis of instruction not only for the
meaning of brother as what brother and sister are
together in a social relationship. Coming-with or
going-together is a social relationship for arriving
at the meaning of brother conversationally between the
interviewer and the child. Amy's answer may be seen as
underscoring what is essential in her domain of interpretation: the sign for a joining-of-two in a mutual
lived experience (brother and sister as well as questioner and answerer). In this act of accompanying
there is no specification of what each must do with
the other in addition to doing it together. Thus, the
effort to arrive at the meaning of the term brother is
itself a way of expressing, exemplifying, and manifes-
ting the meaning of brother to sister. The social act
of joining which is described in going to the park and
library is presented in the way the answer is offered.
The meaning of brother is preserved in the way the
meaning is given. Amy and her brother go together to
the park and library, and here Rona and Amy may go
together to the meaning of brother.

In this interpretation I find that the meaning of
brother offered in Amy's answer is not merely a communicative venture to satisfy a question, but an educa-
tive act. Amy does not simply tell what a brother is,
but offers Rona a way to learn about the meaning of
brother. We can see here the attempt to provide, for
someone who asks, a way of telling which guides the
asker to the signaled entrance of knowing and in so
doing guides the answerer to the same entrance. Descriptions and reference to the concrete are not a constraint for Amy, but a communicative signed procedure
to bring a way of knowing into the conversation.

The Analytic Sojurn of Reflective Discourse

In my effort to understand the meaning of Amy's conversation I have arrived at two interpretations through
three voices of reflective discourse. The first voice
articulated the meaning of my initial understanding of
Amy's talk. The second voice recovered my taken-for-
granted understanding as I turned to my pre-reflective
grasp of what signal was contained in the rupture of
discourse. Here I came to understand how Amy was not
answering the question. But it was the third voice
which offered a recomposition from parts of discourse
to form another conversational possibility. Here I
came to form a conception of the difference between
question asked and answer offered as an element of how
to proceed in the conversation.

   With the second voice I arrive at a conceptualization of child's presence and the distinctiveness of
the child's interpretive domain. But its formulation--
subsuming the child's domain within the adult's--
leaves unattended how meanings may be shared as sharing
is constituted in the way in which an interpretation is
recognized as a reciprocal process in conversations.
The world recovered in the second voice is a world in
which division and dissonance are preserved. The
question of how one would find a meaningful communicative relationship is not contained in its expression.
For in the recovery of the rupture of discourse I come
to a silence. Knowing how I interpret Amy to be an
incompetent conversationalist does not permit me to know
how to respond to her understanding. Instead, I encounter silence within the rupture as a mutual exclusion of
meaning between two interpretive domains. There is no
possibility of transcending silence, no possibility of
an interpenetration of interpretive domains.

213

The third voice addresses that very history as a way of moving forward to recompose from the rupture a form of understanding which offers an entrance to a conversational possibility. Just as the second voice is a bending back upon the taken-for-granted of what is tacit in my pre-reflective understanding, the third voice bends forward from a decomposition of meaning to form a possible interpretation of the conversation. Rupture is the commencement for both analyses. In the analysis of recomposition the rupture is taken as a starting point from the decomposed meaning and for examination of parts of conversation which are cohered into a totality of meaning. In the third voice I build forward from the parts of meaning to form the sense of the conversation; in the recomposition I form a totality from the parts in such a way as to "discover" a meaning which in bending forward can be taken forward into dialogue.

BIOGRAPHICAL NARRATIVE AS
THE EXPRESSION OF EXISTENCE[1]

Vivian Darroch

*Here, Darroch attempts to show a bringing forth of bio-
graphy as narrative in work. This work emphasizes the
languaging of narrative, the translating of narrative's
"visions" into life, and it closes with a conception of
validity which is a necessary one for interpretive
inquiry. The language of the essay is characterized by
its receptivity, which is penetrated periodically by
particular insights of its own words, and so the language here is essentially the language of the "third
voice" to which Silvers refers. Thus the essay represents within it other inherent qualities of interpretive
inquiry: reception and influence through ceaseless
ingress.*

Summary

This essay came to be written when I was attempting a
theoretical consideration of how we might bring our
own biographies as narratives into our work. On one
hand, this essay is a telling about a mother, a Baba, a
father and a self. On the other hand, it is a telling
of my life through which I came to understand that the
power of such telling is in the immediacy by which,
through the response of speech to a vision, our "usual"
introspection is made particular-to-life. A vision
allows a truth of life to recur amplified rather than
diminished by historical facticity. But it is the
affective itinerary of language which is crucial to
understanding the movements inherent in reaching a
conclusion about a vision and which allows the semantic
closure of any telling to be a moment for meaning
rather than an epoch for conviction.[2]

---

1 This paper was first published under the title
"Narrative: A Range of Sense for a Verbal Vision" in
the Ad Feminam section of Atlantis: A Women's Studies
Journal, 1982, Vol.7, No.2. Reprinted by permission of
Atlantis.

2 I am indebted to Barbara Ivan for her discussion with
me about this paper. In the last parts of it I have
included "portraits" of words in response to her advice.
And in these portraits I have often depended on phrasing

Background

The telling of our lives is something about which I
began to write three years ago. At that time I attempted a first telling about a particular vision. Since
then I have come to know that parts of my life are this
vision because this vision is a metaphor living in my
body. And parts of my life are this vision seeking
another expression, an elucidation which would allow
the vision to leave the house of my body and to achieve
the status of a reality-creating force. Parts of my
life are a narration of this vision's movement, a
telling about its seeking, and even a telling about the
telling itself. So these pages are a narration of this
vision's movement, a telling about the telling.

The writing of these pages is never direct. Never
does it provide an explanation of a life. Never does
it show something true about others' lives. But the
writing shows how, as I wrote and listened to what I
said, a vision from which I began to write became
visible to me and then moved through its telling from
life as seen to become life as it is.

So the telling of my life as I have written it is
personal. In that, it is uneffaceable. But the significance of my subjective presence on these pages is not
in what the pages conceal or show about me or my family.
Nor does the significance of my presence lie in any
possibility for generalizing from my narrative to
others' lives, to others' psychological development,
history, or personal evolution. My presence on these
pages is to show that it is only through allowing our
presence to be fully present with our story that we may
move beyond what we may usually call introspection to a
reflective[3] analysis of an external expression of our
mental life. So here, I live and now live differently
in the knowledge shown in these pages. And the yellow
wheat, the silence, the image of my father against the
sky to which the pages refer now live differently in me.

---

she has suggested for the designating of particular
relations between what is carried within the word and
referents to which the word may refer.

3   The idea of reflection as it is used here refers to
the recovery of the origins of our sources of understanding.

The Vision

My father died in a field of wheat. That day I had been
playing in that field but that day there was no wind. No
birds sang. No small animals watched me. In that
terror, in that silence I ran back to the house. My
father laughed joyously. He swung me in the air. Come,
he said, we will make a party for Mihalina. Mihalina is
my mother's name, although she is not called that. My
mother carried the silver tray with her hands that were
cracked and swollen from work. She carried the silver
tray with the tea and sugar and milk to the wheat field.
She put it on a blue cloth in a special place she made
for it in the yellow wheat. Still, no birds sang. No
small animals watched us. My father stood strong smiling
against the sky. In that silence we did not hear him
fall to the ground.

The Telling

Story-telling is a name for something all people do. And
in telling my story I must begin with this, what I have
just told. It is a vision I have known for years, my
whole life. It did not happen. But it is the vision
with which I started my narrative. And so it is an unnamed reality for me from which I cannot escape.

We cannot escape from the story, the narrative of
our life. The telling of it can no more be taken away
from us than can our faces. It is so because, although
that did not happen to my father, and yet that is a
vision which has revealed what my daily life is and so
created myself. For as I told my life, beginning with
what I have told here, an immanence of meaning of its
nature was glimpsed. In the continued telling of it
this vision was decreated. Made. Decreated and made
again. As I wrote, the concealed totality of this
vision, this metaphor, which was and is my life became
visible. It is true that the shape of this totality
was bound by subjectivity, by connections with images
which remained hidden to me. This totality was bound
even by its own weight. So my first telling finished
then, so long ago, with an absence of present meaning.
But even then my writing about the vision began to show
me what was and is at issue in my life.

Another,[4] in speaking retrospectively about her

---

4   Heather Berkeley.

diary, talks of how she believes it is in such telling
about herself she first experienced her identity as a
possibility. That is, while her diary was concrete,
her analysis therein was abstract, and so in the writing
what came to be at issue was the self that was authoring
the diary.

I had always been aware that in the telling of my
life I had been writing in a private moment of anxiety.
I had always been aware that what I was writing was my
knowledge as it is contained within the thought of the
world of my daily life, and so this knowledge was opaque
and often denied itself. This was so. It is so. But
in its being so came to lie the significance of the words
which were appearing on the pages before me. I wanted
to respond to my experience of my life; but although I
attempted it, I could not begin to record happenings and
to turn to logocentric writing. I needed to think in my
usual thinking and to write in my usual language. And
so, although I tried to uncover conceptually the meanings of the meatphor of my vision, the writing on the
pages confounded me, pushed my pencil to the edges of
my sheets of paper. But as I moved from the vision with
which I began, as I continued to write, as I remembered
through my narrative commitment, as I inserted the past
and inserted the future into the instant of the present,
I began to constitute my existence. For it is the
revelation of story which provides that which we were
and that which we shall be. As our narratives are
separated from and returned to our lives, so are our
lives separated from and returned to our narratives.
Our lives are pulled from our history in the telling of
them. And so re-created. And so returned to our
history and our future differently. But for such a
revelation of story the very movement of the beginning
vision arrests the development of the life chosen as
self. And the very expression of narrative elucidation
through offering a vision, through pulling away from
language, and through being most operant in inaccura-
cies, requires tactics of initiation and threshold[5] to
substantiate the experienced range of imaged world.

Through a range of impacted imagery that expressed

---

5 "Threshold" is taken from the Latin *limen*. Its use
here is to point to what is dynamic and processual, to
what moves and is ambiguous between what is recognized
and accepted in the vision and in the telling.

an existence which is truly known by me, my vision
showed me the inevitability of a hyper-truth. I had
written,

> It is true the shape of this totality was bound
> by subjectivity, by connections with images
> which remained hidden to me.

But as I attempted to recall and to describe my image I
became disengaged from the shape, the ambience of this
totality. For, yes, my speech displaced me from the
processes of my vision, but the processes of vision were
covert challenges to what I preferred in speech. So the
binding logic of telling made subjectivity both an agent
and an object of telling which excluded me, the "author"
of my story, from it. That is, the unnamed force of the
reality of my vision required my telling to be aligned
with anxiety rather than with myself because not only my
telling but my vision chastised me for what I saw. What
I saw was an awareness of happening at the wheat field.
But that is not what I told.

Initially, what I told was the range of the knowing
of the vision, masked in my telling by the need for
articulation according to a worthy paradigm through
which I could explain what I would come to understand
through such telling. So although I had written "it is
true the shape of this totality was bound by subjectivity, by connections with images which remained hidden
to me," what I had really told was,

> . . . it is the true shape of this subjectivity. . .
> that the images of totality remained by keeping
> their connections hidden from me . . .

Eventually, however, the range of knowing of the
image was elucidated only because the <u>not</u> truly known
recoiled from my efforts to be accurate and articulate
in what I represented in my story. But this did not
occur before my telling had led me to a beautiful lie
in which the crisis of experience (the vision) which
initiated the ethical intent for a new existence was
masked again by the need for articulation according to
a worthy paradigm.

And as my vision developed and exclaimed, so does a
narrative develop. It also exclaims, it also reveals.
And the narrative explication of a vision demands that

words we use to describe must also be those we see as
combinatorial units for speaking. A narrative's developing is the fixing of a range of affirmation and
negation in words and phrases along a flux of imaging.
Thus, my vision tells of the circumstances which led to
my father's death. It also reveals he did not die.

The Beautiful Lie

In our narrative we must avoid beautiful lies. My
father did not die in a wheat field. He is still alive.
But my grandfather died in a wheat field. No. He did
not die there. But he emigrated from the Ukraine and
did not work. And I only remember we and Baba and my
parents would go once or twice from the town to the farm
where nothing grew. The only wheat was wild and dry.
And we could after all hear the cold creek running. And
I didn't really know then, because the language was
different, how hard my Baba fought for his, my grandfather's survival. Her hands were more swollen than my
mother's. But I remember the roughness of the hands of
them both. And although my own father worked too many
hours each day, it is the continuous physical labor of
Baba and my mother that I remember. They worked in
different places. But they did not work for different
things. They worked for the existence of all the rest
of us. I know how hard my mother is working now. My
hands are not swollen from physical labor. But I know
how hard I fought for the survival of my husband.

The Languaging of Narrative

But I do not really know all this because all our languages were different. Baba spoke Ukrainian. My mother
that and English and I only this. My grandfather was
dead before I was born. My father still lives and works.
The man who was my husband is strong. And although the
languages of my father and my husband are English I
remember them most for their postures of silence. And
yet that party in the wheat field has been a vision in
my mind my whole life. And as my father has been there
in that field, so have been my grandfather, my husband.

Until this year. Until this year my mother's language was that way and mine this way. A number of years
ago I changed my biography and this year my mother's
language is this way and mine that way.

My connections with Baba were scents: of dill, of

220

dahlias, of old quilts, of fresh cream, of the roughness
of the skin on her hands when she held me. And although
Baba is dead I am confident in reconstructing her narrative for it has always been available to me through my
senses. I had no movements of connections with my
mother because the language of my mother is different
from mine. Until this year.

But my narrative is drifting. When a narrative
drifts our sense of our acts is also absent.

Of language I am speaking.

My mother's language matures slowly, grows in battle,
is open and linear. My language is a closed circle, is
self-sufficient, repeats upon itself. Every utterance
of my mother is a speaking of this and that. While we
both came through epics and dramas and dreams, she best
can recognize herself, even in her enforced isolation,
within a collectivity. I am more lyric, more personal,
give monologues of experience. Comparing our languages,
I begin to believe my mother languages a story which is
a reality elucidated and described. I language a story
which, like my vision, is a reality symbolized. My
story is there in that afternoon, in that wheat field.
It is there in that strange party. It is there in that
death. Death that happened there, not here.

The information addressed by my mother's story is
indicative, by mine interrogative. My mother's story
attends to her concrete lived experience, the totality
of her life. My narrative attends to the principle of
my lived experience. In that, my mother's narrative and
mine were unavailable to each other. Until this year.
And now her language is mine and mine hers.

My mother's life has been harder than mine. She has
had to save her self. That is one of the tasks of narrative, to save one's self. Narrative allows reception
of life, informs how life is being used, is to be used.
My mother when she tells her story looks to that very
telling for the rest of her narrative so that she will
know how to continue living it. And so this year my
mother sends to me pages yellow from 1945 and says
Vivian I have had this for many, many years, written
shortly after the war, I went through a traumatic
shock when Dad was missing in action in Normandy, and
later found in a hospital in France badly hurt, then his
return home, very ill, those memories are mine alone.

The following years of my mother's life were described on those pages before they happened.

While a narrative like my mother's will save our
selves, the narrative I attempted intended to save the
world, that is, name the world I lived in. My narrative
told me how and where life is generated. And, although
my narrative powerfully was influencing my life, conscious attending to it was voluntary.

Then in some still-space in time I heard my narrative tell me no life was being generated where I was.
It told me I was at that death in the wheat field, not
here. In another place in time, by leaving my husband
and so by leaving my life which was repeating the life
of my mother, I interrupted my biography. And when I
interrupted my biography both my mother's life and mine
were pulled from our histories, our histories which were
the histories of women and men as I, generationally, had
collected them in that vision.

For my mother, in translating my story as it was
suddenly revealed to her through my own broken biography,
found her own narrative in jeopardy. And the narrative
revelation of that for her, and it was an unconscious
revelation, was to recognize that it is only in biographical jeopardy that one may gain the purpose of truth as
given to the self by the self through vision and telling.
So for the first time she begins consciously to attend to
where life is generated for her. In so doing she may
begin to name the world and she is so doing. And I, in
that same instant recognizing that our biographical
stories had been the same way, may now for the first
time attend to the resting of my narrative, my story
through which I wanted to name the world, which was a
metaphor personal and uneffaceable. In so doing, I may
go on to save myself.

Narrative Elucidation

metaphor . . . . meta-for, the harsh
                            nurture of self-birth

saving . . . . naming as beyond pro-
                            creational prowess

personal uneffaceable . . . a precariousness of
                            experience and identity
                            is expressed

```
per    /  son  / al  /   un    / if / face "t" d
through / child / all / reversed / if /    faced
```

```
exclaim . . . . . . . . . . .. . . ex-claim, the vision
                                   testifies against
                                   itself in order to
                                   maintain its coherence
                                   and to intensify the
                                   seer's (teller's)
                                   experience of outrage,
                                   outraged because
                                   comprehending
```

Narrative elucidation then is as motion of light, as light showing and hiding.

An Aura of Intelligible Seeming

Now whether a narrative is like my mother's or like my own, it cannot be understood unless it is placed within the context of our daily living. Just as our words are, our daily living is ours and others'. Our daily living belongs to a people and is datable. On the other hand our daily living is an absolute beginning. As our narrative is the beginning of our daily lives, so are our daily lives the beginning of our narrative. So I begin this narrative after I have seen the vision again. And in my vision which starts my story my father is the most present one. It is he who stands against the sky. It is my mother who carries. And I who run. And in my life-story here, my narrative here, my father is absent. And this is a curious thing, for anyone who knows the three of us would say my life is as my father's, has been as my father's. And in any way, in all ways, in my daily life my father was very much present.

But I am writing now after I have interrupted my biography. I am writing this now after my narrative has told me to look at my vision again. Has told me to interrogate it. Has told me to hear what I answer to that interrogation. I write here now acknowledging that in all ways in my daily life my father was very much present but that also I have passed close to Baba and my mother. Been pressed close by them. And my understanding is there, not in my father's presence.

I must return again to the vision which is the starting point in my narrative. Come, he said, we will make a tea party for Mihalina. But while my mother is

holding the silver tray with workworn hands my father
falls to the ground. With my parents there never was a
silver tray, there never was a wheat field. Although my
mother's hands are workworn there never was such a tea
party. My narrative has composed these. And although
the composition is imaginal, it is not fantasy. In
being imaginal it is an intensified representation of
my experience of my life and so one to which I must
extend authority. In being presented through the medi-
ation of language it is an expression of my life. And
in hearing what this expression says I hear I have been
wrong in what I have seen in my vision. I have been
wrong in my understanding of the vision. I will not
write all the new understandings here, but I heard my
father say, "Make a tea party for her." I heard myself
say,

party . . . . part-ing, the
bestowal of affective
distance as donum

wheat field . . . . we-field, the genera-
tions of family dis-
placed in time

blue . . . . sky, the color of
faith

imaginal . . . . I-marginal, the
imagery of being
pushed to the edges
by rules of preferred
thought, family condi-
tions as preferred but
ultimately displaced
into the postures of
be-trayal as in

mother carries . . . . is betrayed, the
giving-to is changed
into a taking-from;
and the blue cloth is
laid down as the back-
ground of faith on
which the sacrifice
may rest

a woman feted gets the sky behind her as a cloth
laid down, a child must then "take place"

He said, "Make a tea party for her." It was my
father who wanted to save my mother. And although my
life has repeated my mother's story, it has been my
father's life which until this telling I have always
recounted.

serve . . . . save, impotence
                                because of the abjured
                                centrality in the
                                telling of the
                                "already-possessed" in
                                conflict with "self-
                                birth"

save . . . . the uncoupling of the
                            unity of survival as
                            defense and the de-
                            clining of survival
                            as "serving"

I understand more (not all). But what is relevant
here is that in the end, for myself, and it can be the
only ending, I learned I could not save the world. Nor
did I serve a life.

Gift of Validation[6]

Thus, in the re-seeing of the narrative as it appeared
to me through the tea party in the wheat field, a historical truth was allowed to filter and to absent itself.
And we must know our place in history in order to out-
strip it.

Here, in this narrative, I know that I have seen my
father standing smiling against the sky. And I know
that there, I did not hear him fall to the ground. But
I do not know what his life has been. Yet I weep at my
imagined departure of them, of my father, of my husband.
I weep at their death on that afternoon in the wheat
field. But I do not weep because I imagine them to be
gone from me. I weep because we are also other than
what we imagine ourselves to be.[7] In my vision I have

_____

6 I have taken the phrase "gift of validation" from
Esther Saltzman, who has used it in an unpublished paper
in which she addressed the process of therapy.

7 The idea of that we are also other than what we imagine ourselves to be permeates the work of Simone Weil.

225

murdered them. In my telling I have uncovered that
saving self serves the evil in this vision because in
my telling I was self-directed in volition as well as
intent. I wrote,

dateable . . . . de-bate-able, where
                                  the chronology of
                                  event in life sub-
                                  stantiates the extent
                                  of covert challenge
                                  issued by the vision,
                                  where the truth of
                                  actuality is accepted
                                  as unacceptable

existence . . . . telling, not merely
                                  validity in the sense
                                  of possibility, but
                                  validity in that it
                                  also has the power to
                                  take away existence[8]

Since I have written these pages I have read that
there is a writing which "confuses," "exposes," "shel-
ters nothing." "This writing is a parricidal writing.
It has refused not only to be blinded, but even to take
shelter."[9] I do not know if my writing above as I wrote
it a while ago was this way. Certainly, I doubt that it
was entirely so, for if it were so I would have uncovered
holiness and savagery. I did not uncover these here. I
only uncovered that my father stands. That he falls.

my father stands . . . . . . holiness

savagery . . . . he falls

---

8 "If thought could give reality in the sense of
actuality, and not merely validity in the sense of possibility, it would also have the power to take away
existence, and so to take away from the existing individual the only reality to which he sustains a real
relationship, namely, his own." Soren Kierkegaard, Concluding Unscientific Postcript. (tr. David F. Swenson)
(Princeton, N.J. Princeton University, 1941).

9 Stefano, Agosti. "Coup upon Coup. An Introduction to
Spurs." In Spurs by Jacques Derrida. (Chicago: University of Chicago Press, 1978).

no

savagery . . . . he stands

promise . . . . he falls

I have said I began writing in anxiety. I began
writing from within the darkness of that vision litera-
lized in my body. It is known that the purpose of darkness is to discover the light. In my darkness here, my
words were my "light." They revealed to me the danger
of my vision. They required me to leap with faith from
each one of them to the next. And through this writing
of light, time became for me an experience in which its
changeableness was the only force connecting across the
vacancy which lay between what I knew and what I came to
know.

I heard what I said. I heard what I said fragment
itself. Sometimes, I heard things which are not written
on these pages. But I kept rehearing the writing on the
paper. It is one telling of a life. And it is in such
a telling that the range of sense of the verbal vision
transforms the pleasure of the original visual image
into a situation of crisis where the immediacy of existence in individuality is the paradigm for,

seeing . . . . being, the crisis of
experience is unmasked
through hearing the
words which are spoken
in response to the
vision

validity . . . . it has the power to
take away existence

PART IV

MEDITATIONS ON THE INQUIRY

Here we attempt to address this inquiry reflectively and to discover and formulate the very grounds that make the inquiry possible. Thus these papers are studies of what is essential in interpretive human studies. Departing from the conventional conceptions of methodology and theory, the Silvers paper identifies the contingencies of research and the Darroch paper demonstrates theorizing to be found in the movement of thought. Thus, the papers taken together direct the reader to what is first faced in inquiry, and then to how one moves beyond that engagement.

A SILENCE WITHIN PHENOMENOLOGY

Ronald J. Silvers

*Silvers conceptualizes interpretive inquiry to be rooted
in a silence which marks the limits of shared understanding. Such a qualification of the inquiry separates it
from other approaches of research in the human sciences.
To address this separation Silvers proposes a way to
enter into the imagination and practice of interpretive
inquiry for those who stand in other research domains.
His discussion moves through considering immediate
issues and theoretic discourse, a disclosure of topics,
the primacy of experience, the contingency of research,
and the synthesis of meaning to arrive at a position
that interpretive inquiry as an analytic movement is not
the study of what is social but an attempt to reachieve
the social. Silvers's paper proposes that what phenomenology is can only be shown by demonstrating its
commitment analytically within the text of the paper as
the paper is written.*

Immediate Issues and Theoretic Discourse

In attempting to recover[1] and describe what phenomenology
is as an area of social science, how it is constituted
as a research endeavor, and how research is organized
within its domain, I realize that I am addressing the
very problem that phenomenology takes as its point of
departure: the interpretive focus of phenomenology
directs our attention to how we experience our ordinary,
everyday affairs, how we come to understand those
experiences, and how we make those understandings intelligible to others.[2] The interest in the study of how

---

1 Recovery refers to a return in understanding in which
the practice of self-reflection provides for the sources
or foundations that made the original tacit understanding possible. Thus, recovery is an explication of pre-
reflective understanding through an analytic interpretation. For this paper I attempt a recovery of phenomenology as a practitioner of phenomenological inquiry
who in the very act of research takes phenomenology for
granted.

2 Phenomenology, as a scholarly endeavor with an intellectual heritage, is limited to a tradition of issues

we understand our experience is a concern with the subjective and the conscious in the light of the social:
it is at every point a realization of the dialectical
nature of what is held by a person subjectively and what
is held in common intersubjectively in relation with
others. At every point in this paper I confront the
fact that I live in a world bounded by my own biography--
here my biography as a phenomenological social scientist;
and yet I dwell in a world beyond myself--here in the
pluralistic setting of science.

My biography and the social world around me are
bound in a tensive relationship. The social provides
not only for the common interpretive meanings which I
share with other social scientists but, as well, for the
meanings which are held by others and not by me. Terms
such as functionalism, critical theory, and symbolic
interaction name different forms of life of inquiry;

which are addressed in a systematic manner. Of the
three points just mentioned--(1) the experience of the
ordinary as the focus of interest, (2) the understanding of the ordinary as the analytical pursuit, and
(3) making those understandings intelligible to others--
only the first two may be seen to be clearly and distinctively phenomenological in character. The third
point refers to the dimension of inquiry in phenomenology, which, as a social endeavor, is dependent on the
accomplishment of sense-making within the realm of
analysis, insofar as it may find its place within the
social life of the very society it seeks to know.

Intelligibility has its theoretic side in conceptually framing the phenomenon (see Clifford Gaertz, The
Interpretation of Cultures, New York: Basic Books, 1973,
26). The underlying meaning or the interpretation of a
comment or gesture is provided, analytically, by constructing an intelligible frame. Simply put, the
intelligible frame is a concept which shows the essential features of the understanding of experience.

Intelligibility has its linguistic side. As a
newly constituted form of meaning, it must provide for
its own meaning. It must provide successfully for
itself as a medium of social meaning, so that what is
presented as an interpretation and revelation of a tacit
dimension of society is "immediately" recognized.

beyond these names are exemplified entire realms of what is experienced as real, what is known to be significant, and what consistent concerns are exemplified.

The identification of this tensive relationship between a researcher's biography and social life that I speak of is not the beginning of an attempt to gain agreement for the prowess or appropriateness or certainty of phenomenology. Rather I identify this relationship so that others may recognize in its difference the expression of phenomenology's practices. Understanding a form of inquiry different from one's own is not dependent upon an acceptance of its principles or a moral embrace of its meaning. Rather, understanding among social scientists is a "hearing" of another investigative practice which, as a recognition of difference, brings into view the limits of one's own universals that pre-reflectively have been taken for granted. Here in this recognition we have an opportunity to discover a decisive difference between forms of inquiry and shift our attention to the boundaries of our own knowing and the knowledge of others.

Only in those differences of analytic practice is a recognition of our own work possible; for only in the movement among those differences, and with that movement the encountering of emerging force of doubt, do we begin to face the limits of our own analytic life and raise to conscious thought the totality of that life. The movement among the differences in analysis and theorizing subjects us to the limits of a horizon that we formerly took to be infinite. Only in that consciousness is the presence of others (presence as a distinctive domain of interpretation), of other forms of analytic life, fully present; only in that presence is the underlying significance of a consensible value (rather than a consensual bond) of science fully realizable.

Introducing a form of inquiry in this sense allows not only a first entrance for others but a first leaving for oneself. It is, for those who undertake to recover their own movement-in-inquiry, an attempt through difference and doubt to confront and disclose a silence--a silence which announces itself when we have arrived at the limits of shared understanding. It is an attempt through the disclosure of silence to face the boundaries of one's thought as a distinctive feature of one's knowledge.

The problems in facing that silence are not confined to phenomenology. Outside the historical context, there is no further difficulty in introducing phenomenology than any other mode of inquiry and any other form of theorizing in social science. I do not wish to either elevate it or subordinate it to other schools of thought. The problem of how to make it available is a problem of what I may take for granted that I share with fellow social scientists and what I must recognize that I hold differently. For what I may attend to in my research, what is important and relevant, and what stands as a practice of inquiry may not at all be what others consider as the very essential part of science. Indeed, what we share or differ upon as characteristics of good inquiry and good science lies at the heart of what I face in introducing phenomenology as a form of inquiry.

At this point, there may be a question as to why I begin to discuss the phenomenological imagination[3] in

---

3 My reference to the term imagination is not intended to suggest that there is a faculty that one holds as a matter of life-style or special talent. Nor is the imagination here an evaluative measure to distinguish scientific ability. Rather, I use the concept imagination to account for that which animates the work of phenomenology, and that which stands behind the practices of phenomenological inquiry.

If we conceive those practices of inquiry to be a posture, or mode of orientation, of doing research in collecting materials, interpreting phenomena, and constructing concepts, then the imagination is the central focus of an analytical stance that provides for that orientation.

The attempt to conceive of the focus of inquiry as an imagination within sociology was first conceived by C. Wright Mills in his work The Sociological Imagination (New York: Oxford, 1959). Insofar as the imagination of sociology enables us to understand the relationship of our biography and the history of our society, Mills's formulation of a sociological imagination and my version of a phenomenological one coincide. Insofar as he takes the political issues as paramount for recognizing the history of society, the two do not coincide. The commitments of phenomenology may be located in the political and in other areas, which I attempt to describe in this paper.

this way and why I create an issue over differences of understanding. Why such a preparation? Why not simply state the differences between phenomenology and other schools of thought, and work from there?[4] What prevents me from introducing phenomenology as a methodology, i.e., as a set of rules and principles which programmatically provide a particular direction of analytic practice?

I believe that attempting to approach phenomenology as a method would be both unfortunate and inappropriate for two reasons. Firstly, its design of inquiry and its practice of providing scientific procedures is retrospective rather than prospective.[5] In positivism and related frames of social science the attempt is to construct theories axiomatically, clarify concepts for study, specify hypotheses, choose appropriate phenomena, select a proper sample design, interview schedule, or other data-generating device, and set a design for analysis. The success of such research rests on precision in selecting and constructing prior to field work an effective design to cover all facets of the endeavor.

A key part of the scientific enterprise is to be able to foresee all the main parts of the inquiry and their relationship before engaging in the study and to plan it in as much detail as possible so that all features of theoretical import, validity, and reliability for corroborating or falsifying generalizations may

---

4 Zimmerman, "Ethnomethodology", American Sociologist, 13 (1978), 6-15, as well as James Heap and Philip Roth, "On Phenomenological Sociology," American Sociological Review, 38, 1973, 354-367, attempt in their papers to specify intellectual heritage and recurrent intellectual issues in designating the grounds and characteristics of phenomenology. My purpose here is that rather than describe that heritage and evaluate what is correct or proper for phenomenology and rather than provide a position on the issues, we can only attempt to exemplify the heritage.

5 But it must be noted that while the design of phenomenological research is not prospective, the knowledge is. The phenomenological inquiry called for here is prospective with respect to the formation of newly formed understandings of existence built upon the recoveries of our knowledge of culture and consciousness.

be carried out. While "descriptive" studies depart from this mode, they take their point of departure from a projective attempt to anticipate and exclude intrusive contingencies of field work.

Phenomenology, however, is a retrospective procedure. It seeks to account for the practices that were used in the study by following the biography of inquiry and by providing an account which permits other scientists an opportunity to follow the selection of materials for study, the discovery of practices of interpretation, and the grounding of concepts. Phenomenological research is accountable to others by showing what was at play in arriving at the results of inquiry.

Retrospective accountability as a research practice does not furnish, in the matter of prospective design, a methodology, for it cannot provide what procedures should be used, but only what as used provided for the results. We are prevented from a prescriptive treatment since the conditions for a prescription (as part of what is anticipated and what is to be constructed) are not present. Thus the practices of phenomenology are not prescriptive but scriptive.[6]

There is a second reason for methodology's being inappropriate for recognizing the practices of phenomenological inquiry. To prescriptively offer a set of rules or methods of inquiry would violate the imagination itself in which there is the consistent attempt to recover one's own theoretical grounds. This very stance of phenomenology is to analytically open up the possibilities of understanding, whereas a rule or procedure to be implemented is taken as a prescription for behavior. A rule guiding behavior is not intended to be turned upon itself, as a way of showing itself. For a rule to serve as a rule it must be carried out, not reflected upon.[7]

6 The practice of prescription is to lay down a rule to be followed. But scriptive practices emphasize the discourse between researcher and recipient which requires interpretation of that discourse for understanding both from the writer (as a reflective discourse) and from the reader (as a reflective interpretation).

7 My conception of scientific inquiry coincides with that of Paul Feyerabend, Against Method (London: New

Stepping aside from the domain of methodology to provide an understanding of phenomenology as an organization of inquiry, I must recover through analysis itself the movement of phenomenological research within a study. That movement exists as part of, but in addition to, the intention to uncover the meanings of those I study and seek to understand. That movement points not merely to an understanding of others, but to an understanding of myself as inquirer to recover from my everyday experiences in research my own practices-- as the way I organize observations, assemble materials, provide description, and form concepts.

This second undertaking, as an undertaking to account for research, makes itself present as reflective discourse in phenomenology. This discourse, in which one accounts for one's practices, retrospectively positions the inquirer proximate to the phenomenon and proximate to the reader or hearer. Phenomenological inquiry as proximate knowledge establishes our relationship to those we study and to those to whom we communicate.

In field work I find that observational notes include not only interpreting the meaning of those I observe and interact with, but also seeing what interpretations are at play in my own understandings--which establish my position to those studied and to the research itself. Indeed, the personal understanding of the social scientist as an interpretation of his or her practices in research is basic to the organization of inquiry and basic as well to the claims and assertions of that inquiry. This reflective recovery is central to the organizing of what is known tacitly, central to the organizing of tacit knowledge into thought, central to the organizing of proximate knowledge.

Initially, that organization is confounding for others, as reflective discourse "breaks away" from the researcher to turn and examine his or her own movement-of-attention within inquiry, and to envelop this movement into a meaning that stands behind the analysis which has taken place. Often, upon encountering reflective discourse, the hearer or reader interprets it as an

Left Books, 1975), and Derek L. Phillips, Abandoning Method (New York: Jossey-Bass, 1973).

additional narrator or commentator, a scribe recording
descriptively how the research was conducted. Yet
there is more than description in its expression. In
the enveloping figuration of an account a phenomenolo-
gist discovers and reveals his or her attention which
made the inquiry possible. Reflective discourse takes
the biographical narrative of description as "its
phenomenon" within the question: How is this interpretation possible? In addressing this question and in
going beyond the concrete form of practices in field
work, in examining transcripts, and in conceptualization,
to a movement-of-attention which coheres these practices
into a sensible and reasonable account, reflective discourse establishes a shape of attention for research.

What is beginning to reveal itself in my analysis
presented here is a shape of the movement-of-attention
for recovering phenomenological inquiry. The most
important reason for beginning an introduction in this
way is that phenomenology is an analytical treatment of
the practical: when I begin by considering what is
problematic before me in informing others about the
experience of phenomenological inquiry, I first examine
the organizational grounding (the foundation to meaning)
of how practices of scientific research can be collected
from my own work and related to others. My work in this
paper as a pursuit of understanding is in making explicit
my tacit knowledge[8] by pursuing the difference of phenomenological inquiry from other forms of inquiry as the
limits of its shared understandings of analytical life.

A Disclosure of Topics

While this articulation of the phenomenological imagination points to the recovery of practical issues as a
theoretical interest within one's biography and through
discourse, it leaves unattended how we come to recognize,
formulate, and select topics for study.

We look to the articulation of topics in order to
grasp the problems or questions that a form of research
makes available within its organization of inquiry. What

---

8 Here I draw extensively upon the works of Michael
Polanyi: The Tacit Dimension (New York: Anchor Doubleday,
1967) and The Study of Man (Chicago: University of
Chicago Press, 1958).

238

then are the topics of phenomenology? If we are to
study a dimension of activity, experience, or understanding, what would we ask within research to form a problematic for inquiry which would constitute the work as
phenomenological?

The response for a request to provide a way of
selecting what to study is, in turn, a question which
points to the previous choices of one's research. The
phenomenological imagination becomes dialogical in its
stance by asking always what has made possible that which
is. Turning to the organizational necessity of a topic,
the imagination persists in asking what one has chosen
previously and what those choices disclose. The researcher cannot force a topic within research; instead the
topic possesses a force which confronts the researcher.
For a topic is not a fully conscious, deliberately
willed organization but a realization of interest and
discovered significance from within the tacit confines
of one's biography, a realization which presents itself
within the course of the study. Topic for the researcher
is an acknowledgement and surrender to a moral choice
that has been made and that subsequently must disclose
itself. Thus, beginnings of inquiries are conceived
analytically as recoveries of moral choices as the consequences of placing oneself before one's own biography.
The recognizing of relevance is in what one's own action
discloses as a choice.[9]

Here we are beginning to approach another feature of
the phenomenological imagination: topics are not
established prior to and projected forward to research,
but evolve from and are clarified within the conduct of
research. They are serially revealed to us in greater
specificity.

For this paper the topic is initially identified as

---

9 My explanation of the moral choice within action as
a constitution of the topic is an existentialist one.
See the discussion by Michael Polanyi and Harry Prosch
on thought and intellectual freedom in their work
Meaning (Chicago: University of Chicago Press, 1975).
My version of phenomenological inquiry with respect to
the way topics are established and with the underlying
interest in silence as the finitude of understanding may
be identified as an existentialist phenomenology.

phenomenological inquiry and then, further, as a
silence within phenomenology which is necessary for
phenomenology to recover its distinctiveness in its
contrast to other forms of social science. Yet now
I realize that to turn to that question of topic is
itself an effort to locate the roots of silence as the
silence shows itself in the limits of phenomenological
inquiry. The anticipated questions and issues which I
acknowledge in this paper reveal the dominant perspectives of the historical source of positivism (i.e.,
logical positivism) within the many forms of social
science inquiry. We may see here that rooted in the
topic of silence is an ambivalence to traditions and
conventions that are found in the domain of positivistic thought as phenomenology seeks to recover itself
in its own thought. In confronting silence I must both
point to and point away from positivism in order to show
phenomenology. I must begin with positivism (as found
in the anticipations of a description of a method, posed
throughout the paper) in order to leave positivism.
Phenomenology in its recovery of silence remains close
to positivism as it stands in opposition to that form
of thought.

Yet, further, positivism appears as a boundary or
limit in an attempt to overcome the monistic rationality
of technical thought;[10] only now do I realize that here
in this paper the topic of research itself as scientific
activity is an attempt to move beyond technical thought
to a classical, proximate thought--where we center our
knowledge upon the way we stand in relation to others as
subjects. Here too I realize that the topic of phenomenological inquiry is an attempt to break with the
tradition of technical thought as a duality of a knowing
subject and an object of concern,[11] and further is an
attempt to move, in addressing the appearance of what is
present to us, to a recognition of the encounter between
ourselves as living biographies and the history of our
societies. Disclosed within this paper topically is an

---

10   William Barrett provides an intensive examination of
technical thought within modern society in his The Illusion of Technique (New York: Anchor Doubleday, 1978).

11   Lucien Goldmann, Lukács and Heidegger (London: Routledge and Kegan Paul, 1977, p.5).

attempt to construct knowledge in a relationship proximate to that which I seek to know; I recognize now my desire to discover, within phenomenology, a form of inquiry in which consciousness is joined with Being in the act of reflecting upon that which is immediate to us rather than to distance from ourselves that which is to be interpreted. The movement of this paper topically is to an embodied phenomenology which holds simultaneously the experience to be interpreted and the interpretation of the experience.

A Primacy of Experience

A distinguishing image within the phenomenological imagination is the future of the researcher as experientially receptive. In the previous section of the paper I have described a gradual recognition of a topic and an evolution of a recognition of commitment within that topic. This process suggests patiently waiting within the activities of inquiry for the very experiences that count, and for the revelations that they will permit. In such a practice, there is a priority of experience or an ascendancy of experience in one's research to inform oneself about the focal problem of that inquiry.

When we turn from the discovery of the topic to the discovery of the phenomenon,[12] the same image of the

---

12 For social science, the phenomenon, as that which is studied, is not understanding, per se; the attempt is not to grasp the social meanings as a study of observational materials or texts, for a conceptualization of understandings in itself preserves a subject-object distinction between the researcher on the one hand and that which is under investigation on the other hand. Such a conceptualization of phenomena fails to recover the proximate knowledge of the researcher's relationship to those phenomena. As an interpretive inquiry, phenomena signify a concentration on the reflective grasp of the researcher's attention to meaning as meaning is constituted by the researcher in a shape of attention (i.e., the movement-of-attention) that biographically is located as a cultural memory--what is often referred to as the typifications in interpretation. For sociology, the phenomenon which is studied is the researcher's interpretations of the subject's understanding. Thus, the researcher is accountable in establishing how a particular interpretation of the subject's experience is constructed.

researcher is present, an image which begins to suggest an orientation to the practice of inquiry. Rather than seeking to find what a phenomenon announces or refers to within causality, rather than attempting to establish meaning within an error, fallacy, or myth of another's judgment and view of the world, rather than evaluating another's understanding against a measure of reality that supersedes the one that other holds, the interpretive understanding of another's experience requires that we look to the truth and wisdom expressed in that other's view as a practical feature to which knowing may be applied. Social science ceases to be ironical and iconoclastic in its study of social understandings. We look instead to the unstated foundation from which people experience and embrace the immediate world of an occasion, an unstated foundation which we located through constructing a generous conceptualization which retains the good sense and the reasonableness of their expressed meanings.

But how can that foundation be established? More than that, there is the possibility here that the "good sense" of those we study is a way of formulating science such that the roots of knowledge are handed over to sources other than scientific ones, where we fall into a state of a continual shifting of the ground of the reality that is assumed within the scientific imagination. Put briefly, what knowledge can be generated in this manner, and given its possibility are we not on the way to a naive experience of "whatever is, is" and a confusing nihilism of relativity in establishing judgments about human affairs?

Phenomenology cannot commence from a construction of the world independent of the experience provided; it cannot posit authoritatively the normal and the real-- the actual existence of things against the way people take them to be. To do so would require establishing a basis and order outside the experience of everyday life. A phenomenological imagination orients toward the common-sense understandings of others as complete in their formulation, sensible in their comprehension of the everyday world, practical in their treatment, and entirely reasonable in their judgment. The reason for commencing with this feature is that the intent is to follow the meanings of others in their own completeness insofar as the interpretation of experience may show a version of the world that is not posited authoritatively nor one that is necessarily in keeping with a public version of normality or a single version of rationality. The attempt is to recover the versions of understanding in their own rationality, thereby exploring the social dimensions of the subjective world. Yet, further, the interest in the difference between the appearance of understandings that depart from the normal and conventional, the interest in difference itself, is an attempt to recover the meanings of society's normality and convention. The interest in the experience of others is a prerequisite to a recovering of one's own taken-for-granted understandings as a member of society--that is, the dimension of convention and public normality. A phenomenological imagination secures a starting point in the meanings of the other from which we may examine the interpretive sources of our own culture.[13]

In approaching differences of meanings, we become aware of the multifaceted dimensions of understandings, reality, and rationality. In approaching the horizon of those worlds, we encounter for ourselves a silence, an emptiness within the engagement of discourse, and in that silence we face the limits of what we understand as we face the inaccessible meanings of the other. And it is in this difference, this decisive distinction as I would call it, that we face as researchers the difficulty of how a study may be conducted, how understandings can be shared, and how we can hold those seemingly foreign experiences for ourselves.

Am I simply suggesting an empathetic taking of the role of the other? Not at all. Rather, I am asking for us to see the possibilities of the other's experiences in terms of the differences in our own understandings. By proposing that the other's experiences be seen as full and complete in terms of our own, I call into view our own interpretations as they are typically and conventionally applied (that is, in our social understandings). But I call upon them not for their elimination or replacement, not for seeking objectivity, not as a declaration of bias in order to warn an audience of the contamination of observations and interpretations, and not as an ideological call for awakening

---

13 Michel Foucault's study of madness and psychology exemplifies the importance of the study of the Other as a recovery of an understanding of our own culture. See his Mental Illness and Psychology (New York: Harper Colophon, 1976).

identity. Calling into view our own interpretive conceptualizations is not simply to acknowledge our own set
of understandings, but an effort to place our understandings under the same reflective-analytic scrutiny that
will be applied to the views of others. It calls our
conventions into question, as silence has called the
limits of those conventional interpretive practices into
view.

It is neither practical nor ethical to eliminate
from scrutiny our own membership in society with its
accompanying realm of sense-making. While considering
a distant interpretation from ours, we cannot suspend,
remove, or contain our interpretive practices as a
matter of conscious effort, irrespective of our research
pursuits. Even if we could, such distancing would deny
authenticity to the very realm of experiences that we
permit the other.

The Contingency of Research

Encountering a dissonance of interpretation between ourselves and those we seek to understand emerges in
research not only in what we confront as the problematic
or simply in what we name as the topic, whereby a social
issue defines the problematic and the membership of those
we study. We encounter as well the limits of our sense-
making in the ordinary routines of our research. Here
again we learn from our immediate issues and a theoretic
discourse.

Within the varied forms of inquiry, we find that in
the midst of our field research, in the review of documents, in conducting experiments, or in interviewing, we
often meet an analytical impasse or we discover a phenomenon not yet reported. When we recognize that which we
cannot comprehend and that which can be specified within
a question or problem for inquiry, we turn our research
to a horizon of knowledge and begin investigating the
nearby boundary in an effort to see beyond it. We
experience our newly formed research as a movement
toward and an encompassing of that which we do not know
as part of a community of social scientists. In the
wider context our horizon takes on a theoretical interest which permits us to turn upon it analytically and
to identify it as an existing limit of scientific knowledge. Phenomenology shares with other forms of inquiry
the effort to move beyond the existing limits of scientific knowledge.

Within the movement of research, the limits of knowledge appear in another sense. There are occasions when
we recognize that we do not understand in a very profound
way the people we are studying, and in that recognition
we experience a break or disjunction in comprehending
what is going on. In field work, for example, we observe what we regard as an ordinary activity in everyday
life, and yet we fail to understand why people do what
they do; their motives escape us; their reasoning and
judgment is beyond our interpretation. When we enter
into discussions with them, we often find that we cannot
grasp what they are describing or explaining and their
gestures and general comments appear disjointed. Very
much of the same order, but perhaps less striking, are
the times when we realize that we do not catch the
subtleties of what the activities disclose and we are
kept within a constricting frame of what is meant.
There are times when this separation of understandings
appears to be symmetrical. Those we study do not seem
to understand our questions and requests. They misrepresent our general intent, and they neglect what we
have displayed as being relevant. Since we encounter
these differences in the occasion of research, we often
envision them as a limit of scientific practice and
regard our methodology as deficient or improperly
secured.

The ruptures of meaning between social scientist
and those studied appear to impede the movement of
research. Such interference is most often addressed as
a technical problem requiring methodological attention
and a redesign of inquiry. The limit of scientific
practice is thought to be that of a deficiency of
technique requiring practical attention.

In phenomenology, however, such a limit is itself
a point of analytic attention as a boundary of cultural
knowledge. The practical difficulties of carrying out
the research are reconceived as a theoretic occasion
which permits us to examine the differences of bounded
cultures and which allows us to face a horizon of our
own culture in relation to the culture of others.

If we recognize phenomenology's primacy of experience as the coming to terms with the experiences of
others as they appear within dissonance, and if we
respect the divergence of each meaningful act and seek
to address one act in terms of another, then difference
itself provides for the occasion of analytic interpre-

245

tation by addressing the questions: How is the other's understanding of experience possible? And, further, how is it that we conceive that interpretation of experience as beyond our own life-world?

Thus, the reflective stance in phenomenology is to move from the interpretations of others to our own interpretations, to move through and beyond our own conventional sense-making to its very roots within biography where we locate the cultural and historical dimensions.

Yet the question remains: How can this be achieved in the face of a decisive difference in realities of experience? The possibilities, I believe, are opened to us in what I have described as the breaks, disjunctions, or surprises that appear to us. The most important resources, I find, are the contingencies of research: at the very point of anomalies or where our research fails to work. Where we cannot comprehend the meanings of the other, we reach the limit of conventional understanding biographically, culturally, and traditionally (i.e., tradition as a movement of understanding in history).

Through the breaks we come to recognize our own understanding in reference to others, and in that difference we confront fully the impossibility of our own meanings as the finitude of our world, a finitude which permits a realization of both the totality of that world and, in reflection, the meanings of the conventions of that world.

I have come to appreciate that which is not expected in research, but even more that which stands against the interest of the research itself. Contingencies require that we respect phenomena in the way we take seriously that which is unsuspected and unknown and demands our attention. Phrased dramatically, failed research is the offering of possible experience and possible meanings beyond the conventional ones that we hold. In my research, attention to "failures" has led to those very times of reflective judgment and analysis that were needed to carry the theory forward.[14]

---

14   This is noted analytically in my paper "Appearances: A Videographic Study of Children's Culture," published in School Experience, edited by Peter Woods and Martyn Hammersley (London: Croom Helm, 1977).

The Synthesis of Meaning

But whether it is failed research or uninterrupted research, a discovery is a new way of addressing the ordinary and mundane, a way which permits reconceiving the experiences of the other and the grounds of one's own interpretations. A reconception of the ordinary and mundane may be termed the new image, as an imaginative reconfiguration of what we previously knew conventionally.

Phenomenological synthesis springs from a tension between the conventional image and the new image as we attempt to address the former in terms of the latter. Here in this paper I have attempted to address contingencies of research in terms of the limits of understanding as grounded in silence. We embody the experience both of images and of their conceptions; we grasp at once the anomalous composure of the two together for a recovery; we attempt to discover what practices of interpretation prevented us previously from recognizing the new image.

A synthetic interpretation of conventional understandings is a going beyond our tacit knowledge, which is forced forward by that new image. In a reflective pursuit we search for the concepts which will make available the practices of the understanding of the other that we found so difficult to comprehend at an earlier time. Through the discovery of concepts which formulate the meanings of the other, we identify first by naming and then by interpretation the possibilities of another domain of experience and its meaning. The achieving of an understanding of another life-world is by way of the concepts we construct, the construction as a form of inquiry being part of the imagination of phenomenology.

Yet the naming of the new image (that which may be cast as the unusual within the ordinary) forms only part of the phenomenological task. We have the experience that we first held; that is within the typical, social interpretation. With the named phenomenon and its conceptualization we return to reflect upon our previous understanding to uncover its roots, and through the analysis of these sources we are able to recover the meaning of the conventional which in this new light is an unmasking of its former existence.

It is within this synthesis that phenomenological inquiry addresses a bounded world of silence which, in the experience of the void of meaning, affirms the loss of the social. Phenomenological inquiry as an analytic and synthetic movement in life seeks to reachieve the social by constructing a form of discourse which transcends boundaries of meaning. Phenomenological inquiry, as formulated in these pages, is not the study of the social but an attempt to achieve the social.

BEHIND THE MOVEMENT OF THEORIZING

Vivian Darroch

*Darroch offers an invitation to participate in inter-
pretive theorizing by reflectively addressing how one
would begin to theorize and where one would look for
the sources of theorizing. The beginnings and sources
revealed in Darroch's account are located in the immediate environment of the writing of the paper. Within
the environment, Darroch recognizes the significance of
movement in life which she relates to the movement of
her consciousness in theorizing. The relationship
between what is revealed in consciousness and what
remains hidden from it is the existence of theorizing.
It is this existence that Darroch seeks to recover.
For that recovery, an engagement with the theorizing of
others and with the environment is considered necessary
by Darroch. It is in the movement of others' theorizing and in the movement within the natural world
around ourselves that Darroch discovers her own
existence as a source of disclosing her theorizing.
She conceives her theorizing to be a part of her narrative, her biography, which calls for an engagement
by others and for the readers' examination of their own
narratives. In this way Darroch proposes that for
individuals to theorize they must theorize together in
an engagement with and reflection upon their partici-
patory movement of consciousness and with meditation
upon their biographies, all of which ultimately account
for the way they are present to others in their work.*

In this paper I want to address the idea of beginnings
as they may influence how we come to understand theorizing in psychology, as they may influence how we come
to understand what that theorizing might be and how we
come to understand how to theorize about theorizing
itself. For you, the reader, and for me, the writer,
many beginnings are collected on these pages. You are
beginning to read what I am beginning to write about
the topic. You are beginning to read a paper about
theorizing from wherever you may place yourself within
psychology at this time. And I am beginning to write
from wherever I can locate my thoughts on the topic of
beginnings.[1] By commenting on your beginnings and my

---

1 I bring your attention here to the book Beginnings by

beginning here in this way, I have turned our attention to one kind of beginnings.

But I also want to say this: that in our beginnings here, in how you the reader attend to the reading of this paper, and in how I the writer attend to the writing of it, in these are also how we will express our voluntary movement toward an undetermined objective. And in saying these things I am addressing a different order of beginnings.

A beginning is an idea associated with another idea--for instance, the idea of precedence, the idea of priority. It may be a moment in time or it may be a place, or a principle, or an action. And whichever of these it may be, it will always involve the designation of a consequent intention. So here, for you in the reading and for me in the writing, we will begin to understand theorizing from within an interpretive way, a way of thought which is atypical within the conventions of psychology.[2] Thus, we ourselves may begin to theorize about theorizing. If this will concern us here, in how we begin will be the

---

Edward W. Said (New York: Basic Books, 1975). It was Said's beginning ideas and his meditation on beginnings which first turned my attention to the importance of beginnings as a contained concept which I could use in this paper. Although Said's Beginnings must be juxtaposed with the "beginning" of this paper, which rests in a lived experience of being--mine. As such, the reflections here on theorizing are located outside standard patriarchal scholarship.

2 I take the conventions of psychology today to continue to support descriptive and explanatory theorizing, and the support is of a kind that such theorizing eventually metamorphoses toward the apparently valued goal of reification of the concepts and principles under consideration. A review of these conventions has been prepared by Joseph R. Royce in Canadian Psychological Review, 19(4), 1978, 259-276. Yet while Royce is clearly aware of the limitations of such conventions and, indeed, points to his recognition that theories are constructions of knowledge, in his attempt to address "how to do better theorizing" he does not suggest breaking from the conventions which guide, but which limit, the construction of our theories. The primary

first step in our intentional production of meaning about theorizing in psychology. But although we may begin intentionally to re-understand theorizing, our beginning here, while historical (in that what we might come to understand was once part of the nature of our past) also will always remain present, ready to be shown to others. As I am beginning, I cannot foretell the structure of what I will show you. I can only anticipate that what may be in my telling will be an intelligible structure. As you are beginning, and looking in time toward reading the paper as a document, you can only anticipate what may be an intelligible perception of it. Thus, we move beside each other, although not necessarily together, toward an undetermined place.

Your own beginnings, which will indicate the meanings, the understandings of what you will construct from what happens for you within the context of reading this paper, are present now for you. And I am holding my beginnings, which will allow me to be the only way I can be in the writing of this paper about theorizing. In my writing here, what I will try to do is construct understandings for myself about theorizing, and I will attempt to expose this construction in a way that will permit you to move in the directions I may move. Thus, it is my efforts to discover my understandings about theorizing that will permit you to respond and formulate further about the same topic. For I will try to write in a way that will require a further formulation by you. That is, I will try and write so that no formulation I attempt about theorizing will receive a definitude from what I exclude.

I have said, then, that I am addressing the issue of theorizing but the topic of this paper is beginnings. It is this; for it is in the recovery of beginnings

---

convention which limits our theorizing but which is yet sanctioned by the discipline is that theorists need not account for themselves within their theorizing. Nor, according to this convention, need researchers account for themselves within their analyses and syntheses.

In addition, the conventions for theorizing in psychology leave little place for the contextualized perception and moving patterns which must be admitted to theorizing if it is to "re-create" existence.

that we can illuminate the understandings we may hold in reading or writing a paper about theorizing. It is this; for it is within this illumination that we may move past a "thing-like" attention to theory toward the discovery of theorizing itself. So beginning here offers an opportunity to recognize our own theorizing through a recognition of the theorizing of others. "Beginnings" here is the opportunity to theorize about theorizing. Our theorizing is at each point within the intention and ever presence of our beginnings.

I began writing my notes for this paper in the third week of August at a saltwater farm in Maine. As I began writing them I became aware of the calls and of the circling of many crows. The calls and movement easily could be interpreted as the crows locating a dying animal upon which they would later scavenge. I realized then that during my stay there what I was acutely aware of was the movement in nature. It was the most beautiful thing--and it always meant life or death. (One evening I watched a spider trap and feed on a large pale moth.) Movement is what at this time I am acutely aware of and it is always related to life and death.

But why do I bring this up now, in this way, at this time, in this place, in a paper which is addressing theorizing in psychology? Why do I place the physical environment immediately in relation to my theorizing and my theorizing proximal to that environment? Because when I began thinking about this paper, my attention focused in a hypersensitive way to the movement around me. In trusting that turn of attention I let those perceptions inform me with more clarity of what I think it is important to deal with in this paper.[3]

---

3 To trust that turn of attention was a careful decision by me. On what that trust depends will become apparent as I write and as you read the paper. In anticipation of what will become apparent, however, suffice now to say that I understand freedom, and here freedom of thought to be in attending to where our attention turns. This understanding is specifically within the sense of Gabriel Marcel, who writes, "My attention, I would say, is the measure of my freedom," and who, in

What I am most aware of at the beginnings of my conceptualizing about this paper is the importance to all
of us, to any one of us, of movement. When I say movement is always related to life and death in the skies,
in the tide waters, on the paths where we walk, or in
our minds, movement, any movement is just that important,
exactly that important. And so I find myself writing
that in order to understand theorizing in psychology we
must attend to movement, a movement of our consciousness,
but also a movement beyond our consciousness.[4] So I
watch around me and recognize that it is movement that
binds our existence. So I write that it is in the space
between the movement of our conscious thought and the
movement of our thought which is beyond consciousness
that we may discover the existence of our theorizing.
It is in this space that is hidden the knowledge we
cannot yet tell. It is in the relationship of these
movements with the movements of the untold knowledge
wherein we may locate our theorizing. I find myself
writing that in order to understand theorizing in
psychology we must be able to trace the movement of
different theorists' thoughts. And I find myself
writing that what is most important for understanding
theorizing in psychology is to trace the movement of
our own thought, of our own theorizing as we engage
with the theorizing of others.[5] And why I must show
you this way is because my beginning-to-begin showed me
this. It showed me just this way.

---

saying this, shows that his conception of the relationship between freedom and attention is different from
that of philosophers (including Sartre) who interpret
freedom as fundamentally a privation. I refer you to
Marcel's Preface to his Tragic Wisdom and Beyond (Evanston, Ill.: Northwestern University Press, 1973).

4 By consciousness here I mean our ways of finding our
way through life, our ways of attaining meaning and
defining reality. So the term as I use it departs from
our usual understanding of it as a three-dimensional
intentional structure and becomes a moving, "verb-ing"
phenomenon.

5 The sense of these last two sentences is, indeed,
that criticizing theories for internal coherence or
evaluating theories from the perspective of their implications for practice are insufficient for understanding

By the time I had written all the above, the crows
had quieted. And so had I. I had walked to the water
and back again. And why I am telling you this now is
because again I am trying to recover and describe the
movement of my thought. It is not enough for me to
write that we must approach theorizing from our beginnings. To explain why I want us to develop our thought
this way is only to take us away from doing so. If I
merely explained why, I could finish writing this paper
and you could finish reading it, and we would still not
understand <u>how</u> our thought lives. But if I can show
myself the writer and so show you the reader partly,
even partly, the movement of my thought, then, through
our personal responses to that--that is, through our
intellectual and emotional responses to that--we will
come to begin to do with this paper what I believe it
is important to do with others' writings about theory.
If I can show you even partly the movement of my
thought, then you will witness that I believe what I
understand and that I only come to understand what I
believe. And that is what I want you to understand
about yourselves with respect to our theorizing in
psychology, that we can only come to understand what we
believe and that we believe only what we understand.[6]

So, in Maine, at the moment when I want to write a
brief paper on theorizing I hear and see the crows. I
hear their calls. I see their circling. I remember
the movement of other natural things. What I hear and
see in nature in Maine is a presencing of my own knowledge. Seeing the movement informs me, shows me that
I know theorizing to be a way of moving in thought

---

them. After all, a theory essentially says, "Conceive
of the world in the following way, and in this conception of the world these courses of action may be taken."
A critique will provide an idea of the logical structure
of that world and the action it prescribes. But only
our own theorizing as we engage with the theorizing of
others will allow us to locate or see our own experience
within that which is provided by the theory. Not
entirely as an aside, I point to the moral implications
of adopting practices prescribed by a theory in which we
cannot find our counterpart.

6 And here I admit that in showing this desire I am
assuming you are a reader at a particular point in your
psychologizing, a point at looking back perhaps to the
consensual boundaries in which, so far, our work has
been contained.

inasmuch as that movement is what I attend to and what I organize my theorizing around.[7] Seeing movement shows me the way in which I theorize. Hearing and seeing the crows as the beginnings of my theorizing repeats by reflection for me what I have already experienced, what I have already thought, what I already know. The crows show me what has preceded the beginnings of this theorizing and they show what, for me, could only be a beginning of this theory of theorizing. And when I took the moment of attending to theorizing as a beginning, the use of the word theorizing pointed me to the experience of seeing movement. And this may seem to be a circular thing. But, rather, it is a spiraling record of my past thought wherein at each turn my beliefs become more and more subtle and my understandings become more and more an expression of the immanence of my beginnings. So, for example, here I would need to pursue all this further to understand that in addressing the world theoretically I notice a physical response to it. I would need to pursue further the point that in the moment of beginning to theorize about theorizing I have a physical response to the world. And I would not pursue this as something I recognize which should allow an abstract sense-making by me. Rather, I would pursue it as an attending to my senses, as a life-world relationship from which my understanding will move and return and move again. For all my senses respond to this movement around me which is ending in life or death. To admit this totality of response into my work, I need to admit that the movement of theorizing for me is physical. But I would need to go on and account for what kind of movement of thought such a physicalness would allow. I would need to account for what kind of formulating and theorizing and understanding would come from such movement, and so on.

So I try to show you that some phenomena in nature in Maine informed my thought, my conceptualizing about what it is important to attend to and understand about theorizing in psychology. And it is a spiraling thing, for why didn't I choose to see something else which might have as equivocally informed my understanding of

---

7 I use the word "know here with a sense that knowledge is what we hold within ourselves which provides what we will begin to attend to, work with, and ask questions about when our work and our beginnings are our own and not a "beginning" necessarily prescribed by others or even by a discipline of study (for example, psychology).

theorizing? That is not unraveled yet. For that is in the origins of that one and only possible beginning.

But I know this. The origins of that beginning, of beginnings of theorizing as I will do it, can only be found in my history, in my biography. And I do not mean to disclose private states. Instead I am suggesting a kind of personal disclosure in discourse which will also disclose the human condition. I am suggesting a personal disclosure by an author of theory which will require others to interrogate their own experience.[8] There is already something I know and understand about theorizing in psychology which informed my perception at that time and place, at that beginning in Maine when I began thinking about this paper and when I saw movement. If in subsequent weeks I were to write or to teach from this perception, that understanding about theorizing would be unraveled, because the understanding would come into awareness through my personal focus on movement. Although that focus, that beginning, is from my history and therefore is personal--personal in the sense that it is attached to my biography--it will account for my relationship to what I am trying to understand. My attention to that beginning allows me to admit my narrative of my biography into my work. My narrative then may be present in my work as an existential elucidation. But for the moment, the implications

---

8 Here I want to affirm my understanding that all know-ledge--be it in our personal lives, in the social sciences, or in the physical sciences--is a social construction; but as the paper moves forward I will also try to show my understanding that all knowledge is a personal construction, more personal than social, and is so whether or not it is seen as that. Yet, the word personal as I intend its use here has a strong social connotation (i.e., social as in knowledge shared). Calvin Schrag in his book Existence and Freedom (Evanston, Ill.: Northwestern University Press, 1961) addresses the responsibility of the theorist to use indirect communication "to show us what it means to exist." And others, too, now, in psychiatry (for example, David Cooper) and many in Women's Studies (for example, the collection of essays by Charlene Spretmak, The Politics of Women's Spirituality (New York: Doubleday, 1982) talk of the need to "speak the un-speak-able." Also, see my "A Response to Radical Reflection: Mediating the Irreconcilable" in Reflections: Essays in Phenomenology, Vol.2, No.1, 1981, 27-39.

of how my beginning informs my theorizing and my understandings of others' theories are not yet accessible.

And I had a moment of apprehension as I wrote these last lines here, for I knew that at this moment when you the reader read them, you may be apprehensive that I am asking you to apprehend something in this paper that I myself do not freely apprehend. Yes, that is what I am asking of you. And I am asking it of you because none of our understandings of anyone's biographies as they bear on our understandings of their theories will depend on the same beginnings. Nor will any of our different beginnings provide, through addition of whatever moving thought, for the same shapes of theorizing. The bases for our comparing theorists and their theories, which will give that comparison its consistency, will always be ourselves. Thus, there is no point in writing only about what I now know, for in order for you to come also to understandings, I must acknowledge the authority for theorizing which you the reader also hold. For the admission of my narrative to my work requires me to respect your examination of your own narrative. And your questioning of your own theorizing will yield what is different from mine. And it is in the recognition of the nature of this relationship of differences between theorizing where we may come to shared understandings.

But from my beginning I can continue to try to show what we may do so that we may come to our own understandings and thus be able to construct knowledge about theorizing in psychology. From my beginning I must suggest that we must read others not for what they know but for the movement of their thought. That is, we must read them for what they said, said, and said again to come to understandings about the psychological processes. So we read them not to find out about psychological theory but to find out how they proceeded, how they made different psychological processes clear for themselves. And from that we will come to our understandings about what they said; yes. But from that we will also come to understandings about what we already know, for it can only be ourselves that we bring to their work. We begin to come to understandings by locating our experience or the absence of our experience in what others disclose. And it would not be sufficient for us to merely decide to accept or reject what was said and written by others in their theorizings. Rather, we must take the responsibility to struggle with what is

said and written until, through following the movement
of our thought, we can transform it until it becomes a
different thing, our own understanding.[9]

Now, once more to point out to you the movement of my
thought. I stopped writing here and read the last
little piece. I see that I am talking about beliefs
and understandings, about spiraling thought processes
and, again and always, about understandings with respect
to learning and un-learning about psychological theories.
Yet I know that when you read most of the theoretical
writings about most psychological processes, the talk
in them will be of explanations, of normative descriptions, of reliable predictions, of applying techniques,
and so on, and most of it will be presented through
dualistic thought. So why am I emphasizing this other
way? I have already said that it is not enough to be
informed about theories. It is more important to
understand them. And so from my beginning I try to
show that it is only in tracing the movement of our
thought that we can come to understandings.[10] But what
is understanding?[11] Again I prefer not to provide a

---

9 I am beginning to refer to movement of thought again.
I will not define what I mean by this, but I will talk
around it. Certainly, I do not mean a description of
thought in the sense of knowing only structurally or
topographically wherein one is located at any moment;
but, yes, I do mean at any moment appreciating the primacy of the process of the movement. So the important
thing is not the thought-decision but understanding in
terms of appreciating the totality of the movement of
thought as non-relational--non-relational to anything.
And you will come to see where I think this leads.

10 Actually, and especially recently, and especially
within the professional and applied areas of our discipline, there are attempts toward understandings which
begin with practical programs or deliberate moral
stances. But these attempts, though sincere, fail. It
is only through attempting to understand, through understanding, and through what we do come to understand that
we will find what is practical and what is moral. Unfortunately, in the presentation of most psychological
theories, the theorists themselves are absent.

11 First, understanding is not eventually accepting a
little of this and a little of that for whatever

finite, complete definition. Rather, I will talk around the word and you will have a sense of what I mean, enough so that you may continue to develop through an interpretation of my meaning a conceptualization of the word. Essentially, understanding provides for the place of our biographies within our comprehension of what we are attempting to comprehend. Understanding is a movement <u>within</u> our biography which shows a movement <u>of</u> our biography. It is that which points to our life-world relationships. And that is all that tracing movement of thought leads to. And that is why movement of thought is so important. It renders our theory and our biography understandable as we recognize the experience of that theory in our narrative.

So, essentially, understanding must provide for our narrative. Our histories, our narratives, cannot be <u>not</u> considered when we look at the topics about which we seek understanding and when we look at the meanings we discover about such topics. Our narratives provide for what we choose to select to understand and for how we eventually come to understand it. Yet the latter represents a simplicity of symmetry of which we must be suspicious, for understanding is always, always more complex than we can understand. Paul Ricoeur has noted that understanding is a very dense word, a richly ambiguous word, and as such it designates our apprehension of discovering how we belong or not to the whole of what is under consideration. And perhaps this is why we as theorizers in psychology generally would rather describe and explain than understand.[12] The knowledge which comes into awareness through understanding is not merely acquired and used as in a methodic process such as

---

rational or intuitive reasons and concluding that we are eclectic. Nor is it accepting a school of thought in its entirety or not, or almost in its entirety or not, for whatever rational or intuitive reasons. For in these ways not only is there compromising with our thought and, perhaps, with the consensus of the psychological community, but also there is no taking of responsibility for our own capacity for theorizing.

12 Here I note my own affinity for (and refer you to) Ricoeur's description of explanation and understanding, although I also note my own difficulty in accepting his description of the dialectical relationship between

explanation. Rather, knowledge acquired through understanding becomes embodied in us. We understand this
when we come to understand our own understanding. And
when knowledge is embodied in us, it is evident to
others that the knowledge lives in us and that we live
in the knowledge. To embody knowledge is not something
that can be deliberately attempted. That is, we cannot
decide beforehand that because something appears func-
tional, or because something appears needed, or even
because something is ideologically attractive to us,
"that something" is the knowledge we will embody. It is
only through understandings that knowledge becomes
embodied, and that is why we will never know what the
knowledge is until after it is there. And I repeat,
from my beginning, from my beginning here, I understand
that it is only through tracing the movement of our
thought that we will discover what knowledge is there,
what we understand, what we embody. And we are able to
share the knowledge embodied in us with others when we
can show precisely how we belong to the whole of it and
it to us. And so embodied knowledge can only be shown
to ourselves and others through reflective thought.[13]
As I realized that the movement I responded to in nature
was my knowledge about theorizing, so must I realize how
my thoughts open into and through all parts of each other.
And the doing of reflective thought requires us to place

---

them. Of the concepts themselves he says, ". . . only
explanation is methodic. Understanding is rather the
nonmethodic moment . . . it precedes, accompanies,
closes and thus envelops explanation." The starting
point for the two are, of course, different. Ricoeur
specifies that explanation is dependent on descriptions
of initial conditions and statements of general laws,
that understanding always responds to specific uniqueness and has a lacunary structure, so that the "why"
may spontaneously come from the "what." So he suggests
that it is easy to go to explanations from understandings but almost impossible to go to understandings from
explanations. These ideas are discussed in chapter 11
of The Philosophy of Paul Ricoeur: An Anthology of His
Work, Charles E. Reagan and David Stewart (Boston:
Beacon Press, 1978).

13 My reference to reflective thought here is a plain
one. I refer to the idea that the logic of the thought,
whether rational or of other form, simply bends to turn
back upon itself.

our biographies in our theorizing just as I have admitted my narrative to this work. Thus, we come "to
know" as our beginnings enfold upon another's understanding, and we come thoughtfully to knowledge as we
unfold our biographies within other's theories.

In theorizing it is typically thought and accepted
that our histories, our cultural contexts, and our
socialization are known to be the enemies of theorizing.[14] And the challenge is not to detach from this
personal context but to fully account for it in one's
work. I am paraphrasing Alan Dawe in the next several
sentences, for he has differentiated the personal, to
which I too want to refer, and the way he refers to it
is present in our work: not as a confessional, apologe-
tic preface to our work, but rather presented and
shown through the kind of work, of psychology, we do.
Dawe shows that in theorizing, "the personal turns on
a representative articulation of what is historically
grounded." For me, that articulation depends on the
presence of our narrative in our work. It depends on
our acknowledging our own, our personal existentialist
thought which is guiding our interpretive thought. It
depends on accounting for our interpretations. Dawe
goes on to describe how the personal can be presented
and shown through the kind of theorizing one does, a
theorizing which will not only provide insights about
a phenomenon in psychology but will also conceptually
account for the personal historical interpretation
brought to bear on the psychological phenomenon in
question and will conceptually account for the analytic
practices used within theorizing about it.[15] I would go

---

14 A recent issue of Journal of Personality and Social
Psychology (36(11), 1978) published four articles (by
Allan R. Buss, Ralph L. Rosnow, Edward E. Sampson, and
Kenneth J. Gergen) which as a special topic addressed
the status of psychological theorizing. While these
articles contained insights I respect, my serious concern with them was the fear, implicitly or explicitly
expressed but thematic in them, of the interaction of
cultural and personal values with science. Yet if we
are beginning to accept now that our psychological
theories are social organizations of knowledge, then we
must necessarily admit they are expressions of value,
and better that these expressions of value (of desire)
are conscious rather than unconscionable as they are now.

15 For the articulation of the conceptualizing I am

further, I suggest we need a theorizing which will transform the phenomenon under investigation and the psychologist making the inquiry--thus, a theorizing which will transform psychology.

I have already said that the beginnings for theorizing which attempts understanding differ from the beginnings for theorizing which presents explanation. Understandings always respond to specific uniqueness. They have a lacunary structure so that the answer to why spontaneously comes from what. In the lacunary structure of understanding, it is in the spaces, the places where one momentarily glimpses an absence or lack, that discovery and construction, and creation and meaning around that discovery, occur.[16] And it is in this space, if we attend to it, where we may find what we need to account for ourselves and our place as theorists in our theorizing.

So if I take theorizing to be understood in this way by me, for me, with what do I begin such theorizing, a theorizing which is an interpretive theorizing? To begin it is first of all to know with what to begin.

In this case here it is simple. Just as we will need to formulate in words for ourselves what we come to understand about psychological theory, we will need to depend on theorists' words to understand what it is they come to understand about psychological phenomena.[17] Just

attempting here, I was greatly aided by this article of Alan Dawe: "The Role of Experience in the Construction of Social Theory: An Essay in Reflective Sociology," Sociological Review, 21, 1973, 25-55, and would refer you to it for a fully developed sense of these ideas.

16 I am recalling here again words of Ricoeur. Yet others too have given power to lacunae, to spaces. For example, one is reminded of Maurice Merleau-Ponty's idea of silence, and Jacques Lacan's discussion of the rupture, the split, the opening. And in this paper, "discoveries" about theorizing are occuring "in" the space made by the "absence" (in our usual theorizing) of the consciousness to which I am attending.

17 My own teaching now is always from the original sources of theorists. For it is only their words which can show the movement of their thought. Even though the

as I have needed to use words to show you what I understand, you will need words to show yourselves what you understand. And if you begin to theorize in the way I have been talking around, you will come to see that our words do not merely serve to communicate our analyses, our theory, but our communication of our theory becomes a part of our theorizing. So only when we are finished speaking or writing will we know the knowledge we embody. From the beginning we must depend on our language and use language as the norm of all other manifestations of speech, including our physical movements. Of course, you will protest that we often know things we cannot put into words. This is so, but it is so only in one sense, only on one turn of the spiral. For instance, as for my perception of movement in nature in Maine as symbolizing something I already know and something about which I can already begin to write and to teach but which I have not yet apprehended: I could move in that circle forever if I did not begin as I did here today. We cannot hold an understanding to ourselves if we cannot name and begin to interpret and recover it. When I discover and name my new understandings, I will move from this circle upwards or inwards or outwards, to another. This discovering and naming of new understandings would be the articulation of and accounting for intuition. It may also be an attempt of articulation and accounting for what we believe we might glimpse in a desiring unconscious which we might never come to know. And when you name your present understandings, you will be able to move upwards to another circle of theorizing.

In coming to an end here I am still beginning, and I am formulating for you some ideas about the forces within and the changings of theorizing in psychology. These words are bearers of some of the qualities of my beginnings, and I can produce them insofar as they are causes of these qualities. Again that circle spiraling upward.[18]

---

writings of secondary sources describing a theorist's works are often more self-evident, the conceptualizations shown therein are someone elses interpretations to the theorist.

18 Shelley Woodall, a doctoral candidate at the Ontario Institute for Studies in Education, in an unpublished paper has written that ". . . in the beginning wasn't the word, but the nervous system material that would describe

But in the saying of the first word of my theorizing is the realization that the words have always dwelled within me. So another beginning different from our corporeal one and different from our metaphorical one must be acknowledged--one placed in speaking/hearing.

Here, in placing the topic of beginnings with the issue of theorizing, I have wanted to show the immediacy of readers in their relationship to any author's theorizing. Beginnings in this paper point to the presence of the personal in the theorizing behind the introduced theory and in the theorizing behind our responses to an intro- duced theory. Thus, beginnings in this paper point away from what is formulated by us to how that formulation is recognized by ourselves and by others. Thus, beginnings for both of us, reader and writer, mark the source of a movement of theorizing which we experience in any com- prehension we may attempt. But beginnings as an ever- present force within movement return us to the reali- zation of the significance of movement itself, a movement in theorizing which is the movement of one's own thought in the presence of the movement of the thought of an other.

    In this paper I have placed my existential response to physical nature immediately in relation to my theori- zing. If in this way I have chosen to talk about begin- nings as a source from which and way in which psycholo- gical theorizing may be understood, it is because in this context for me a beginning is thought possible.

---

and inscribe circles of meaning." She says, "In the metaphorical beginning was the word . . ."

ABOUT THE AUTHORS

Vivian Darroch is an Associate Professor in the Department of Applied Psychology at the Ontario Institute for Studies in Education and is appointed to the School of Graduate Studies of the University of Toronto.

Ronald J. Silvers is an Associate Professor in the Department of Sociology in Education at the Ontario Institute for Studies in Education and is appointed to the School of Graduate Studies of the University of Toronto.